the
kids
are
all right

The four of us, with Berry (l–r: Dan, Amanda, Diana, Liz)

the
kids
are
all right

A MEMOIR

....

DIANA WELCH AND LIZ WELCH

with Amanda Welch and Dan Welch

Harmony Books / New York

Published in the United States by Harmony Books,
an imprint of the Crown Publishing Group,
a division of Random House, Inc., New York.
www.crownpublishing.com

Harmony Books is a registered trademark and the Harmony Books colophon
is a trademark of Random House, Inc.

All photographs are from the Welch Family Collection.

Library of Congress Cataloging-in-Publication Data available upon request.

ISBN 978-0-307-39604-4

Printed in the United States of America

Design by Chris Welch Design

10 9 8 7 6 5 4 3 2 1

First Edition

Our parents on their wedding day

IN MEMORY OF MOM AND DAD

AND AUNTIE EVE

Dan with Auntie Eve

contents

a note on the text

This book is a true story. Or rather it is several true stories. Really, it is a collection of memories, and in the process of writing them down, and comparing them, we have learned that memory is a tricky thing. It's like returning to the house in which you lived as a child. The staircase you remembered as that monumental thing you crawled up slowly on your hands and knees is now something you can run up, hands free, two steps at a time. Well, you weren't wrong then, and you aren't wrong now. Perception may have changed, but the facts remain. Those stairs were big. Now they're small. Go figure. In the following pages, you'll see that we disagree about certain things, as most siblings do. Over the last few years of writing, researching, and interviewing lots of people, we have learned that truth is subjective, always. That goes for every character in the book. Our interpretations of other people's actions are locked in a time and a place. An eight-year-old who has lost her parents sees the world in a much different way than that same girl twenty-five years later. The same is true for a sixteen- or twenty-year-old-girl and for a fourteen-year-old boy. Some people in these pages insisted on using their real names, but other names have been changed, along with identifying characteristics, to protect people's privacy. Other than that, we have each told the truth, and each truth is our own.

the
kids
are
all right

Does it feel that your life's become a catastrophe?
Oh, it has to be for you to grow, boy.

—"Take the Long Way Home," SUPERTRAMP

introduction

OUR MOTHER DIED three times. We have the first death on tape, recorded the day it aired in 1976: Morgan Fairchild, wearing a trench coat and pale pink lip-gloss, shot her in the back. Over the past thirty years, we've each watched the tape several times, pulling it from dusty cardboard moving boxes and crossing our fingers it doesn't get eaten by the VCR. It's our only copy.

The scene opens with Morgan, as Jennifer Pace, hiding in a darkened hallway. Our mother, playing Eunice Wyatt on the soap opera *Search for Tomorrow*, is kissing actor Val Dufour good-bye at their apartment door. His square jaw and dimpled chin are powdered an orangey tan. As John Wyatt, Eunice's cheating husband, Val is dressed conservatively in a suit and tie, but we know him as the guy who once wore a kilt and a feather boa to our parents' annual Christmas party.

The music swells. Commercial break.

Back at the apartment, our mother turns away from the camera, and there is a loud bang. A tiny circle of dark red appears on the back of her pink satin robe. The next shot is a close-up. Our mother's face fills the screen in a death snarl revealing upper teeth.

And so our mother's decade-long run as Eunice Gardner Twining Martin Wyatt came to an end. It was her third soap gig, and her longest. She started out in 1962 as Erica Brandt on *Young Doctor Malone* before making her name in 1964 as the original Dr. Maggie Fielding on *The Doctors*. Born in 1965, Amanda is the eldest of the four Welch children. She was

introduced to soap fans in a splashy *Dialing the Daytime Stars* magazine spread
as "The Baby Who Took Ann Williams off TV." We still have the article,
now yellowed with age, tucked away in the same manila folder where Mom
stuck it more than forty years ago. When Liz was born, in 1969, Mom had
been playing Eunice for three years. Instead of getting written off entirely, Eunice had a breakdown and was temporarily sent to a mental institution. By
Dan's birth in 1971, Eunice was so popular that the pregnancy was written
into the show. But Mom wasn't pregnant when Jennifer shot Eunice; rumor
had it that Mary Stuart, the show's diva and Dan's godmother, was jealous of
Mom's fan mail. That's what Mom told us, anyway.

Diana was born in 1977, a year before Mom landed the role of the vil-
lainous Margo Huntington on *The Edge of Night*. Which brings us to our
mother's second death: Margo was bludgeoned with a fire poker off-camera
in a whodunit story line that continued for weeks after her body was discovered. Margo had a lot of enemies; she was a successful businesswoman who
owned the only TV station in Monticello. Her story line involved an illegit-
imate child, a sham marriage to an ex-cult leader, and pornography.

During the Margo years, as part of their after-school chores, Mom enlisted
Amanda and Liz to record her episodes on our VCR, one of the first, which
was the size of a stuffed suitcase. At night, when she came home from her day
of shooting, Mom labeled each tape with the date, show name, and episode
number and placed it chronologically on a bookshelf in her study.

Today, only five tapes remain, the labels peeling off from the dust that has
weakened their glue, their images scratchy and worn. Amanda is the reason
we have any tapes at all: After our mother's third and actual death, the one
that followed our father's by three and a half years, Amanda carted those
tapes around in boxes, stored them in a friend's garage, and drove them
across state lines. They have been packed up, unpacked, sent parcel post, and
popped into VCRs in New York, Virginia, and Texas. They're our family
heirlooms, a fuzzy, dusty connection to the person whom waitresses at
Chock full o'Nuts recognized as Eunice or Margo but whom we knew as
Mom. Watching them now, we see bits of our lives on the screen. The diamond ring Eunice wears is really the one Dad gave Mom when he pro-
posed in the early sixties, just a few months after meeting her. The red mug
ringed with fat white hearts that Margo drinks out of spent the eighties

stained with coffee in our kitchen sink at home in Bedford, New York. The yellow organza dress that she wore to announce her engagement to the cult leader is the one that Diana wore, fifteen years later and tripping on acid, to the junior prom. Though the ring was stolen years ago, and the mug is long gone, Amanda saved the dress, as she did the tapes, and the grandfather clocks, and the Etruscan trunk. Like Mom, she keeps the clocks wound to chime on the hour, and she fills the trunk with sheets and blankets. And, like Mom, she saved the manila folder that holds magazine clippings documenting the highlights of our mother's career.

"Ann Williams: 'I Relate to Children and Animals Better Than to Adults!' " shouts a bold headline across the opening spread of a 1976 article from *Day TV Gossip*. It chronicles life at Twin Meadows, the fourteen-acre estate where we grew up. In it, Mom describes Amanda, then ten, as a "serious human being" who likes to ride her pony and wants to be an animal trainer someday. "Lizzie," six, is a "backgammon whiz, you can't beat her!" and also the "most giving of people," one who would gladly give up her dessert so that another child wouldn't be left wanting. Daniel, four, is a "lover" who "practices his best Clark Gable moods" on Mom. He also has a "vivid imagination" and likes to go "elephant hunting in the backyard with his Daddy," she says. "They shoot them out of the trees." Diana wasn't born yet.

In one of the photos accompanying the article, Amanda, Liz, and Dan are all piled on Mom's lap. In another, Amanda and Dan pose with their stuffed animals. There's one of Dad, his salt-and-pepper hair elegantly parted on the side and slicked back, like a Kennedy. He has a kind Irish face, freckled and dimpled, and smiling eyes. They described him as an investment banker. He was on TV with Mom only once, for a *Newlywed*-styled show called *Tattletales* that Amanda, Liz, and Dan remember watching when they were kids. Every time Dad got an answer wrong, Mom would swat the air, smile big, and shrug her shoulders. Diana has seen the photo someone took of the black-and-white television set the day the show aired. Mom is sitting on Dad's lap, biting her bottom lip. He looks nervous and serious, though in real life he was neither.

Amanda has that picture in one of many family albums, glued beneath a thin plastic sheet alongside other images, proof of where we come from, of who we were before everything changed: our parents at fox hunts, regal in their red coats and top hats; childhood birthday parties with frosted cakes, lit candles, and paper hats; horse shows with ribbons and trophies; beach picnics and Thanksgiving dinners. Amanda also has several grainy 16-millimeter home movies that Mom and Dad made, the sounds of which have gone wobbly and deep.

One year, as a Christmas present, Dan edited the films together and layered sad-but-funny songs like Motley Crue's "Home Sweet Home" and Elvis's "Don't Cry Daddy" on top of their slow, distorted narration. After five long years apart, it was the eighth Christmas we had spent together as a family; our separation and subsequent reunion had reinforced the importance of childhood rituals. That Christmas Eve was spent the same as the ones before it: We prepared a dinner of Yorkshire pudding and roast beef, hung the four patchwork stockings that our mother had made, our names hand-stitched in white rickrack on each cuff. We dressed the tree with old family ornaments and placed the gold papier-mâché crèche at its base. Then, in keeping with another Welch tradition, we each opened one small present. Amanda opened one from Dan—our new home movie.

On that Christmas Eve in 1998, we watched our father hold Amanda up in the window of their apartment in New York City so she could see the Macy's Thanksgiving Day Parade drift down Central Park West, and we watched him hold her at her christening at St. Patrick's Cathedral, and as she sat in his lap on her first birthday and tried to eat her card. We watched our mother, puffy from giving birth, wave to the camera and smile, holding a fat newborn Liz in her arms. We watched a determined Liz tromp up a grassy hill in tights and fancy shoes, struggling to hold an Easter basket nearly as big as she was. We watched Amanda wave at the camera and pat Dan's back as he lay belly-down in his bassinet, her mouth forming the words "Hi, Mom." We watched Liz help Dan take off his tiny terry-cloth robe at the beach in Cape Cod before she left him sitting in the sand and ran to catch up with Amanda in the waves. We watched the three of them splash around in our pool, held up either by Styrofoam floaties or by Mom in a bikini and a big sunhat. It wasn't until the tape finished that we realized Diana wasn't in any of those warm, sun-splattered scenes that our parents recorded and Amanda saved and Dan edited and scored. It made sense. Those home movies recorded the idyllic times, and Diana doesn't remember much of those.

part one

. . . .

SPRING 1982 – SUMMER 1983

Diana and Dad

LIZ

I WANTED TO be an actress just like Mom. In the fall of 1981, I came close to getting the part of Jon Voight's daughter in the movie *Table for Five*, but then Ricky Schroeder was cast as the son. We were both blond, and the director wanted the daughter to be a brunette, so I was out. At least, that's how Mom explained it to me.

The following spring, I had another audition. This time, I was up for the part of Mariel Hemingway's younger sister in *Star 80*. Mariel was playing Dorothy Stratten, the *Playboy* playmate killed by her jealous husband. Mom thought I had a good chance because I looked like Mariel, same blond hair and blue eyes, dark eyebrows, and square jaw. Even strangers told me so. Some said I looked like Brooke Shields, but she had brown hair and brown eyes so that never made any sense to me.

Mom picked me up early from school to take me into Manhattan. Usually, her coming to get me would be an endless source of embarrassment. She'd barge into volleyball practice dressed in too-tight velour sweatpants tucked into gardening boots, her big dip sunglasses perched on top of the silk scarf she'd wrap around her hair instead of brushing it. Worse, she'd holler "Yoo-hoo" in a falsetto across the court, waving her arms at me as if I didn't know she was there. She was impossible to miss. During the winter months she wore a floor-length coat that looked like a skinned dead collie turned inside out. It was mortifying.

But that afternoon, waiting in the parking lot, she looked glamorous. Her brown hair was curled under and combed into a chic bob, her gardening outfit replaced by a silk shirtdress and burgundy knee-high boots. This was her city outfit.

Usually Mom liked to help me prepare for my scenes during the hour-long drive into the city, but this afternoon, she had other things on her mind. "Lizzie Bits, you'll be the decoy," she said as we pulled out of Fox Lane Middle School's driveway. "You'll distract your father as I set up."

She was planning a surprise party for Dad's fiftieth birthday that weekend, and she had invited old college friends from Johns Hopkins, business associates from Houston, Dad's brothers and sisters, as well as friends from the Bedford Golf and Tennis Club and the Goldens Bridge Hounds. More than fifty people had RSVPed, but Dad had no idea. "I'll make eggnog," she said excitedly as we drove down Bedford's packed dirt roads lined with stone walls and ancient oaks. "We'll use the big punch bowl," she added. "We'll use all the good crystal."

Mom started her cut-glass collection when she married Dad in 1964, and over the last eighteen years, she had managed to fill the shelves of the butler pantry that lined the narrow hallway between our dining room and kitchen. She had cake plates and platters and champagne glasses, too, plus a dish designed specifically for celery and another for deviled eggs.

"I'll make lamb stew and Irish soda bread," she continued, turning onto Interstate 684, her diamond engagement ring catching and releasing the midafternoon sun. "And an angel food cake for dessert."

Angel food cake was Dad's favorite, and mine too. For my thirteenth birthday, only one month earlier, Mom made me an angel food cake with strawberries and whipped cream.

She wanted me to keep Dad away from the house for three hours that Saturday afternoon. I gazed out the window at the messy paintbrush stroke of pine trees. I needed to come up with a good plan. Dad was smart. He paid attention to detail. He wore pressed shirts and pants, even on weekends. Duping him would be hard.

After several minutes of silence, I asked, "What if I ask him to take me shopping?"

"Ehhh," Mom made a sound like a game show buzzer. "Wrong answer. Try again."

Typical. Mom never wanted to take me shopping, and when she did, she'd let me buy things only if they were on sale. Dad, on the other hand, would deposit me at the Stamford Bloomingdale's and tell me to meet him at the cash register in twenty minutes. It's because of him that I was the first girl at Fox Lane Middle School to own Jordache jeans. On our last spree, I got the kelly-green Ralph Lauren cable-knit sweater I was wearing that day for my audition.

"How about tennis?" I offered. "I'll ask him to play a set." I had been taking lessons that winter at Chestnut Ridge, an indoor tennis club in town. I could show off my new and improved overhead serve. It was the perfect ploy, Mom agreed.

Soon we reached the outskirts of the city. Dingy buildings replaced trees along the parkway, which had doubled from two lanes to four. Suddenly, the buttery sweet scent of vanilla biscuits penetrated the diesel and gas fumes; then, minutes later, the Stella d'Oro factory whirred by.

"Lock the doors, Lizzie," Mom instructed as we approached the Third Avenue Bridge. She always said this here—not back in Bedford or anywhere in Westchester County, but here, as we were about to enter Manhattan through Spanish Harlem.

After we parked the car, we passed a blind man selling pencils. "Can we buy one?" I asked.

She shook her head and then said under her breath, "He makes more money than you do." I wondered if that was true. Other than the five-dollar weekly allowance I got for feeding the dogs and loading the dishwasher, the only money I had ever made was one hundred twenty-five dollars in seventh grade to model for a Macy's catalogue, and five hundred dollars for a Jell-O pudding commercial I did when I was eight. I'd had to eat so many bowls of chocolate pudding that I got a stomachache. After the twelfth take, when the director said, "Action," I looked into the camera and instead of saying, "It's delicious!" I said, "I think I'm going to throw up." And then I did.

For the *Star 80* audition, I had to do a sad scene. The waiting room was chaos: Young girls dabbed their lips with gloss and brushed and sprayed their hair into place while their mothers filled out call cards and handed in head shots. Mom and I found a quiet corner in the back stairwell to go over lines. She was more interested in craft than in cosmetics.

"Never rely on your looks, Elizabeth," she warned. "They'll only get you to thirty."

People always said Mom was beautiful, and in her cast photos and head shots pinned on the wall of her study at home I could see she once was. My favorite photo was of Burt Reynolds, signed, "To the prettiest girl in all of New York, love, Burt." Mom had guest-starred on his cop show *Hawk*. This was before *Smokey and the Bandit* made him famous, before Loni Anderson. There was the cast shot of *Pajama Game*, Mom in a silk nightshirt that just barely covered her tushy, and a close-up of her where she looks like a young Ingrid Bergman, the curl of her chestnut bob kissing her full lips, her big brown eyes hypnotizing the camera. In another photo, she's in Lauren Bacall's dressing room in *Applause*. Lauren is wearing a caftan and holding Mom's hand, and they're both laughing. But those photos were taken in Mom's twenties—when her skin was taut, her hair a natural dark brown, her eyes sparkling and bright. Now, at forty-six, her hair had turned brittle, a lighter, unnatural shade from two decades of perms and dye jobs, her skin was puffier, like unbaked bread. Once a size six, Mom now struggled to get into a twelve and blamed her bad luck with booking jobs on being middle-aged. "I'm too young to be a grandmother and too old to be a mother," she'd often lament. Still, it didn't stop her from working on her craft. She went to the Actors Studio weekly to workshop scenes and often asked me to read lines with her back home. She had studied with Lee Strasberg, and she taught me what she knew. It was called Method acting. For this audition, my character had just learned that her sister had been killed. Mom asked me to imagine the most terrible thing ever.

"Like when we found Frodo?" I asked. Frodo was my cat. He was black and purred when you looked at him. He had gone missing for several days that winter, and we finally found him on West Patent Road, roughly fifty yards from our driveway, his skull smashed against the pavement, his fur crusted with dried blood.

"Even sadder," Mom urged. "You have to inhabit the character, Bitsy. Imagine if Frodo were somebody you loved."

I closed my eyes and replaced Frodo's smashed skull with Dad's, and real tears began to simmer deep inside me. They slowly began to bubble up as I read the lines.

"Good, stay there," Mom said as the casting director popped her head into the hallway.

"Annie?" she said. All the casting agents in New York knew Mom. "He's ready for her."

I walked into the audition room and sat on a couch facing Bob Fosse. He had intense eyes and a full beard that made up for his thinning hair. No one else was in the room. "Whenever you're ready," he said kindly. As I read, hot tears streamed down my face. I looked up at the end and saw that Mr. Fosse's eyes were glistening, too. "Very good," he said. "Very, very good."

I left the audition feeling, for the first time, like a real actress. Maybe duping Dad wouldn't be so hard after all.

Several days later, on the morning of the party, I trotted downstairs to ask Dad if he wanted to go play tennis. He was sitting at the breakfast table, scanning the *Wall Street Journal*, his reading glasses perched halfway down his nose. He kept his head bent toward the paper but moved his eyes so they looked over the glasses and at me.

"So, you think you can beat your old man?" he said with a wink.

Dad didn't look old. The biggest difference between him at fifty and him in his wedding photos at thirty-two was that now his hair went from black to salt-and-pepper, though with the same reddish-brown highlights. His body may have thickened up a bit, but it was still athletic—cut calves, broad chest, and not an ounce of excess fat. He was only five-feet-eight-inches, yet he had been captain of both the football and the basketball teams in high school. And he watched his weight carefully, priding himself on always leaving a bite of food on his plate at the end of every meal. "Self-restraint is a virtue," he liked to say.

That afternoon, we both dressed in our tennis whites—Dad in shorts and a polo shirt, his arms and legs a spotty tan from freckles grown together with age. I had Mom's skin—a spotless pale that turned golden brown in the sun. I wore a sweatband on my wrist, and as I got into the front seat of the Mercedes, I saw Dad was wearing one, too.

"Like father like daughter," he said with a smile, and off we went.

We hit back and forth for two hours. I won the first set, and Dad won the second. Even though I was leading the third, midway through I started to worry about time. As much fun as it was to have Dad all to myself, I knew I had to get him back home by six o'clock. That was the whole point. "Should we call it quits, Dad?" I shouted over the net. The score was two to one, and it was Dad's turn to serve. "I'm pooped."

Dad had one ball in the front pocket of his white tennis shorts and one in his hand, which he bounced several times before saying, in a disappointed tone, "Elizabeth Morgan Welch, what's my motto?"

"If you're not going to do it right, don't do it at all?" I said meekly, embarrassed that I hadn't thought that through. Of course, we'd finish the set. Bob Welch's kids were not quitters! That was another one of his favorite sayings. So was "The only things you have to do in life are die and pay taxes," which I never quite understood.

"Right," he said. "Ready?"

He aced the serve. And the next one. I returned the third, and we had a good rally hitting back and forth, hard. I won that point and the third set and still wonder to this day if he let me.

By then, it was six and we were late. I kept a cool facade, but by the time we turned into our driveway, the butterflies in my stomach had morphed into slam-dancing frogs. Dad was still talking about tennis, and about how I should consider joining the Bedford Golf and Tennis Club's junior team that summer, as we began the ascent up the narrow, quarter-mile-long strip of tired pavement that had cracked in the middle like a messy part. Dad didn't see the cars until we drove through the opening of the privet hedge that set our house, with its gray shingles and hunter-green shutters, apart from the rest of the property. They were parked not only on the gravel circle in the front of the house but also to the right, beside the garage, and even on the lawn out toward the pool and down near the swing set. He pulled up to an empty spot by the front door, turned to me, and said, "Elizabeth, what is going on?" not in a serious way but with a smile as though he had a hunch.

I shrugged and said, "Let's go find out." I had practiced that moment in my head and was impressed by how coolly I pulled it off.

As we got out of the car, I could hear the hushed silence of the people waiting inside. Several silhouettes flickered across the drawn window shades in the living room. One shadow was hunched over, perhaps a person crouching down, another was walking toward the front door, and another looked like a four-headed blob. I walked ahead and flung open the front door. The lights flicked on, and "Surprise!" resounded throughout the house.

Mom rushed toward us wearing a floor-length chiffon gown the color of lemon meringue pie and pale peach high-heel sandals, the ones I always wore to play dress-up. Her hair was swept back off her face with two tortoiseshell combs. "Happy birthday, my darling," she said as she threw her arms around my stunned and smiling father.

Everyone who was important to Dad was there—his sisters and brothers and old college friends. My siblings stood in a line in front. Diana was dressed in green velvet. Her unruly red curls had been coaxed into two ponytails that bounced off her tiny shoulders as she shouted "Surprise!" in her sweet four-year-old voice that sounded more like a Sesame Street puppet than a human being. Dan stood next to her, and they looked like twins, despite the six years between them, with their red hair, freckles, and dimples that pierced their cheeks whenever they smiled. Everyone in the packed room was smiling, even Amanda, who usually wore her scowl like a badge of honor. A chubby sixteen-year-old with a Pat Benatar shag haircut, she hated dressing up, preferring her ripped jeans and concert T-shirts. Tonight, she was wearing a skirt.

I turned and looked up at Dad, who was beaming. "Nice job, toots," he winked, before being swallowed whole by the crowd of outstretched arms. I went upstairs to change, and when I came back down, the party was in full swing but Dad was gone. He then reappeared dressed in tartan slacks and a crisp white button-down shirt, a bow tie, and navy-blue blazer. Mom burst out into "For He's a Jolly Good Fellow," and the whole crowd joined in.

An hour or so later, Mom clinked a champagne glass to get everyone's attention. It was time for presents, she said, Amanda and Dan's cue. They entered the living room holding a large rectangular gift between them, which they handed to Dad. He was seated on our gold brocade couch, and the whole party gathered around to watch as he neatly untied the bow and then slid a finger beneath the taped corners, careful not to rip the paper. It was a family tree. Ever since she saw *Roots* on TV, Mom was obsessed with genealogy. She had spent the past six months in the New York Public Library working on our family history, unbeknownst to Dad, who thought she was going on auditions. She used gold and silver pens to painstakingly mark each name, birth date, and place.

At the top of the two-by-four-foot sheet of thick ivory paper, Mom had written "Ann Morgan Williams married Robert Daniel Peter Welch on September 19, 1964," in her near-perfect curly cursive. Our names and birth dates: "Amanda Gordon Welch, August 15, 1965," "Elizabeth Morgan Welch, February 3, 1969," "Daniel Merryman Welch, March 24, 1971," and "Diana Rebecca Welch, September 30, 1977," floated above our parents' names like tethered balloons. Dad beamed. On the bottom right, you could see that his family came to Boston from Ireland in the early 1900s. On the left, in a longer entanglement of roots, you saw that Mom's family came to Maryland from Scotland and Wales in the 1600s. One ancestor, Mary Ball, married Augustine Washington. They had a son named George.

"Bob, your children are descendants of the first president of the United States," Mom boasted as Dad studied the tree.

"Not from your side, Bob," Aunt Barbara shouted out above the crowd. She was Dad's older sister, and she pronounced his name with a thick Boston accent so it sounded like "Bab."

"You got that right," Uncle Russ, Dad's brother, chimed in, and all his siblings laughed their distinct Welch laugh that sounded like a drunken, jolly Dracula.

Aunt Gail, Dad's youngest sister, gave her gift next. It was a potato that she had written a poem on with a calligraphy pen, decorated with small green shamrocks and shellacked.

"To keep you connected to *your* roots, Bobby," she said.

The room grew quiet, someone murmured "How sweet," and then Barbara gave him her gift. It was a book called *Sex After 50*. All the pages were blank. The room filled with laughter again.

AMANDA

I HAVE OUR family tree hanging on my wall in my house in Virginia, where I have most of our family heirlooms—the two grandfather clocks, the hand-carved wooden Etruscan trunk, even the unfinished oil painting of some cows on the beach that our great-aunt did when she was at the Corcoran Gallery of Arts in Washington, D.C. It's funny, because back then, when I was sixteen, I couldn't have cared less about our genealogy. I didn't even like the family I had. Why would I care who came before them?

That was around the time I stopped going on family trips. A month after Dad's birthday everyone went to Myrtle Beach for spring break, except me. I used the animals as an excuse. Mom was a sucker for strays. In addition to the three dogs, two cats, and a litter of kittens, we had a stable full of horses. "Who's gonna feed the horses and muck out their stalls?" I argued.

But really, I just didn't want to do any of that family bullshit. I was a junior in high school, a fat misfit who wanted to ride my horses, listen to my records, and smoke pot with my friends. I certainly didn't want to go on a family vacation. To do what? Play miniature golf and go to the beach? I hated the beach. What do you do at the beach? Get sand in your bathing suit and up your crack?

So Mom and Dad agreed to let me stay home alone. It was great. I had a party. We drank gin and tonics and did shots. It was the first time I ever blacked out.

LIZ

MOM AND DAD may have been sad Amanda wasn't coming to Myrtle Beach, but I was relieved. Amanda hated me. She called me Big Shot and a dumb blond and tattled on me for talking on the phone with my friends, which I would do for hours on end. A week in Myrtle Beach without her meant I could work on my tan in peace and quiet, and put lemon juice in my hair without her sneering at me or putting her finger in her mouth and pretending to throw up. Or singing that Carly Simon song "You're So Vain."

Auntie Eve was coming instead. We all adored Auntie Eve. She used to be our live-in nanny, but when Diana turned two, she moved to Yorktown Heights, twenty minutes from Bedford, to live with her son and his family. She still came twice a week to clean the house and do the laundry since Mom wasn't keen on housework. "It's not my forte," she'd say. Auntie Eve was in her seventies, I think, but if you asked her how old she was, she'd always answer, "Old enough!" Dad joked that between Auntie Eve and Mom he had the perfect wife.

"Why aren't we flying?" I asked Dad as he strategically stacked Mom's golf clubs on top of a cooler in the back of our Jeep Wagoneer. "Isn't it far?"

"Road trips are fun!" he bellowed, rearranging two suitcases to fit the last duffel bag, this one full of beach toys. "Plus, we'll get to see a bit of the East Coast."

Dad hopped in the driver's seat, and I sat directly behind him. Mom took her place in the front seat, and Auntie Eve took hers, behind Mom. Dan was squished in the middle, and Diana bounced from my lap to Eve's to Mom's before crawling in the back and making a nest on top of the luggage, where she fell asleep, her pale cheek smashed against Mom's leather golf bag, forcing her lips into a pucker. By the time we crossed the George Washington Bridge and entered New Jersey, I was bored stiff. We'd only been driving one hour and had thirteen more to go. Dad started a game of punch buggy, and then Mom suggested the capital game and we all moaned. Then Mom started singing, "Fasten your seat belts, it's going to be," and everyone sang the part that sounds like human horns, "eh eh eh eh eh," before she finished the line, "a bumpy night." It was the song she had a one-line solo in when she did *Applause* on Broadway with Lauren Bacall. The solo went, "She's laughing a bit too loudly, that's how the last one began."

After that song, Mom tried to get me to sing "Tomorrow" with her, but I refused, having sworn never to sing that song ever again, not after auditioning for *Annie* on Broadway the year before. The casting director asked me to do the part that goes, "When I'm stuck with a daaay that's graaay and lo-onelyyy, I just stick out my chiiiiin and griiiin and saaay . . . !" They were the highest, hardest notes in the whole song. My voice strained to reach them and then cracked when I got there. The director yelled "Cut!" before I could even sing the refrain. "I'm sick of that song," I said, rolling my eyes.

Mom caught me doing it out of the corner of her eye and frowned. "Don't be a bad sport, Bitsy," she said. "It's unbecoming."

DAN

MYRTLE BEACH WAS like a carnival, with all these rides along the boardwalk in town. After standing in line forever to ride a roller-coaster, I stood on my tippy-toes to pass the height requirement. I was so excited until I got in the seat and realized I was going to fall out for sure. As the ride started, I held on for dear life, and when it turned upside down, I closed my eyes and fought hard not to cry. When it was over, I felt sick, like I was going to puke. I had eaten an ice cream right before and told Mom I had a stomachache from that, but really I just didn't want to go on any more rides.

So Mom took me to the Ripley's Believe It . . . Or Not! museum. I loved that kind of stuff: my favorite TV show was *In Search Of* . . . with Leonard Nimoy. I loved seeing all these photographs of impossible-to-believe things that actually existed in the world, like those African tribes that wore rings to elongate their necks. I also liked all the gory stuff, but it scared Mom. She couldn't even look at it. But she did like this grain of rice that someone had written a poem on so tiny you had to use a magnifying glass to read it. And her favorite thing was a matchbook that a man had taken and cut into a long, one-hundred-foot strip without breaking it.

We stayed at a condo right on the beach, and Dad taught me how to throw a perfect spiral football there on the sand. He told me to use my left hand to point to the sky in the direction I wanted to throw the ball. With my right hand, I was to keep my fingertips on the laces at all times, breaking my wrist just as the ball passed my face and then letting go. I tried really hard, but I couldn't do it. My hands were too small. Dad didn't make me feel bad about it, but I never wanted to disappoint him. I wanted to grow up to be his carbon copy.

The next day we all got into the Jeep to go to this sculpture garden. As we pulled up to the entrance to the parking lot, there were these two giant statues of fighting stallions. They were up on their hind legs, lashing at one another with their front hooves and biting each other's necks. I was the only one in the family who didn't like horses. I'd been terrified of them ever since Rascal, my Shetland pony, rolled over with me on top of him when I was eight. He nearly crushed me to death. It was awful, but Dad made me get back on him right away. I did what he asked because I wanted to please him. Still, I've hated those beasts ever since. As we drove beneath the statues, I looked up and saw their huge marble testicles, and I just knew: This was not going to be fun.

LIZ

AFTER SPENDING FOUR hours looking at boring statues, I was desperate to get back to the beach to work on my tan. We got back into the car—Mom in the passenger seat, Dan and I in back with Diana strapped in the middle. Auntie Eve had stayed at the condo, claiming statues were "not her thing." Dad started the ignition without any cause for concern, but as soon as he put the car into drive, it lurched forward, then groaned, and then we all heard a gigantic thud. Then the car let out a big sigh and went completely silent.

Dad quickly got out of the car and down on his knees to look beneath it. We heard him mutter, "God damn it."

"What is it, Bob?" Mom called from the passenger seat.

"It's the drive shaft," he shouted back, still under the car.

Mom turned in her seat and looked at us quizzically, "The what?" she asked, unsnapping her seat belt and opening the door.

"The thing that holds the car together," Dad said quietly as he got up off the ground and brushed gravel from his hands and knees.

As he went in search of a pay phone, I climbed out of the car and sat on the pavement, determined to get some sun before it set. I pulled the bottom of my T-shirt up through its neck to make a bikini top, rolled the sleeves up on top of my shoulders, and leaned back on my arms with my face and body lined up with the sun. Eventually, the cab came, taking Mom, Dan, Diana, and me back to the condo while Dad waited for the tow truck. The following day, while our car was still at the shop, Aunt Barbara called Dad to say Grampy was in the hospital. He had pneumonia; his lungs were filling with liquid. His doctor gave him only a few more days to live.

Dad flew to Boston the next day to see his father one last time, leaving us three kids behind with Mom. Suddenly, the vacation was less fun. Mom didn't know how to throw a perfect spiral football with Dan, and she kept telling me I was spending too much time in the sun. Worse, I had given up the chance to be in *Star 80*. Three days into our vacation, my agent had called to say that Bob Fosse was considering making the sister older for me and would I fly back for another audition. I had told Mom that I didn't want to, that I was having too much fun. Now I wasn't so sure.

The Jeep got fixed, and the ride home seemed twice as long without Dad. He liked to play punch buggy, and he let us eat at Burger King. Mom only liked word games and made us eat soggy tuna fish sandwiches on Branola bread that Auntie Eve made the night before. Plus, we were all worried about Grampy. Mom said she wasn't sure we'd ever see him again.

We made it back to Bedford by nightfall. I was happy to be home, happy to see Max, our German shepherd, who jumped up to look inside the car as soon as Mom parked. We had dropped Auntie Eve off at her son's house in Yorktown Heights, so I helped Mom unload. I already knew that I wanted to wear my white button-down shirt to school the next day, since it would best show off my tan, so I emptied all of the suitcases and started a load of whites. An hour or two later, just as I was ironing my shirt, the phone rang. It was Dad.

"Hiya, toots," his voice boomed through the receiver.

"How's Grampy?" I asked.

"He's a fighter," Dad replied. "He's going to make it."

We chatted a bit more, and then he said, "Tell Amanda not to pick me up at the airport. And tell your mother I'm renting a car and driving home."

And then, "Kiddo, don't worry about a thing. I have everything all figured out."

And with that, he hung up.

Amanda's room was on the third floor. I walked up the two flights of stairs and knocked gently on her door. It had a sign on it that read, DO NOT ENTER UNDER PENALTY OF DEATH in chunky block letters. Supertramp was blasting on the stereo. "Take a look at my girlfriend / She's the only one I got" wafted through the closed door.

I pounded harder, and then heard the scratch of the record needle and a gruff "What?"

She wasn't going to let me in, so I shouted through the door, "Dad says don't pick him up. He's renting a car."

Instead of answering, she put the record needle back down.

DAN

I WOKE UP to Mom sitting on my bed, crying, her hands covering her face.

It was a clear night. I remember the blue glow of the moon reflecting off the wallpaper and the silhouettes of my hobby toy cars and planes and my battery collection.

"What's wrong?" I asked.

She told me Dad died. She said that Dad was never coming back, and that God wanted him. And I started crying. We hugged and stuff like that. And that was that.

LIZ

AMANDA DECIDED TO go to school the next morning, but the rest of us stayed home. Every time the doorbell rang, I'd shout, "I'll get it!" I was grateful to have something to do besides wander aimlessly through our suddenly huge and foreign house. Even Max sensed something was wrong. He accompanied me to the front door each time growling softly, his hair on end. It was either a deliveryman with another arrangement—lilies, tulips, roses, and carnations, all in muted shades—or a concerned neighbor dropping off a tuna casserole or a pineapple upside-down cake.

Mom remained in her bedroom all day, mostly on the phone. I eavesdropped, standing in her doorway or sitting outside on the steps going up to the third floor, and listened to her tell the story over and over again: "It was a car accident . . . He was on his way back home from Boston . . . He fell asleep at the wheel . . . He was only two exits from home."

No matter how many times I heard the words, the reality of what she was saying never sank in. I kept waiting for him to pull up the driveway, tooting the horn, laughing, "Ha! Ha! Ha! I really had you all going!" Dad was a joker. He loved a good prank. When the phone rang and he was home, he'd answer by saying "Ku-Ni-Chi-Wa" in a ridiculous *Saturday Night Live* Japanese accent. Or "Vinnie's Pizzeria," winking at whoever was nearby to include that person in on his joke.

Plus, he was still everywhere. His brown leather slippers were sitting at the foot of the green corduroy ottoman in his bedroom where he had last kicked them off, and his blanket-soft baby-blue cardigan was hanging on a hook in the mudroom. I couldn't resist grabbing it, burying my face in its soft folds. It still smelled of pipe tobacco and Colgate toothpaste, Dad's scent. If his scent was still alive, how could he be dead? In the fridge there were three cans of Ballantine ale and a half-eaten wedge of Stilton cheese wrapped in cellophane, which would stay there for weeks until someone realized, I'm not sure who, that Dad was the only person in our house who drank ale or liked Stilton cheese. And then there was the note, written in his choppy, left-leaning scrawl, all sharp angles and straight lines, pinned to the bulletin board near the phone: "Annie, I'm out in the barn."

I floated and fumbled through the day, lurking in hallways and listening to conversations, hunting for clues that would prove my hunch right. Dad was in the barn! That was what the note said! Or perhaps he actually took the plane and was waiting at the airport! We need to send someone to JFK! Or maybe to Newark? Or maybe the man who had died in the car crash was someone who looked like Dad. Uncle Harry, Auntie Eve's boyfriend, identified the body. He told Mom that Dad was unrecognizable. I overheard him say that Dad's head was so badly smashed that the only reason he knew it was Dad was because of the red, brown, black, and silver mustache smeared across his lip. I thought, lots of men have mustaches! And Uncle Harry said he was unrecognizable. So maybe it wasn't him. It couldn't be him. How could it be him?

Later that afternoon, after Amanda came home from school, I sat midway up the stairs that led to her bedroom, listening to the conversation she was having with Mom. The DO NOT ENTER UNDER PENALTY OF DEATH sign had been ripped down from her door, but the sentiment remained, as did two paper corners beneath pieces of stubborn tape.

"You cannot wear leather pants to your father's funeral," Mom pleaded. She sounded exhausted. I crawled silently to the top of the stairs and peeked through the crack where the door was ajar. Mom was sitting on Amanda's bed, just beneath the poster of a half-naked Jim Morrison, his arms outstretched in a slacker crucifixion pose.

I loved Amanda's leather pants. She bought them with money she got for her sixteenth birthday, and said she was going to wear them to concerts. She was so proud of them, she even invited me into her room one afternoon to show them off. She had ripped out the lining to get them to fit, and still she had to lie down on her bed, suck in, and tuck her stomach to one side, then the other, in order to zip them up without catching any flesh. Once she was in them, she looked amazing.

"They're black," Amanda said, scowling.

She was slumped in her desk chair, arms crossed.

"We'll go shopping tomorrow," Mom suggested.

"I hate shopping," Amanda said without moving. She was staring out the window, with her back to Mom.

That's when panic first struck me—I had nothing black to wear to the funeral. I ran down to my room and ransacked my closet. Dad had just bought me a cotton sundress for the eighth-grade spring dance, but that was white with purple and turquoise stripes. I also had a Gunne Sax dress, a Christmas gift, but it was pale gray calico with a white lace collar, not remotely somber, not close to black. Dad prided himself on his attire. He always dressed appropriately. Even though he didn't like to ride horses all that much, he had a dashing red coat with a black velvet collar and a matching top hat he wore to go fox hunting with Mom. I needed a black dress.

I ran to tell Mom, now back in her bedroom, her eyes raw but still leaking tears.

"You're too young to wear black, Elizabeth," she said quietly.

A lightning bolt of anger shot up from somewhere deep inside me. "If Dad were alive, he'd buy me a black dress," I said through clenched teeth, my bottom lip stuck out at her instead of my tongue, my top lip clamped down holding back the tears whirling in my chest.

Mom looked as if I had slapped her in the face.

"Well, I'm sorry," she said. "Your father is not . . ."

I don't know how she finished the sentence because I was already running, my hand covering my mouth as my lips were parting against the howling pressure now in my throat. I slammed my bedroom door and flung myself on my bed. For the first time that day, I cried.

AMANDA

YEAH, I WENT to school the next day. I had to get out of that fucking house. Everybody was all crying and weird. And Mom was driving me crazy; she cried nonstop from the time Dad died until after the funeral. It's like, you cry, and then you stop. You don't cry, cry, cry, cry, cry. Don't get me wrong; I cried. I just didn't sit around all day doing it in front of everybody. Also, when Dad died, Mom and I didn't have a very good relationship. I was in the middle of my sixteen-year-old angst, and she was . . . well, she was really annoying. That morning, I just couldn't deal with her, so I drove Dad's Mercedes to school.

Up until that day, I had been trying to lose weight by walking the four miles to school and eating only every other day. I wasn't obese, but I was fat compared to other kids. I mean: I had to rip the lining out of those leather pants because I couldn't get my fat thighs in them otherwise. It was Mom who taught me to make up my own hare-brained diet schemes. I was seven when she first brought me to Weight Watchers. By the time I was a high school junior, we were doing the Shaklee diet together because Mom was out of work and started selling the disgusting meal-replacement shakes. I flavored mine with maple syrup extract and ended up smelling like pancakes for the entire semester.

Then, the day Dad died, food was dropped off on the hour, like, whole baked hams and ziti, just casserole dish after casserole dish. There was food everywhere. And I thought that was so funny, like, what, our dad died so we're not going to eat? Nobody's going to open the refrigerator? But I guess they just wanted to do something. Anyway, when I came home from school that afternoon, I ate an entire pineapple upside-down cake. It was the best thing I had ever eaten in my life.

DAN

I DIDN'T GO to school for the longest out of everybody; I just hung around the house for about a week. It felt big and lonely even though there were all these people coming over to say they were sorry. Then my friends Curtis and Jeremy came over after school one day. We stood in the driveway, right in front of the house. It was awkward. We were only eleven and we didn't really know what to say to each other, so we just hung out. But it was really nice of them to come.

When I did go back to school, some kid made a joke about my father being dead and I started crying in class. Curtis stood up and hit the kid. And that felt good, seeing him do that for me. It made me feel less alone.

LIZ

AMANDA WOUND UP wearing her leather pants to the wake. I wore my gray Gunne Sax dress and sat in a folding chair, cocooned by seven or eight girlfriends who had pulled their chairs around me. Their eyes were fixed on me, but mine were set on the coffin, only ten feet away. Mom thought I was too young to wear black, but I guess she figured I was old enough to help her pick out Dad's coffin.

Just the day before, I sat in the undertaker's wood-paneled office listening as Mom answered a series of questions. A man in a dark suit and white starched shirt sat behind a large desk and wrote her answers on a clipboard.

"Do you want him cremated?" the man asked.

"Do you have a funeral plot?"

"Will it be a religious wake?"

"How many people do you expect?"

"Do you want an open or a closed casket?"

Mom sat straight up in her seat and cocked her head to one side, confused. Now I understood why she brought me along. This man might as well have been speaking Cantonese. This was a new role for her: Dad was the one who handled practical things. He paid all the bills, filled out all the forms, hired the handymen. So she answered each question hesitantly, with a shaky voice, her bottom lip quivering.

It hadn't stopped quivering since Dad died. I had seen this expression before, but mostly on TV. It was her trademark: She'd bite her bottom lip and wrinkle her forehead, and then her chin would shake. It always irritated me, and I never once thought it was sincere, until now. I wanted to reach over and hold her face between my hands to steady her chin, to wipe away her tears. Instead, I just sat there, feeling useless. I was no help at all.

Then this man asked, "What type of coffin?"

Mom stared at him and shrugged, prompting him to pull out a three-ring binder filled with glossy photos, which he placed in front of us. I flipped through until I saw a shiny, deep purple-y red mahogany casket with a royal-blue velvet lining.

"This is it, Mom," I said. "This is what Dad would want."

In a way, it felt as though we were shopping for a celestial car, one that would zoom Dad to Heaven. He had only ever driven a Mercedes-Benz as long as I could remember, so mahogany with brass hardware and a royal-blue velvet lining seemed fitting. It was the Mercedes-Benz of coffins.

Nodding his head, the undertaker agreed and said, "Your daughter has excellent taste."

Mom sighed and said, "She gets that from her father." Then she asked for the price, and I felt instantly ashamed. How could she be thinking of money at a time like this?

The figure he quoted was high enough to shock Mom out of her sad stupor. "That's ridiculous," she said, then softened. "It's more than we can afford."

She continued flipping through the book, her hands shaking along with her lower lip, tears splashing onto the laminated pages, and I wondered if that was why they were laminated. She finally settled on an oak casket with no lining—a waste of money as, even the undertaker agreed, Dad's face and body were so badly smashed up that a closed coffin was the only way to go.

Sitting in the funeral home staring at the casket, I wished it were mahogany. But then I saw Mom, standing an arm's length from her husband's body, thanking people for coming, nodding her head as they told her how sorry they were, and agreeing with others about how awful it was. I realized it simply didn't matter.

I spent most of that night comforting my friends, especially Adrianna, the girl who addressed all notes to me throughout seventh grade as "MBF," short for My Best Friend, and signed them "YBF." We were no longer close friends, but Adrianna was crying so hard that her face was slick with tears and snot, her wailing mouth webbed with saliva. "It's going to be okay," I told her, over and over. I didn't mind, though. It gave me something to do.

My siblings were like zombies. Dan stood with two friends, kicking at a spot on the floor, his hands shoved in the pockets of his gray flannel slacks. Amanda sat with her best friend Anna in one corner, stony-faced. And Diana stayed home. Mom thought she was too young for such sadness and instead brought a photograph of her and Dad to place on the casket. It had been taken the summer before: Dad standing in the shallow end of our pool, waist deep in water, with Diana on his hip, her pale arms wrapped tightly around his neck, her freckled face smashed against his as if she wished she were clay and wanted to mold into him. They were both smiling so hard, it was surprising the frame could contain the happiness of that moment, surprising that it didn't shatter into a million pieces, floating all over the funeral home like dust.

DIANA

I REMEMBER WHEN that picture was taken, the one that took the place of both Dad and me at his funeral. It was a sunny day, and we were by the pool. I was wearing a hand-me-down bathing suit that I had inherited from a cousin, a brown calico number with large circular cutouts that left one vertical strip of material to cover my belly button and one to cover my spine. I had put it on that morning, all by myself, in the bathroom I shared with Liz. All those holes made the suit difficult to negotiate. Bare ass on the cool tile, I stuck my feet through the wrong holes and yanked the suit up my thighs. I had to get up and sit down three times before I got it right. I thought it was the coolest thing until my sisters told me it was hideous. This was after Dad, towel slung over his shoulder, had scooped me up for the camera that Mom held beneath the wide brim of her straw hat. I squeezed his neck, smushing my cheek to his. He laughed and said I was getting big. Then he threw me up in the air and into the pool.

DAN

DAD NEVER CRIED. I cried a lot when I was little. I was a momma's boy, always hiding behind Mom's legs because I was scared of a bunch of things: cats, horses, geese—you name it. This one time, Dad and I were walking down the driveway, and I was crying and acting spoiled. Finally he said to me: "Stop crying, or I'll give you something to really cry about." He never told me that men shouldn't cry, but it was implied.

Like in the movie *The Great Santini*, there's a moment where Santini's wife has died. He and his son are in the hospital, and he says to his son, "Okay, you have fifteen minutes to go cry. And that is it." The son went into the hospital room and cried for fifteen minutes and that was it. The mourning was over. That stuck out in my mind. I thought, "That's what I should do. That's what men do."

When the pallbearers walked down the aisle, each holding a corner of Dad's coffin, I saw a tear roll down one man's face. For the first time, I thought it was okay for men to cry.

DIANA

I DON'T REMEMBER much else about the four years I spent with Dad. I now know he was one of seven, born in Quincy, Massachusetts, three girls and four boys, raised by a widower. He was the quarterback for North Quincy High, making the local paper a couple of times for his handling of the pigskin. He worked, got fair marks in school, and teased his sisters mercilessly. My grandfather, known to us as Grampy, was a drinking man born to a long line of drinkers, and after school, our father and his brothers were often greeted in the kitchen by their surly and slouching dad, his bottle half empty on the table in front of him. The unlucky son who was ordered to the basement for a bout with his old man would glumly descend the wooden stairs, strapping on some gloves. Uncle Russ, an artist and interior decorator who died of liver failure in 2003, got it the worst.

It was Russ who held me the day Dad's coffin was lowered into the blazing green earth of the cemetery grounds. I hadn't been at the wake or the funeral, but Mom brought all of us up to Massachusetts for the burial. There were people crying all around, looking at the coffin, the hole, the grass, their shoes, the sky. Russ looked at the grass. My hands gripped the back of his neck and patted his puffy, prickly cheeks. I looked at his eyes, red and wet. They looked as if they hurt. I looked at his big ear and at the hairs that curled from the waxy hole.

"Is my daddy in there?" I whispered to him in the silence. He ignored me, so I leaned in closer, my lips touching the hairs, and asked him again. Then I saw his eyes spilling and shut my mouth so hard I bit my tongue. I could taste the blood, metallic like the water from the fountain at school, licking its way to my teeth. I started to cry and put my hands to his cheeks once more, just like the cheeks I had touched in the sunshine by the pool, in the dimly lit hallways of our house, in my bed before I fell asleep.

"You look just like my daddy," I whispered. "You look just like my daddy." My uncle turned his head and began to sob as some gray-haired lady took me from his arms, my hands scraping his stubble as I was carried away.

LIZ

DAYS LATER AND back home, the flowers had begun to wilt, and their stems turned slimy. The smell of rot made me nauseous as I gathered and threw them out. I was glad that the people and their baked ziti and tuna casseroles and spiral hams were gone. I was sick of comfort food and would be for many years.

I was also sick of Mom and her quivering lip. More than a week had passed, and there was lots to sort out, lots to do. But Mom continued to cry long after my aunts and uncles had gone back to Boston, and we kids were the only ones left to console her. I wanted to put up a DO NOT ENTER sign on my bedroom door because Mom wandered in every afternoon, glassy-eyed and whimpering, "What are we going to do? What on earth are we going to do?" I wanted to scream, "*I don't know!* Figure it out! You're the mother! Remember?" But then I remembered that this was a woman who banged her head against the wall every Thanksgiving when her pie crust fell apart before she could flip it from the counter into the dish. If she couldn't handle baking a pie, how on earth was she going to raise four fatherless kids?

One day, after she had wandered zombie-like in and out of my room yet again, I was desperate. Mom was acting like she was the only one who had lost someone, like it was harder for her than for us kids. We were all in Dad's car as it veered out of control. Instead of reaching over and grabbing the wheel, instead of trying to slam on the brakes and steer the car to safety, Mom was still buckled into the passenger seat, screaming, and I knew that if we all screamed with her, we'd crash and die. Grief had rendered Mom useless, and it was terrifying, adding another layer to my own sadness. Panic.

I walked up the carpeted stairs toward Amanda's room and stood silently outside her closed door for several minutes. This time Elton John was playing. I took a deep breath and knocked. No response. I knocked again, this time more forcefully. I knew she was crying. I heard the stifled sobs behind Elton's lyrics and imagined the pool of saliva on the pillow and the stringy strands of mucus as she lifted her head to shout "What?"

"Can I talk to you?" I said into the doorjamb.

I heard her blow her nose and the mattress squeak as she sat up and got off the bed. She unlocked the door, looked at me with red eyes and a slight frown, and headed straight back to her bed. She flopped down and stared at the ceiling, her hands behind her head. I sat in her desk chair and listened to Elton sing "Benny and the Jets."

"How's school?" I finally ventured. She had gone to school every day since Dad died. I took a whole week off and felt naked and ashamed my first day back.

"Fine," she said, her eyes never leaving the ceiling.

"Goodbye Yellow Brick Road" started to play. We listened to the whole song without saying a word. It felt good to sit there, listening to Elton sing. I scanned Amanda's room. The cork wall was lined with ribbons she had won at different horse shows; there were two red plastic milk crates filled with records; and George, the Steiff teddy bear Dad got her when she was born, was lying next to her on the bed. He was wearing one of Dad's black bow ties and had concert pins stuck to his furry chest. Above Amanda's bed, there was a window that looked out onto our yard. The swing set with its monkey bars and seesaw looked so still and sad, as did our pool, empty except for the carpet of decomposed leaves that had collected over winter. Cleaning the pool and getting it ready for summer was Dad's favorite task. He would shovel out the leaves, then power-wash the pale blue walls, patching any cracks or holes, before filling the pool with the garden hose, a process that took several days. Then he would add chlorine, big tablets like aspirin for monsters, which came in an oversized plastic bucket. He'd throw a few in, wait a day or two, then test the water using a special kit, dipping plastic tubes into the deep end and then adding different liquids from tiny droppers. We were not allowed in until the pH balance was just so.

"I wish it was Mom," I suddenly blurted out.

For the first time since I had entered the room, Amanda looked right at me startled. "Me, too," she said quietly.

It was the first time in our lives we had ever agreed on anything.

AMANDA

TWO WEEKS AFTER Dad died, his business partner went missing. He was the vice president of Dad's oil company and had given a heartfelt eulogy at the funeral. He even broke down in the middle of it, sobbing. Then the motherfucker showed up at our house a week later and told Mom that Dad's company was in trouble and that he needed fifty thousand dollars to get the company back on its feet. She gave it to him, he took off, and the company went bankrupt.

Soon after, the same people who sent condolence cards started calling Mom, demanding money. Dad's investors somehow held Mom accountable for the company's failure. Even Uncle Buzz, her own brother, asked for his twenty-five-thousand-dollar investment back. That really pissed me off, because Uncle Buzz was such a cheapskate. I always hated that guy. When I was fourteen, Dad, Liz, Dan, and I went to the Grand Canyon with him, and we hiked seven and a half miles to the bottom because Buzz said there was going to be this great steak dinner at this ranch at the end of the trail. When we arrived, they served us some disgusting Salisbury steak. Dad and I were expecting filet mignon the way Buzz talked about it. I could tell even Dad was pissed, and he hardly ever got mad. Then, on that same trip, we all went out to dinner with some of Buzz's friends in Flagstaff, Arizona. Buzz was being so petty about the bill—at Bob's fucking Big Boy!—Dad just paid for the whole thing himself. He didn't make a big deal out of it, but I noticed that Dad ended up paying for everything of Buzz's on that trip. Mom never saw any of this, though, because she stayed home with Diana, who was just a baby. Mom loved Buzz; he was her brother. So of course she gave him back his damn money.

Then the Bank of New York called. It turned out that Dad had taken out a loan for $250,000 six months before he died to buy an oil rig that he was going to use in Honduras. And he'd had Mom cosign for it. Suddenly, she was responsible.

Mom had no idea Dad's company was in such bad shape. No one did. He was good at hiding things. But there had been subtle signs. A few weeks before he died, I overheard him talking to his lawyer on the phone. He was like, "Wait a minute. Are you kidding me? How did we not know this? There has got to be a way to fix this." Something about the oil in Honduras belonging to the government and how he was not going to be able to drill after all. He was in the kitchen talking on the phone, and he had this tall glass in front of him. He had given up alcohol for New Year's, so I assumed it was Fresca. When he wandered out into the hallway to talk out of earshot, I took a sip from his drink and wound up spitting it out all over the kitchen floor. It tasted like turpentine.

LIZ

OUR MOTHER WAS convinced Honduran hit men killed our father. She was sitting at the end of our long wooden kitchen table, leaning toward Amanda and me conspiratorially. We stared back, arms crossed and stone-faced.

"Two eyewitnesses," she said breathlessly, "told police they saw a car sitting in the middle of the highway with its lights off." She grabbed hold of the table's edge with both hands and leaned in closer. "Your father came upon the idle car and swerved before bashing through the highway median and into an abandoned car on the opposite side of the road."

"That explains why Dad was heading north instead of south?" Amanda asked. At least she was trying to follow Mom's logic. I was completely lost.

"Or was killed," Mom replied, her voice deep and dramatic. She continued the story in a throaty whisper as if someone might have been listening, hiding in the rhododendron bushes just beyond the breakfast-room windows. "One eyewitness told the police that the car was filled with four Hispanic men," she went on. "After your father crashed, the idle car sped off into the night."

This theory was in stark contrast to our father's obituary, which had run in the local paper only a week before. According to *The Patent Trader*, Dad had fallen asleep at the wheel and smashed into an abandoned car on the other side of the road.

On the actual day of Dad's funeral, however, there were other rumors.

"Wasn't he in terrible debt?" a blond woman in a black velvet headband asked another woman in a black cashmere twinset. They were standing at our kitchen table, picking at a platter of cold cuts when I came up behind them.

"I heard his company was near bankruptcy," the twinset lady said before spotting me and quickly changing the conversation.

That happened more than once. People would be speaking in hushed tones, chins pinned to their chests, eyes nervously darting from right to left. The word "suicide" was never actually spoken, but the notion sucked any oxygen from an already claustrophobic room. Time and time again, I heard "poor Ann" and "those poor kids."

The Honduran story was better than falling asleep at the wheel, certainly better than suicide, and it made some sense, considering Dad's mysterious work. He called himself an entrepreneur. At thirteen, I had no idea what that meant. I knew that he had been to Honduras several times, and that every time he came back he brought us presents. We'd all gather around him in our parents' bedroom, wiggling like puppies waiting to be fed. He'd plop his suitcase on the king-size bed and unzip it slowly, then pretend that the zipper was stuck or that he had forgotten to get us anything. But we knew he had something special for each of us inside. Then, with the dramatic flair of a magician, he'd pull one present out at a time, handing each of us a gift with a smile and a wink. On his last trip to Honduras, only two months before he died, he had given Dan a small wooden carved Inca statue, Amanda a leather bracelet, Diana a small doll with black braids, and me a carved wooden jewelry box lined with red velvet. I still have that box.

We also got stories. Dad had loads of them. Usually they were funny, about strange food or trying to pronounce the name of the capital city— Teg-u-ci-gal-pa—and always getting it wrong. But this time his stories were scary.

"There's gunfire in the streets," he said that night at the dinner table. "It's mayhem." He had hired a bodyguard. Someone had tried to shoot him on his way to the airport. It was dangerous, and that night he told us all that he did not look forward to going back. He never did.

While I was sitting at the kitchen table several weeks after Dad's death, Mom's theory tumbled through my brain as Amanda tried to connect the dots out loud: "Did the Hondurans not want Dad to take their oil?" "Did he ever find any oil?" "Why on earth would anyone want to kill him?" Then Mom dropped another bomb.

"Girls," her voice dropping to an even quieter whisper. "Your father worked for the CIA."

"The CIA?" I repeated, flabbergasted.

"Shhh. You mustn't tell anyone," she continued. "It's top secret." Diana wandered in, hungry for a snack. Mom looked at us and pressed her finger to her lips and opened her eyes wide. We never spoke about it again.

DAN

THIS WAS WHAT I took as fact: There was a car parked on the highway, and Dad was speeding. He didn't see it until it was too late. But then there was the rumor that he was assassinated, something to do with the rebels in Honduras. Supposedly there was oil down there that would set us up for life. That's what Dad told me. There were rumors that the Honduran government seized his oil well after a huge strike. Then there was a rumor that he was supplying guns and technical support to the guerrillas in El Salvador. I didn't know what to believe. I still don't.

But this one afternoon, I was running errands with Dad when a car slammed on its brakes right in front of us. Dad grabbed me, swerved, and sped off, tires screeching. He seemed scared, and when I asked him what was going on, he said that just as the car stopped in front of us, another car was speeding up behind us, like a trap or something. That happened right before he died.

After Dad died, I found this box in the attic that kind of looked like a tackle box, but from the World War II era. There was an old gas mask inside it. I was looking for evidence that Dad was a spy, and I convinced myself that this box was his Morse code–type telegram machine. I kept it for years and played with it when no one else was around.

AMANDA

I'M SURE IT was one of Dad's crazy siblings who started the assassination stories. And the suicide rumors that ran through the Bedford Golf and Tennis Club crowd? Those people didn't know us, and they certainly didn't care about us. They just liked a bit of good gossip. Dad never really fit in with that crowd anyway; he always seemed more comfortable joking with the caddies and the staff than socializing with the actual club members. Mom was the reason we went to that club in the first place. She loved to play golf and was really good at it. Her name is engraved in gold letters on some plaques that still hang in the clubhouse. She was ladies' club champion in 1975, 1978, and 1980.

I hated that club. When I was younger, Mom and Dad made me go, but by the time I was a teenager, I refused to spend all day sitting by a pool with preppy assholes. But I do remember going to one dinner several summers before Dad died. Something pissed Dad off, and he threw his napkin down and stormed out of there. I think Dad hadn't paid his dues that summer, and the manager pulled him aside and asked him to pay or leave. So we left.

Screw them. It was a car accident. End of story.

LIZ

ONE AFTERNOON, MOM called Amanda and me back to the breakfast table. "Girls," she said in a deep and dramatic voice. "I have something to tell you."

Amanda and I slouched in our seats, wondering what on earth it could be now. I doubted anything could shock me. It was late May; Dad had been dead for one month exactly. I had finally wrapped my head around the notion that he was not going to drive up the driveway, that his seat, at the opposite end of the breakfast-room table from where Mom sat now, would remain empty, and that the pool probably wouldn't get cleaned out and filled that summer. Dad may have been a CIA agent, he may even have been killed while doing secret work for the government, but that did not change the fact that he was never coming home. But I didn't expect what came next.

"I have cancer," Mom said.

"What?" Amanda seemed to spit the word rather than say it.

What happened next is fuzzy, but I think Mom said that the tumor was the size of a grapefruit. She also said it was in her uterus. I'd just taken health class the year before, so I understood what that was. It was the fruit analogy that bothered me the most. A grapefruit? I had only just gotten my period that spring and was still uncomfortable with the size of a tampon. Plus, we were sitting at a table where we had eaten many grapefruits, a family breakfast staple. We even had special spoons with serrated edges that doubled as short knives to carve out the sections once the fruit had been sliced in two.

"A grapefruit?" I asked.

Perhaps the phone rang, or Diana came home from school, but I remember Mom getting up, leaving Amanda and me sitting there stunned.

Our mother was healthy, or so she had always seemed. She never smoked and rarely drank. She played golf and mowed the lawn and rode horses. She even owned a juice machine and made us all drink celery-carrot-apple-and-beet cocktails, claiming they were "good for us" as we held our noses and gagged down the pulpy purple swag.

"Could it be chocolate?" I wondered aloud.

Amanda squinted her eyes and thought hard before agreeing, "Well, it's her only vice."

It was true; our mother was a self-confessed chocoholic. She claimed hot fudge sundaes were the reason she put seventy pounds on her five-foot-nine-inch frame while pregnant with Amanda, topping the scale at two hundred pounds. Snickers were to blame for the ninety pounds she gained with me, and it was a family debate as to whether or not they had in any way contributed to the fact I weighed eleven pounds at birth, so fat that Dad's first words upon seeing me were "When will the swelling stop?"

Our mother's affair with chocolate always resurfaced when she was between jobs. She'd go on binges, eating not one but six chocolate-glazed donuts without shame. She loved devil's food cakes and could eat whole bags of Hershey's Kisses in one sitting. It was a catch-22: She'd get depressed that she had to be thin for work, which made her want to eat, and then the more she ate, the more fleshy and dimpled her thighs and upper arms became. Then her chin would grow a twin, and she'd dread going to auditions. In 1981, after Margo was killed off *The Edge of Night,* Mom put on twenty pounds. She was still trying to lose the extra weight when Dad died. She had tried every kind of diet—Scarsdale in 1976, juice-fasting the summer of 1978, and that horrid Shaklee diet that she and Amanda did in the fall of 1981.

During these diets, she banished all things sweet from our house. Even raisin bran was contraband. I blame the authors of *Sugar Blues.* She read it when it first came out in the early seventies, and I can still feel the burn of humiliation from when Mom brought whole-wheat cupcakes sweetened with apple juice into school for my eighth birthday. Natalie Brown took one bite, made a face, and spit it out into her hand. It was bad enough I was being punished, but my entire second-grade class? If sugar was as bad as Mom claimed, it certainly could have caused her cancer. Maybe it was the reason that only one month after Dad died, she was scheduled to go for a radical hysterectomy.

She explained the procedure to Amanda and me a few days later. "They will take out my uterus. Not that I need it anymore!" She was trying to sound upbeat, but to me it just sounded awful.

The only person I knew who had cancer was Mom's acting friend Diana Hyland. She was the original mom on *Eight Is Enough*, and she dated John Travolta after playing his mom on *The Boy in the Plastic Bubble*. Mom named our Diana after her. Cancer had killed Diana Hyland. Could it kill Mom? After days of stomach-sick worry, I decided, No, it couldn't. If it did, then we'd be orphans. And that wasn't possible.

AMANDA

ACTUALLY, MOM HAD cervical cancer and the tumor was only three centimeters wide, the size of a quarter. The grapefruit-size tumor came later.

DIANA

THERE IS A dream I remember from when I was little. In it, Mom and I were walking together in the desert, over rolling yellow hills with green scrubby shrubs and black scorpions. The sun was hot and gold, and my sneakers hit the sand hard when we started running toward a rusty red and white swing set, its two wooden swings hanging perfectly still. I was good at swinging. I jumped on and started pumping my legs back and forth until I was soaring. I liked to go so high that the chains coughed, losing their tension for a second when my face was even with the sky. I turned to see how high Mom was, but she was just sitting, her swing twisting gently, her shoulders slumped.

In the distance, I saw a figure walking toward us. It was a big beast-man, a warrior. Mom didn't see him; she was looking at her shearling slippers in the sand. Her head was getting sunburned because her hair was so thin. I could see her scalp. It was turning pink and some skin was flaking off. The beast-man was closer now, beefy and veiny in his leather skirt and wide metal suspenders. He reminded me of *Clan of the Cave Bear* and *Conan the Barbarian*. Mom stood to meet him, pulling her shawl tight around her shoulders and holding it there with one hand at her throat as her other hand reached for a sword within its folds. She raised the sword above her head, her eyes still on the ground. The warrior walked toward us, and Mom took two steps toward him, bringing her other hand up to hold the sword above her head as her shawl fell to the sand by the swing set. Her sword seemed so heavy.

There were rocks all around. I jumped off the swing and picked one up. I was going to hit the warrior in the head, but Mom brought her sword down on his head hard and pulled the blade toward her slowly, leaving a thin line of bubbling blood along his crown. His hair was animal-like, tiny clumps of curly wire on a greasy scalp that was dark and bumpy. He took a blade from his leather skirt and raised it above his head, grunting. Mom lowered her head as he brought his blade down, cracking her skull open. He grunted and walked away. She fell to her knees, hands in the sand. Her head was a quartered cantaloupe. I saw the rind of her skull and the melon of her brain and the seeds in the middle. I put my cheek on her bony back, and I felt her sobs moving her shoulder blades together and apart. We stayed like that until she got up, picked up her shawl and we began to walk.

LIZ

MOM WAS SITTING upright in the hospital bed, wrapped in the white Christian Dior silk robe Dad gave her when Diana was born. I'd always loved that robe. It was decorated with purple irises with long green stems— Mom's favorite flower and mine too, to this day. It was early June and the window in her private room was open, letting in fresh air. Despite having had a radical hysterectomy, Mom was in remarkably fine form. Her lips were firm and upturned, her eyes sparkled bright, and her chin jutted out in defiance as she cracked jokes about kicking this cancer in the rear end.

"Eviction time is here," she said, raising her fist triumphantly. "Screw squatters' rights, pack your bags, and go!" For the first time since Dad died, she seemed hopeful, even happy.

She was staying in the hospital for a few days to let the scar heal. The crooked rag-doll's mouth across her belly made it hurt to laugh, but with Dan around, it was impossible not to. He was a joker like Dad and would do anything for a laugh. He had just formed a break-dance crew with two friends and wanted to show Mom his latest moves. He was a "popper." This meant he could make his arms look like a liquid stream, beginning at one end of his finger tips, popping at his elbow, bubbling up through his neck and then down the other arm, another elbow pop down to his fingers, which ended with a wrist flick. He performed for us while rapping "Roxanne Roxanne" by UTFO. For the line that went, "Yo, Kangol, I don't think you're dense, but you went about the matter with no experience," he moonwalked in his army pants across the hospital room floor. For the line "You should know, she doesn't need a guy like you, she needs a guy like me with a high IQ," he did the Robot, jerking his skinny upper body from one side to the other, and bent his arms upright like a soccer referee calling a goal, ending with both pointer fingers aimed at his red French legionnaire cap, part of his crew's outfit. It had black felt letters in a medieval font that read "Danny D." We all were cheering him on, laughing. Amanda was doubled over, holding on to the bed railing as she guffawed, Diana was lying next to Mom on the bed, hugging her belly, her eyes magnified, happy slits beneath her pale pink glasses. Mom was laughing so hard she snorted, which made us all laugh even harder. We laughed and laughed—tears streaming down our faces.

Then Mom screamed, "Ouch!"

She had popped a stitch. And as awful as it was, we kept laughing. We had to. It was the first time we had all laughed like that in over two months, and it felt too good to stop.

DAN

THAT SUMMER MOM got sick, I had just graduated from elementary school. It was right across the street from our house, so me and my crew—Curtis, Jeremy, and Sean—would walk over there and go straight to the roof. There was always a stray ball that someone had kicked up there during recess, and we'd use it to play basketball, kickball, whatever. Or sometimes we'd hit our fists against this brick wall to see who was toughest. The bricks were concrete with this coarse sand that would rub off like the salt from a pretzel. My knuckles would be bleeding, but I would not stop hitting the wall. It was cool. I was always the toughest.

Curtis was my best friend. He lived with his mom in a low-income apartment complex in Mount Kisco. It was like we came from two different worlds. The differences really hit me that summer when I invited him to the Bedford Golf and Tennis Club to play tennis. I walked onto the court, bouncing the ball and talking shit. When I turned around, I saw that Curtis hadn't set foot on the court. He was just standing there, and his eyes began to well up with tears. He was looking at a sign that said WHITES ONLY. He thought it meant black people weren't allowed. Even though I felt so bad, I just laughed it off and explained that the sign referred to clothes. But I hated the club from then on. Later, I heard that the club, the Bedford Golf and *Tennis* Club, wouldn't even let Arthur Ashe join.

One evening, this kid Kenny, Curtis, and I were walking back to Curtis's house from the Bazaar Mall, and this Puerto Rican gang of older kids drove by and almost hit us. The car stopped. Kenny backed off, but Curtis and I stood our ground. One of the Puerto Rican kids rolled down his window and was like, "Give me your jacket." Curtis said no. We stood there, glaring at them, and they drove off. That night, I learned that you have to stand your ground with things like that. You have to be tough and stand your ground.

LIZ

MOM CAME HOME from the hospital with a bandage on her belly and a mission: to find Dan a male role model.

"He's surrounded by women!" she declared one June morning, sitting up in her bed as if she had just realized yet another tragic impact of Dad's death. The bills that lay in messy piles scattered on her blue chenille bedspread were one; the crooked scar that underlined her belly button was yet another. Although she could do little about the unpaid bills or her missing uterus or her dead husband, she could find a man to kick a soccer ball with her eleven-year-old boy. That seemed doable.

But it just added to the cast of characters who constantly streamed in and out of our house that summer, "friends" I'd never heard of or seen before Dad died. They appeared in droves, locusts buzzing up our long driveway bearing casseroles and furrowed brows. In a way, I think our sad story soothed them, made them feel better about their own lives. Every time a new stranger appeared in our kitchen and embraced me, each time I saw the same tense-eyed and tight-lipped expression, I couldn't help but think: You don't know me. You could not possibly care as much as you are pretending to.

Duncan showed up that summer with an altogether different expression. He was the son of a friend of Mom's, another instant friend. Since Mom thought it would be nice for Dan to have another man around the property, Duncan was welcomed with great enthusiasm. He was twenty-eight, with long wavy dark hair, chiseled features, and intense dark brown eyes set deep into his skull. He wore dirty jeans and slip-on leather boots despite the summer heat. He lived in Greenwich Village and started showing up on Saturday mornings with his guitar and always a knapsack full of records. Every weekend, he would bring a new assortment to play. Amanda was in awe. Instead of Supertramp or Elton John, Jimi Hendrix and Cream wafted down the stairs from her room. She made a mix tape that started with Janis Joplin singing "Mercedes Benz" and played it loud in the tape deck of her car, Dad's Mercedes.

I spent most of that summer listening to music too, either up in Amanda's room with her and Duncan or downstairs in the living room with Liz Subin. Liz was my best friend. She was my twin in reverse—she had jet-black hair and olive skin. And she was Jewish, which as far as I could gather meant no presents on Christmas or jelly beans on Easter. Being Jewish sucked. Her parents called us Liz One and Liz Two, like Thing One and Thing Two from *Cat in the Hat*, only we never got into any trouble.

Liz often spent weekends at my house, where we'd pick fat blueberries from the row of bushes that lined our side lawn and make blueberry pies or muffins or pancakes. On weekdays, we'd spend afternoons playing a game of tennis or hitting a bucket of golf balls at the Bedford Golf and Tennis Club. I would have much rather rented a golf cart to play nine holes, but Mom said we couldn't afford that anymore. She even closed our account at the pool snack bar. That would have put me off going to the pool altogether, if it were not for the new lifeguard, a cute high school senior.

Brad had broad shoulders, narrow hips, and short brown hair golden-tipped from the sun. He was the reason I showed up for swim-team practice every morning and afternoon that summer. I'd swim a hundred laps at eight in the morning, then again in the afternoon. He was also the reason I signed up for swim clinics. I didn't need much help with my strokes—I had records in butterfly and freestyle—but I pretended my flip turns needed help. I struggled with them on purpose, hoping Brad might place a hand on either side of my hips to show me how they should turn.

The afternoons Liz and I were not at the club we'd be at my house, lying on the living room floor listening to the Doors. We'd spend hours dutifully inking the Doors logo on the soles of our Tretorn sneakers, our forearms, and our inner thighs. That summer, I had two crushes, Jim Morrison and Brad. And Amanda had one. It was Duncan. She talked about him all the time: "Duncan gave me his Cream album." "Duncan is going to take me to the city." Duncan, Duncan, Duncan. And Duncan responded by spending most of the weekend sitting on her bedroom floor playing his guitar or his records, or helping Amanda in the barn. Summer passed, and no one seemed to notice that he never once kicked a soccer ball with Dan.

I started freshman year at Fox Lane High School that September. Amanda was a senior and I knew, without ever discussing it with her, that I was to avoid her at all costs. She thought my preppy friends, with their flipped-up collars and their penny loafers, were lame, and I was scared of her tough-looking smoking-lounge crew. Even if I passed her in the hallway, as I did every day on my way to my English class, which was right next to her locker, I knew to avert my eyes, to busy myself in a notebook or in a conversation with a friend.

But at home it was a different story—we had begun experimenting with RIT dye. Amanda and I raided Dad's closet, taking his old Hanes T-shirts, twisting and rubber-banding them into deformed snowballs, and then plunging them into Tupperware trays of purple or red dye. As our spider-web designs improved, we graduated to Dad's Brooks Brothers button-downs, his crisp tuxedo shirts, which Amanda wore into the city to go see concerts with friends. I wore mine with black leggings in my bedroom and danced by myself, Billy Idol blaring, my side ponytail whipping my cheeks as I practiced moves I'd seen on MTV.

That same fall, Amanda's colt, Bartholomew, was scheduled for castration. Amanda was nervous, worried that the surgery would be painful. Bartholomew was still so young, knobby-kneed, and skittish. He had been born in May just weeks after Dad died. He was a small, skinny version of his mom, Berry, with a toast-colored coat, black mane and tail. When Amanda told me that Duncan wanted to be there during the procedure, I thought it was nice. I certainly wasn't going to volunteer to watch her pet's balls get chopped off. Just the thought made me woozy.

The next afternoon, as I was reaching into the kitchen freezer for a tub of Breyer's mint chocolate chip ice cream, I saw a Ziploc bag containing two bloody hunks of meat. I pulled out the package.

"What's this?" I asked Duncan and Amanda, who were sitting in the kitchen.

Amanda repressed a smile, shrugged her shoulders, and said, "Ask Duncan."

I thought it was a prank. I think Amanda did too. Then, in a very matter-of-fact way, Duncan said, "They're Bartholomew's balls."

Once he said those words—Bartholomew's balls—I could see that it was true. Veins ran through the grayish purple rounds of frozen flesh. I shrieked and dropped the bloody bag back on top of the frozen peas and spinach.

"Why are they in our freezer?" I asked. Amanda's contorted smile exploded into a full-on belly laugh. So they *were* playing a joke on me, I thought.

"Because I am going to eat them," Duncan said.

Amanda stopped mid-"Ha" as if the second "Ha" got stuck in her throat. "Eat them?" she asked, her face going from good humor to horror in a split second.

"They are a delicacy," he explained calmly. "Sometimes called Rocky Mountain oysters, they're good for virility."

I had my back to him, but I could feel his eyes. I had felt the gaze before but had brushed it off or made up an excuse for it. This time it was direct and impossible to ignore—partly because of the way he said "virility," all smooth and creepy, and partly because of the silence that stemmed from Amanda's realization that this man she had a crush on wanted to eat her pet's balls.

"That's gross" was all I could muster.

"You slice them into thin pieces and sauté them," he was saying to a silent Amanda as I left the room, not fast enough. I felt sick to my stomach and wasn't sure if it was the balls or just him.

Several weeks later, Amanda and I went grocery shopping, and Duncan came along. We whizzed through the aisles, picking up things on Mom's list—tuna fish and brown rice—and things that were not—ice cream and Oreos, perks of having a distracted mother.

As we waited in the checkout line, Amanda remembered milk.

"I'll be right back," she said and took off before I could say "I'll get it," which would have been code for "Please don't leave me alone with him."

I watched her run, in her tie-dyed Levi's jeans and her Pop Rocks T-shirt, her Converse low-tops squeaking as she ran past the deli and racks of Hostess cakes and Thomas' English muffins. She hooked a left and disappeared down the dairy aisle. As soon as she was gone, I felt his eyes.

I was in the middle of a busy grocery store. A woman was unloading a full cart of groceries onto the moving belt two feet in front of me, yet I felt totally alone with this man I did not trust and did not like. I took a step away from him and toward a nearby magazine rack to look at Kim Alexis on the cover of a magazine. She was so pretty. Ever since I had done the Macy's catalogue, I'd become obsessed with supermodels. Everyone in the eighth grade at Fox Lane saw it and thought it was so cool, and I even got to take home the clothes I wore for the shoot. I wanted to do more modeling, maybe even be a model when I got older. As I was scanning the racks and fantasizing about being on the cover of *Seventeen* one day, Duncan took a step toward me and pointed at Paulina Porizkova on the cover of *Modern Bride*.

"One day, you'll be in *Modern Bride*," he said.

I froze. Then he added, "One day, you'll be my bride."

The hair on my neck hupped to attention. Goose bumps covered my body as if trying to provide a protective layer between him and me. I felt queasy and faint. I knew I should say something. I should turn around and say, "Never, no way. I hate you. I hate you. I *hate* you."

But then Amanda appeared, flushed from running. She was carrying a gallon of milk and smiling. And the lady in front of us had paid. It was time to unload our groceries onto the belt.

Back home, I was standing in the pantry, placing boxes of raisin bran and Wheat Thins and tins of tuna on the shelves but really just dawdling. Amanda had gone out to feed the horses, a chore Duncan usually helped her with. But this time he said he was going to help me with the groceries. I told him it wasn't necessary, and Amanda shrugged and walked out the door. Mom was upstairs in her bedroom—even though her cancer was in remission, she still spent an awful lot of time in bed.

We were alone again, me in the pantry and Duncan just outside the door, sitting on the counter and kicking the kitchen cabinets softly. I could hear the thuds over my racing heart. And then he said, "Liz, I have a secret."

My body froze up. I did not answer, hoping he would simply disappear. Instead he said, "I dream about you. I dream about you at night, every night." I said nothing. I closed my eyes and wished for a machine like the one on *Star Trek* so I could beam him somewhere far, far away. Then he said, "I love you."

The only man who had ever said those words to me before was Dad, and he said them in a different way entirely. Duncan's words made me feel sick, so sick I thought the wave of nausea boiling up in my stomach would swallow me whole and drag me out to some sloshy, dark sea.

I kept silent and he stopped kicking the cabinets. The only sound was my heart pounding hard and fast, so loud I was sure he could hear it, and I hoped he would understand its Morse code, telling him, "You scare me." Perhaps he did, because he quickly added,

"But you mustn't tell your mom. She wouldn't understand. She would make me leave. It has to be our secret."

I heard the kitchen screen door squeak open and then someone's foot-steps, and I felt safe enough to get out of the closet without having to look at him. I ran upstairs. Mom was in bed, surrounded by piles of paper-work. She looked tired, but when she saw me in the doorway and sensed I was upset, she patted the rumpled sheets beside her. I plopped myself down, fighting back tears. My heart was still on fast-forward as I told her what Duncan said. Every last word. Then I looked in her face. It was pale and her bottom lip started to tremble. Her eyes grew moist before she grabbed hold of me and hugged me tight and said, "I'm so sorry, I'm so sorry, I'm so sorry." She told me to wait right there, and I did. She got out of bed, pulled on her robe, and marched downstairs, and I never saw Duncan again.

Later that evening, I was reading in my bed when Amanda popped her head through my doorway. This was it, I thought. She would hate me for-ever. "Can we talk?" she asked rather gruffly. I patted my mattress as Mom had done only hours before. Amanda sat down next to me, the look on her face teetered between anger and utter disappointment.

"What a jerk," she said

I wanted to throw my arms around her and squeeze her tight and tell her how much I loved her. But instead, I played it cool, shrugged my shoulders, and said, "I know, right?"

AMANDA

I DID HAVE a crush on Duncan, so I was disappointed that he turned out to be such a creep. I even spent the night with him at his apartment in the West Village, but he never got weird with me. I was too old for him, I guess. After Mom kicked him out, I never heard from him again, which was good.

That whole castration thing really messed with me. Up until that moment, my plan was to become a veterinarian. I applied to Cornell, Tufts, U-Penn, and Wesleyan for their pre-vet programs, and I was sure I'd get into at least one of them; I was thirteenth in my class and had a 91 percent average. But when I saw the blood dripping out of Bartholomew's empty ball sack, I was like, there is no way could I do this for a living.

That fall, Mom gave away Precious Little, her favorite horse. At that point, we had only Berry and Bartholomew and Pony, and we rented the empty stalls out to boarding horses. Mom was downsizing. She decided to sell the seven acres with the house, pool, and pool house but keep the remaining seven acres with the caretaker's cottage and the barn. We'd build a brand-new house there from scratch. Mom said she wanted to move because the house held too many memories and felt too big and lonely without Dad, but I knew the truth. We were broke, totally broke. After Mom tallied it up, she realized that Dad had left us $1.2 million in debt.

Mom told me that, although she hadn't known it at the time, Dad had been struggling for a while. I guess he really thought the deal in Honduras would solve all his problems, but when that fell through, we were completely fucked.

Dad had taken out a five-hundred-thousand-dollar life insurance policy right before he left for Myrtle Beach, filled out all the paperwork, and left it for his secretary to send off. The insurance company had cashed the check but then claimed that the policy had not been "certified" or some bullshit. Mom tried to fight it, but her lawyer warned that the insurance company would take us to court and would play hardball. She told me they would put people on the stand to question Dad's drinking. He'd already had two DWIs, and Aunt Barbara said he'd had a couple of martinis before he left her house in Hanover the night he died. Mom said that the insurance company was going to say that he was drunk or, worse, that he had committed suicide. And she said that they were going to want to put us on the stand, too, the kids. She didn't want to put us through that. So she decided to let it go and sell the house.

That was the beginning of the end. We never even celebrated another holiday in that house, and in our family, Christmas and Thanksgiving were always such a big deal. We'd dress up for Thanksgiving, after helping Mom, who would cook all day. For Christmas, we always went and picked out a live tree with Dad while Mom put electric candles in all the windows and hung our stockings from the fireplace mantel.

But that Thanksgiving, we flew to Portland, Oregon, and drove up the coast to bum-fuck nowhere to see Aunt Gail, Dad's youngest sister. We couldn't really afford the trip—I remember Mom complaining about how expensive the airfare was. But we were still rich compared to Aunt Gail. She and her two kids lived on welfare, but she told us it hurt her feelings that Mom sent her our hand-me-downs when she had her first kid. She said she'd expected Bergdorf Goodman the way Dad bragged about how well-off he was. Mom tried to explain that things had changed, and that Dad was not as well-off as Aunt Gail thought, but it was useless.

On that trip, for the first time, I saw my family in a new light. I saw how Liz took care of Diana, always holding her hand and watching out for her, making sure she was included. And I saw how Dan seemed lost, with this vacant look in his eyes. And Mom was just a mess. I saw that she was lost, too, without Dad.

For Christmas, Mom decided to take us to Disney World. All I remember is waking up on Christmas morning to presents under the fucking TV. Everything about it was horribly sad and depressing. We were in a dingy motel room where I had to share a bed with Liz. Diana slept with Mom, and Dan slept on a roll-away cot. I just couldn't understand why that was supposed to be better than being at home.

DIANA

THERE WERE GHOSTS in our house. Mom said she saw them, too, late at night while everyone else was asleep. She said I had ESP. Me and Dan both. She had weird people come to the house and look at our auras, and when they agreed that we were special, Mom looked so happy.

Dan said he didn't see ghosts like I did. He said that maybe his aura was different from mine. And he said he didn't think he had any special powers, but he liked it that Mom thought so.

"I have warts all over my hands," he told me one afternoon in Mom and Dad's room. He held out his hands, and there they were, nestled in the webbing between his fingers. The ones on the back of his hands blended in with his freckles, but if you looked close enough, you could see them, little snow-capped mountains, scaly and pink.

"And one on your face," I told him, and reached over to touch his upper lip with my finger. His face was covered in tiny leopard spots, like mine, and his lips were thin and curly, just like Dad's. His red hair was straight and cut into the shape of a bowl.

"Don't!" He flinched and jerked his head away, grabbing my wrist. "They're contagious." Then he started rubbing his warty hand all over my face, giggling as I squirmed. His grip was strong.

"Don't!" I yelled, panicking. "They're contagious!" His hands were clammy and smelled like sweat. Mom poked her head around the corner of her bathroom door. She was rubbing cream on her cheek.

"Daniel," she said softly. "Do not rub your warts all over your sister's face." Dan dropped my wrist. As I ran over to Mom, I turned to stick my tongue out at him, but he had already turned away. He was staring out the window with both hands in the pockets of his camouflage pants.

DAN

I DIDN'T HATE Mom, but I couldn't love her anymore, either. The cancer scared me to death, and the thought of losing her was too much for me to handle. But I did love her. Of course I did. I just lost respect for her for some reason. She seemed so pathetic. One day, she came to pick me up at the Bazaar Mall in Mount Kisco. I had been playing PacMan there all day, and she had to drag me out. When we were leaving, there were four or five pennies lying on the pavement in the parking lot. She bent down to pick them up.

"Don't pick that up!" I said, embarrassed. "It's like you're a bum!"

She was quiet from that point on. I had hurt her feelings, and I couldn't say I was sorry. I knew I should apologize. I felt horrible, but I couldn't do it.

DIANA

I ALMOST GAVE Mom a heart attack. It happened when I was walking home from my new school, West Patent Elementary. It was different from my old school, Rippowam Cisqua, because you didn't have to wear a uniform and there were more kids.

Every afternoon, Mr. Tagliano, the gym teacher, organized the bus lines in the atrium, blowing his whistle and shouting out names alphabetically. I loved Mr. Tagliano because he looked like the Fonz, and I liked it that his nickname was Mr. T, who was on my lunchbox. So when Mr. T shouted "Welch, Diana!" I happily gathered up my Snoopy pencil bag and coat and rose from my spot in a clump of first graders on the floor. I had a note in my pocket from Mom saying that it was okay for me to walk home from school on my own, which I presented to Mr. T, who waggled his eyebrows at me and told me not to get lost.

I made my sneakers squeak on purpose, twisting them on the white linoleum tile as I left all those bus-riding babies behind. Once outside, I tried to twist and squeak my sneakers some more, but the smooth pavement just rubbed my soles like crumbly erasers. As I hung a right to crunch down the gravelly edge of West Patent Road, there was Mom, at the end of our driveway, waiting for me. When she saw me turn the corner, she straightened up and started waving and smiling. The sun was shining on her and on the leaves on the trees above her head. Excited, I waved back and picked up my pace and hooked my thumbs up under my backpack's straps near my shoulders to hoist it up a little. It was starting to feel heavy, full of my new textbooks that we had spent the morning in homeroom covering with brown paper grocery bags. I had drawn some balloons on mine. I was going to have homework, like Dan and Liz, also a first, also grown-up. So I began to yell to Mom that I was going to have homework, and her arms began moving in big, frantic waves, and I thought, "Wow, she's really excited to see me!" And it felt great. Then, when I started to cross the street, Mom started screaming, and then—*whoosh!*—a big yellow school bus flew between us, its current knocking me back a step or two.

After the bus had passed, Mom was still yelling and crying, her eyes wildly searching up and down the road in the directions from which the bus had come and gone. Finally, she waved me over to her and clutched me to her legs, then crumpled to the ground, squeezing and rocking me and saying "Oh, God, oh, God" over and over. After we had made the long, sobbing walk up the driveway and were back in our kitchen, Mom got on the phone to my school. As I sat on the counter banging my legs against the cabinet and eating boysenberry yogurt, she clutched the receiver with two veined hands and yelled, "She could have been killed!"

Now every afternoon I had to take the bus home from school, like everybody else, only it was a stupid, short ride. And every time, as I prepared to take the giant steps down from the bus to the asphalt, the bus driver, a nice old guy with milky blue eyes, warned me to look both ways. I did.

LIZ

IT WAS SUDDEN. One day, late that winter, Mom got out of bed, got dressed, and decided to take charge of things. She went from depleted to energetic, as if she were coming out of a grief-induced hibernation. She started going to the city looking for work in earnest and was thrilled when she booked a commercial for Brim decaffeinated coffee. Her line was "Fill it to the rim, with Brim." She had practiced it the morning of the shoot in our kitchen as she filled her coffee cup, experimenting with different intonations. She finally settled on "Fill it to the rim" in a high, cheerful pitch, followed by "with Brim," deep in her throat and low as if she was in on a secret. Satisfied, she smiled at me, and it was a real smile, the first I'd seen in months. But that was only the start of her good news. When she learned she'd been cast as June Slater on *Loving*, a brand-new soap opera, she could not stop smiling. She was thrilled! A full-time job, back on TV! We celebrated like it was New Year's Eve: Mom made prime rib and Yorkshire pudding, everyone's favorite, and strawberry shortcake for dessert.

Things were going well for me at school, too. I made the junior varsity volleyball team and had lots of friends, which made it a bit less painful to be totally ignored by Amanda. She still wouldn't even look at me at school. I doubted anyone, other than my close friends, knew we were sisters. She even refused to drive me there, forcing me to take the bus.

One sunny afternoon, I walked up the driveway and saw the Mercedes parked in front of the garage. Before I opened the kitchen door, I could hear David Johansen's raspy voice singing the Animals cover "We Gotta Get out of This Place." Then Amanda shouted my name from the den. I popped my head into the den and saw her sitting on the couch with Anna, her best friend. Anna lived across the street and had blond frizzy hair that she wore big, like an Afro. She was big, too. Nearly six feet tall, she could pick me up and twirl me around like a baton, which she did, once.

They were both smiling at me in a conspiring way. I looked at the TV and saw David Johansen prancing around, chest and chin thrust out, wearing only a vest, no shirt, with skinny striped pants and high-top Nike sneakers. Amanda had taped last week's *Saturday Night Live*. She loved David Johansen the way I loved Jim Morrison, but after watching that video for the twentieth time, I was starting to fall in love, too.

"We need your help," Amanda said with a mischievous smile.

"Yeah, come here," Anna instructed, suppressing a cackle and sliding over to make room on the couch.

Hoping to not get twirled like a baton I sat between them. Amanda pulled a small pipe from behind her back. "We're going to get you high," Amanda said.

"But you're not going to actually smoke or anything," Anna chimed in. "That would be irresponsible." They both laughed as if that was the funniest thing either of them had ever heard. Then they made me pass the pipe between them as they each took long drags, held their breath, and then exhaled into my face.

The kitchen door opened and closed, and a little voice shouted "Hello!" Diana was home from school. I jumped up to fix her a snack. She wanted peanut butter in celery, her favorite after-school treat. As she munched away, sitting at the breakfast-room table, I realized that I was hungry, too.

I knew there was a roast chicken in the fridge because I had made it the night before. Mom worked most afternoons and left Amanda and me in charge of things. I babysat Diana and cooked everyone dinner and helped Amanda with the grocery shopping. I ate a cold chicken leg, but that wasn't enough. I searched through the food closet and pulled out a package of Oreos and then got the Cracker Barrel cheddar cheese from the fridge. I pried apart the chocolate wafers, scraped the sweet white cream off with my teeth, and replaced it with a slice of cheese. I thought I'd discovered the best new snack and brought a plate of them into the den. Amanda teased me about how absolutely revolting it was but ate them anyway. Sitting there, surrounded by smoke and Amanda and Anna's laughter and David Johansen singing, I was happy.

Then Amanda invited me to go with her to see David Johansen play at the Ritz that weekend. The pot had been an initiation. I passed, and Amanda decided without telling me that she was going to mentor me in the ways of pop culture and New York City and rock and roll. It was 1983. I had just turned fourteen, and I was game.

But when Amanda suggested I wear her orangey brown suede Frye cowboy boots, I was suspicious. "Are you sure?" I asked. They were her favorite. This must be a test. We were up in her room, getting ready for our evening out. Amanda was sitting at her desk, using a handheld mirror to apply eyeliner to her lower lids, extending the line beyond her eye for an Egyptian effect. She was already wearing her black leather pants, having squeezed into them only moments before. She looked like a rock star. "I mean, what are you going to wear?" I asked tentatively.

"My ankle boots," she said, flashing her eyes to the short slip-on black leather boots in the corner. "My cowboy boots will look cool with those jeans." I could tell she was sincere.

I slipped them on, tucking my pants inside so you could see the fancy swirled stitching. I felt like a rock star, too.

That night, Amanda, Anna, and I piled into the Jeep Wagoneer. First, we went to Times Square for fake IDs. The bright lights and seedy people scared me, but I kept cool, quickening my pace to keep up with Amanda, focusing on her and not on the homeless man sitting cross-legged on the dirty pavement, or on the man in the shiny suit handing out flyers in front of a GIRLS! GIRLS! GIRLS! movie house, or on the woman in short shorts and a rabbit-fur coat sucking her teeth and looking bored standing on the street corner. Amanda turned into a brightly lit storefront. Inside, there was a wall of fake ID cards to choose from, and my eye went straight to a pretty pink one from the Manhattan College of Arts and Crafts. I pointed it out to the man behind the counter and gave him my birth date, February 3, but instead of 1969, I said 1964, which made me eighteen—old enough to get into the Ritz.

Amanda chose the same card. We realized this only after the cards were laminated. We decided it made sense that two sisters would go to the same college. But it didn't make sense to the bouncer at the Ritz, a big man with a handle-bar mustache and tattoos that crept above the neckline of his tight white T-shirt. When he asked for my ID and then for Amanda's, he examined both closely and called over to the other bouncer, "Get a load of this." Then he turned back to us and said, "You two sisters?"

"Yep," Amanda answered. I nodded.

"You go to the same school?" he asked.

"Yep," Amanda replied coolly, as if she had done this a million times before.

"Your mother in the *Guinness Book of World Records*?" he asked.

We stared back, confused, and then he pointed to our birth dates. If I was born in February 1964 and Amanda was born in August that same year, we were only six months apart. "So you're a premature Irish twin?" the bouncer asked Amanda, then threw his head back to laugh so hard I could see the tattoos on his neck skipping with each guffaw.

It was apparently so funny he let us in.

"What's an Irish twin?" I shouted above Billy Idol screaming "Rebel Yell" on the stereo system. The place was packed with people dressed in black with spiky hair, some wearing dog collars, others in wide-necked *Flashdance* sweatshirts with leggings, short boots, and glittery eye shadow.

Amanda shrugged and shouted, "Want a beer?"

I nodded and stood in the middle of the dance floor, turning slowly in my big sister's Frye boots, soaking it all in. The disco-ball lights poked holes through the smoky haze that hovered just above the sea of bobbing heads. Small packs of people hopped from one foot to the other, their shoulders and arms following in fluid motion, their shaggy haircuts bouncing with the beat, their big hoop earrings playing hopscotch on their shoulders.

"This is awesome!" I shouted at Amanda as she handed me a plastic cup full of flat Rolling Rock beer.

We found a spot close to the stage and put down our beers as the music quieted down and the lights above the stage came on, pinks and blues and yellows. The crowd surged forward, slamming Amanda and me against the stage. The drummer wandered out and took a seat behind his set. Then David Johansen came out. We lifted our chins toward the flashing lights, and there he was, so close we could see the frayed threads of his hand-cut sweat-shirt vest. His bow tie was pre-tied and attached to the silk ribbon around his neck, not hand-tied like the ones Dad wore. "Hello, New York!" he screamed, and we screamed back.

I began to really dance, fists pumping in the air, boots stomping and kicking, shoulders thrusting and shimmying. I bumped and slammed into strangers lost in their own worlds, some with eyes closed, others wide-eyed and ecstatic. I pounded the floor so hard I thought I'd bore a hole through the Ritz floor, and I was sad when David started bellowing, "Good night, New York!"

Then I remembered the rose I had bought for this moment. I had stuck it underneath the stage with my beer while I danced. I reached down to grab it and then thrust it up toward David in his top hat and tight leather pants. He grabbed my wrist instead, hoisting me onto the stage. He put the rose between his teeth and his sweaty arm around me as the crowd went wild, yowling and screaming and vibrating with applause. He spit out the rose and shouted, "I love you New York!" Then he turned and gave me a long, wet sloppy kiss that tasted like cigarette smoke and stale beer. It was my first kiss ever. It made the peck on the cheek from Brent Lupone in eighth grade insignificant. When he pulled away to take his bows with the band, I felt as if I was floating above the crowd. The noise grew loud. I snapped to attention and suddenly felt ridiculous. I scurried off the stage, nervous that Amanda would be pissed. She should have kissed David, not me, but instead of laying into me she threw her arms around me and screamed, "That was so cool! That was so cool! Oh my God! That was so cool!"

AMANDA

BETWEEN DAD'S DEATH, Mom's cancer, and our money problems, we completely forgot about the Chilean exchange student. I had signed up for him before Dad died, and when Mom got the letter announcing the date of his arrival, she freaked out. She said it was the last thing she needed. But I told her I'd take care of him, and, well, what could she do? His name was Andres, and he stayed with us for eight weeks, maybe not even that long.

His eighteenth birthday fell on the same weekend Mom went to play in a celebrity golf tournament in Florida. Now that she was back on TV, she thought the exposure would do her good, so she took Diana for the weekend and left me in charge. Before she left, I asked her if it would be okay if we threw Andres a surprise birthday party, and she said she thought that was a great idea. So I invited everyone at Fox Lane, bought a couple of kegs, and charged at the door.

LIZ

ONE AFTERNOON, AMANDA offered me a ride home. I was so excited I followed her to the senior parking lot practically skipping. "So I have an idea," she said once we were both in the car. "You know how Mom is going away this weekend? Well, it's Andres's birthday. I thought we should have a keg party."

"I love that idea!" I shouted and put my hand up for a high five. Amanda greeted it with an eye-roll. I felt badly for Andres. He probably expected sit-down dinners and Sunday church services when he signed up to come to Bedford. But Amanda made up for that by taking him to New York City nightclubs, teaching him important phrases like "What's up?" and schooling him in cool American music. He particularly liked Depeche Mode, the Psychedelic Furs, and Public Image Limited. A keg party was the next step in his American teen indoctrination.

"I'll get a couple kegs," Amanda said. "And you start spreading the word at school: Party at the Welches', Saturday night."

I got to work immediately. By Friday afternoon everyone at school knew. Our property was perfect for a keg party. High school parties usually got busted because of the long lines of cars clogging up cul-de-sacs, but our driveway and lawn alone had space for more than a hundred cars.

That Saturday afternoon, Amanda bought three kegs, which her friends helped roll onto our back porch. She also bought plastic cups and placed them on the glass porch table and ordered me, Dan, and Liz Subin, who had come over to help set up, to follow her into the den, where she had set up her stereo system and records.

"The den is for dancing," she explained as Liz and I followed, making mental notes. "The kitchen and porch are for drinking, and no one, under any circumstances, is allowed in the living room or Mom's room."

By nine o'clock, the kitchen was packed. I followed a couple up the stairs and watched in horror as they opened the door to Mom's room, clearly looking for a place to fool around. I marched in after them saying "This room is off-limits" just as the phone rang. I picked it up.

"How's the party, Bitsy?" Mom's voice chirped through the receiver. "Was Andres surprised?"

My heart began beating and my pulse quickened as I said "Yes, totally!" in a high-pitched voice.

"Did you bake him a birthday cake?" she asked as two kids stumbled in, bong in hand. I covered the receiver with one hand and made wild batting motions with the other, crude sign language for "Get the fuck out of here!" They quietly backed out, closed the door, and stood guard until I was off the phone.

More than two hundred people showed up. Amanda worked the door like a pro, charging football players nearly double and flat-out refusing Patrick O'Casey, captain of the football team. When he arrived with his cheerleader girlfriend, Amanda simply said, "Sorry, we've reached maximum occupancy." The couple turned away, dejected. But I was already slightly tipsy and thought Patrick was cute. I ran around the hedges to meet him on the other side.

"Follow me," I said, and he smiled wide. Unfortunately, his girlfriend followed too. I led them around back to the porch, where two senior football players were holding a sophomore girl by her ankles over a keg as she drank beer through the nozzle until it started spewing out of her mouth and nose. I thought she might drown.

"I think it's called a keg stand," Liz Subin shouted in my ear as I looked at her, alarmed. Another group of seniors were chugging beer through funnels with long spouts.

Patrick joined in, pinching my cheek beforehand, muttering, "You're one cool girl." I watched in awe as he finished an entire beer in three gulps, roared like the Incredible Hulk, and then did weight-lifter poses. Liz and I both wandered into the next room to join the mad tangle of people slam-dancing in the den.

Not too long after that, Amanda started to worry. "Who let that fucking asshole in?" she screamed when she saw Patrick with his buddies splayed out drunk on our lawn furniture. Her eyes darted straight to me, and I shrugged my shoulders, feigning innocence. Things were getting out of control. Someone had broken a glass pane in the French door that led to the TV room, and people were making pancakes with ingredients from our cupboard. Amanda approached Tom Granger, a six-foot-four-inch senior who wore a black trench coat all year long and had a scar that ran diagonally from his left temple to the right side of his chin. She offered him fifty bucks to help her clear the place out. He went room by room, clenching one of Dan's baseball bats and shouting, "The party is over. Everyone out!" People did as they were told.

AMANDA

THAT WASN'T TOM Granger; it was Matt Garrity. He was a mild-mannered, funny guy who was wearing a Hawaiian shirt. He did grab a baseball bat to clear people out of the rooms that they shouldn't have been in, but I didn't have to pay him. I was freaking out. There were too many people in the house, and I had just found Dan wasted on peppermint schnapps with those Neanderthals Liz let in. I'm still pissed about that.

LIZ

THE PARTY DIDN'T end until two in the morning. By then, those who could drive home had, and anyone else had passed out on every horizontal space our house offered. As Liz Subin and I went searching for a place to sleep, we found four girls asleep in my bed, two Chileans passed out in Andres's room, and Andres asleep in Mom's room with a girl from the drama club. Both twin beds in Diana's room were occupied, even though one had collapsed into a heap on the floor. Dan was asleep, fully dressed, on top of the covers on his bed, his snores mingling with those of two senior football players passed out on his floor. Liz and I ended up sleeping together, wrapped in a twin-size fitted sheet, the only thing left in our linen closet. We made our makeshift bed in the foyer, next to a table.

Not until the next morning did we realize how badly our house was destroyed. There were plastic cups everywhere—on the counters, on the floor, some crushed and empty, others half full with cigarette butts floating in flat beer. The linoleum floor, which Mom had just had redone so she could sell the place, was covered in an inch-thick brown scum that stuck to our bare feet. Liz and I went upstairs to put on shoes. On our way up, we noticed that the banister was wobbly and that there were sneaker marks on the wall. When I came back down, I found Amanda standing among the ruins.

"Fuck," she said, standing in the kitchen. "Fuck, fuck, fuck." In hopes of cheering her up, I told her I'd make breakfast for everyone.

"Good luck," she snarled.

I opened the fridge. It was empty except for a box of baking soda, a can of Crisco, and a few old onions. I went to the kitchen walk-in closet and found it empty except for a few canned goods. Even the flour was gone.

"They ate all the condiments," Amanda said. "Who eats condiments?"

Amanda sent her friend Rasheeda, who had spent the night, on a donut mission and then took Liz and me around the house for a reconnaissance tour.

"We are so screwed," she kept saying. "Mom is going to kill us."

It was Sunday morning. Mom would be arriving that night. We had to
get busy. As the kids who were too wasted to leave the night before slunk
out of the house, we scrubbed, mopped, vacuumed, and filled trash bag
after trash bag with plastic cups, cigarette butts, empty mustard jars, and
the occasional used condom.

By the time Mom arrived home that evening, we had done an amazing
job. But there were still cigarette burns in the crushed-velvet couch in the
den and in her brand-new linoleum floor. We had no idea how to fix the
broken pane of glass leading into the TV room or the wobbly banister, so
we just hoped she wouldn't notice. If she did, she didn't say.

Weeks later, Mom called me into the den, using my full name, which
she did only when she was angry. I walked in sheepishly.

"Where's my gnome candle?" she demanded. She was standing in front
of the fireplace, her arms crossed, her eyes narrowed.

"Excuse me?" I stammered. I had no idea what she was talking about.

"My gnome candle!" she shouted, her voice shaking. She pointed to
an empty spot on the mantel.

Then I remembered. Dad had bought Mom a candle the Christmas before he died. It looked more like a wizard than a gnome and was made
entirely of wax—even the long, flowing white beard, the blue hooded
cloak, and the brown staff. After Dad died, Mom placed the candle on the
mantel and claimed that the gnome was our guardian angel.

The candle was gone. I could see that was true, but I had no idea what
happened to it. Maybe someone knocked it off while dancing, or maybe
someone stole it. I didn't have the answer. All I knew was that I could
never replace it. And that made me feel terrible.

AMANDA

WHAT MADE ME feel terrible was when Mom got rid of Pony. Granted, I wasn't riding that much then. It was the classic "As soon as you get your driver's license, you forget about your horse." We still had Berry and Bartholomew, but Pony was my first horse. Mom and Dad had given him to me on my fourth birthday. Everybody, Liz, Dan, and Diana, we all learned to ride on him. Worse, she did it behind my back. I came home from school one day, and Pony was gone. When I confronted Mom, she told me that she found him a good home on Old Wagon Road, that the family was really nice and said that we could visit him anytime. So that afternoon, Anna and I drove up and down that damn dirt road looking until we finally saw him grazing. As I stood in that paddock, petting Pony's nose, I cried harder than I ever had in my life. I cried harder saying good-bye to that horse than I did when Dad died. It just didn't seem fair. At least I got to say good-bye.

After that, it didn't take long for the gray house to sell. Mom sold it for a half-million dollars to an English family called the Chisolms. Mom said we were going to move into the cottage until the new house was built, which would take about a year. By then, I had heard from colleges. I didn't get into any of my top choices, the vet schools. Dad had been the hard-ass about grades, but once he was gone, I didn't care anymore and my grades started to slip. The only school I ended up getting into was NYU, my safety. I wasn't too upset about it. I didn't want to be a vet anymore, and I was psyched that I was going to get to move out of the house and live in the city. I was so glad that I wasn't going to have to live in the cottage. Going from the gray house, which was practically a mansion, to a tiny three-room shack, would have sucked. In the gray house, we all had our own rooms. In the cottage, Mom and Diana were going to share a bedroom, and I was supposed to share the other bedroom with Liz when I came home on weekends. But it was so teeny you had to walk sideways between the bed and the dresser to get in and out. I figured I'd just sleep on the pullout couch in the main room, which was living room, dining room, and kitchen all in one. Meanwhile, Dan was going to have to sleep in a walk-in closet, which was really lame. But it's not like any of us really had a choice.

part two

. . . .

FALL 1983 – WINTER 1985

Christmas 1983 (l–r: Diana, Liz, Dan, Amanda)

LIZ

EVEN THOUGH THE new owners would not move into the gray house until Christmas, Mom thought it best if we all started our new school year in the cottage. So we began our slow move late in the summer of 1983. We could bring only what was necessary, so I packed all my clothes, records, and Mom's hot curlers and sent my swim team trophies and childhood dolls and photo albums to storage.

The last day of our move was a sunny Saturday in September, and Mom decided I was old enough to drive one load over by myself. I already knew how to drive. Dad had taught me when I was eight. Coming back home from an errand, he had pulled the Mercedes into the driveway, pushed the driver's seat as far back as it could go, and said, "Okay, toots." I climbed onto his lap and took hold of the steering wheel as he instructed—left hand at nine o'clock, right at three—my shoulders scrunched to my ears, my knuckles whitening as I tightened my grip. I steered straight as Dad accelerated, his voice firm but kind, "That-a-girl, nice and steady."

For this trip, however, my fourteen-year-old legs were long enough to reach the gas without having to scoot forward and point my toes, and I was driving the Jeep on my own, down the driveway instead of up. Midway, there was a dirt road that led out to the cottage just above the horse paddock. I pulled the blinker arm down to signal a left even though there were no other cars in sight and pulled gently on the steering wheel. Amazingly, the whole hunk of metal followed my lead. As I drove alongside the pasture, Berry and Bartholomew galloped beside me until the post and rail fence ended. They stopped, but I continued through a thick forest patch to the cottage on the other side. Mom was already there, waiting for me. She shouted "Brava!" as I awkwardly backed the Jeep toward the garage doors. With each brake pump, glasses and bowls rattled in their boxes, poorly packed with down parkas and pillows as padding. Dad never taught me how to drive in reverse.

Once the gray house was finally empty, I made another trip by myself. The only sounds were the crickets and the wind rustling through the still-full September trees. As I drove through the small thicket separating my old life from my new, I had no idea that I wouldn't set foot in that house again for more than twenty years.

Yet I would walk past it every day on my way down to the bus, at times turning my head away from it, sitting there, up on top of that hill, taunting me. Those mornings, I'd wake up after Mom left for work. Diana would already be dressed—in her OshKosh overalls and her favorite rainbow sweatshirt or in her purple corduroys and a hot pink unicorn T-shirt—watching morning cartoons with a bowl of Cheerios balanced on her lap. Mom would leave notes, "I'll be home by 7 p.m.," sometimes a grocery list, and always "Love, Mom," in her loopy cursive. I'd make Diana lunch—peanut butter and jelly on Branola bread, a box of apple juice, and a granola bar—and tell her when it was time to make the trek down the driveway to wait for the bus.

Dan and I took the bus together—he was only in seventh grade but his middle school was on the same campus as my high school. I always showered and washed my hair the night before because there was only one bathroom in the cottage. My morning ritual took time: I desperately wanted a perm, but Mom said I was too young, so I used her hot curlers instead and applied my makeup as they cooled. Mom thought only blush and lip-gloss were appropriate for a high school sophomore, but since she was gone most mornings, I raided her makeup. She kept it in a red leather suitcase that looked like a fancy fishing tackle box, embossed with her initials, AWW, in gold. It was filled with tools of her trade: pots of foundation, compacts of blush, brushes from tiny to large, and dozens of pencils for both eyes and lips. Her Ultima eye-shadow kit, which looked like a painter's palette with twenty-four different colors, was my favorite. I experimented with gold and peach one day, pale blues and grays the next. Face done, I unwrapped the curlers and placed one hand on my dresser and the other on my bed before whipping my head back and forth several times, unleashing the tight coils into loose lassoes. I'd read somewhere that this was what Farrah Fawcett did. Pleased with the results, I used a can of Aqua Net to spray my frothy locks into place and headed off to school.

Hardly anyone at school knew I was living in the cottage because I never invited anyone over. Ever. It was small and cramped and uncomfortable for my family, let alone friends. We were living on top of one another. If everyone wanted to watch TV, someone had to sit on the floor. It was embarrassing. I hadn't told anyone Mom had cancer, either. I kept that a secret, too. She never even seemed sick, just sad. I wanted to protect her and my siblings from people passing judgment on us as a family. To lose our dad was painful enough. To lose our way of life added a layer of humiliation—for me, at least. So I only told my closest friends that we had even moved. No one else needed to know.

I spent lots of time at friends' houses or babysitting. No one seemed to notice how drastically my life had changed. I still wore the same preppy clothes from the year before. Mom still drove the same cars, and we even used the same turnoff on West Patent Road to get to our driveway, as the new one didn't split off from the old one until just below the pasture. For months, it was simply a rough line dug into the earth where the bulldozer tire had carved a herringbone pattern into the red-gold dirt that would eventually fade with use. But no one could see the new driveway from West Patent Road. The only good thing about the cottage was that it was hidden.

When Amanda came home, she slept on the couch. Sharing a twin bed was uncomfortable, and if we pulled out the trundle, there was no room to walk. To help Mom out, we'd do the grocery shopping or run other errands together. Mom still left a check made out to ShopRite, but she had stopped leaving lists because by now I knew what we needed.

One weekday afternoon, I wanted to make meatloaf for dinner and realized we didn't have any ground beef. Amanda wasn't due home for two days, Mom was at work, and we were running low on milk and eggs. I went through the cupboards and the refrigerator and made a list—we needed tuna fish and mayonnaise and graham crackers, too. As always, Mom had left a check on the counter. Dan was probably at Curtis's house; he was never home anyway. Diana was busy coloring in Mom's room, so I shouted, "I'll be right back, Di," grabbed the check, and walked out the door.

The Mercedes was parked out front. I got in the driver's seat, started the engine, and caught a glimpse of myself in the rearview mirror. I was only fourteen but I could pass for older. I had begged Mom for braces to fix one errant tooth that popped out of line, but she insisted it gave my smile personality, explaining, "Perfect is boring, darling." I knew she just didn't want to pay for them, and on this particular day, her stinginess worked in my favor. Girls with braces were generally too young to drive cars. I was almost five-foot-six and my feet were size eight. One more size up and I'd be able to wear Mom's shoes. I put the car in reverse.

Driving down the driveway was easy, as was taking the left onto West Patent Road. Then I saw a car speeding toward me. My chest expanded—I thought I might explode. But the car passed, and I was still alive and not smeared on the street or smashed against the windshield. My fear dissipated until another car appeared ahead, barreling toward me. I remembered Dad's words, "Steady and straight, toots, steady and straight," and I kept on, clutching the wheel, my knuckles almost popping through my skin.

I made it down our road and another before I came to the one that poured into Mount Kisco's busiest intersection. The road was steep and narrow and had such sharp, blind corners that I honked as I rounded each and stayed so far to the right I heard branches scrape against the passenger's side. Thankfully, the light at the bottom of the serpentine hill was red, giving me a moment to breathe and strategize. ShopRite was just across the four-lane road.

The light turned green and a stream of cars started moving toward me, some turning in front, others whizzing past. I imagined Dad guiding me, "Okay, kiddo, make it through this intersection and you're golden." A horn hollered from behind, jolting me into action. I lifted my foot off the brake and began to cross. As I maneuvered the Mercedes through the labyrinth of metal and wheels and horns, I held my breath and fought the urge to close my eyes. Once safely in the lot, I parked far away from the shopping carts and people and cars and got out shaking. I kept waiting for someone to bust me, to ask, "Where's your mom?" or "How did you get here?" I was slightly disappointed when nobody did. I did the grocery shopping and added an extra twenty-five dollars, the limit, to the total of the bill, pocketed the cash, and then drove home. Dan was sitting in front of the TV, watching *One Day at a Time*.

"Hey," he said, barely turning his head.

"Hey," I answered back and started unpacking groceries, giddy. If no one noticed I was gone, then I wouldn't get caught. But then vague disappointment set in: No one was there to pat me on the back and say, "Nice job, toots."

I started driving all the time. To grocery-shop, to buy candy at D's variety store, to Mount Kisco to drop Dan off at Curtis's house, and to go try on dresses at the Bazaar Mall with my friends.

One evening, Mom called me to her bedroom. She was just home from work, and I was in my room, doing homework. "Elizabeth," she said, concern coloring her voice.

I froze for a moment before going into her room, only a couple steps from my own. "I just got off the phone with Mrs. Vucovick," she continued.

I was standing in her bedroom doorway, and Mom was sitting on the corner of her bed, unzipping her knee-high burgundy boots. Her hair was set and sprayed into a puffy bob, and she still had a thick coat of makeup from her day on the set, but she looked tired beneath the foundation and eyeliner and blush. She looked worn-out and a bit deflated beneath her stiff hair. Her eyes caught and held mine.

"She called to say she thought she saw you driving the Mercedes by yourself down Springhurst Road."

The panic I felt during my first drive started to uncoil once again. How could I talk my way out of this?

Mom was now bent over and massaging her left foot, which looked puffy and swollen beneath the beige pantyhose. It was bigger than her right foot, I could see.

I stood in silence for a moment, thinking hard. Mom always said she could forgive anything except a lie. So I said, "How else are we supposed to get groceries, Mom?"

She stopped rubbing her foot and looked up at me. Her face, which was taut yet weary, suddenly shifted. She crinkled her nose as if she were about to sneeze and thought for a moment before she said, "Good point, darling." She said it again and smiled. "Good point." I saw a fleeting spark in her eye and her lips soften. I saw the mom who sang lines from Broadway show tunes in the midst of conversations, who insisted on playing levitation with my friends at slumber parties, and who used to take me and Dan to school in a horse-drawn carriage until the police stopped her on West Patent Road and said she needed a special license. I saw a glimpse of the mom who used to embarrass me and whom I now missed terribly. And so I kept driving.

DIANA

THE WALK UP the driveway was even longer now, since I had to pass by the gray house and walk between my old swing set and pool before I got to the cottage. The people who lived in our old house were called the Chisolms, and they were English. They had an Auntie Eve they called "Nanny," and they called mud "muck." They also put sugar on their grapefruit. Hugh and Laura were around my age, and they went to Rippowam Cisqua, my old school. Their little brother Mark looked like a tiny old man, and he tried to follow us everywhere. It was fun to not be the youngest, and they were nice about sharing the swing set that I still considered mine although Mom had explained to me that it wasn't any longer, even though it was closer to our new house than it was to theirs.

Nobody was playing in the yard that afternoon, so I kept walking until the cottage appeared from behind the pine trees. Since we had moved, Mom had very little time to do the things she used to. Everything seemed harder, a chore. Even my birthday. Mom didn't want to have a party for me because things were "so up in the air." That's what she said. I heard her arguing with Liz about it in the kitchen. I was lying in the new bedroom I shared with Mom, making purple spirals with my Spirograph set. My pen kept cracking through the paper because the carpet was too soft, so I used a Pay Day board game box as a table.

"We have to do it, Mom," I could hear Liz say, and then Mom's low murmur. "Every little girl deserves a birthday," Liz answered back, fast and hard.

My sixth birthday fell on a Friday, and Liz surprised me at school with cupcakes for my whole class. That afternoon, Amanda took me to the music store and let me pick out three tapes: I chose Huey Lewis and the News' *Sports*, Depeche Mode's *Speak and Spell*, and Yaz's *Upstairs at Eric's*.

Then Liz took me to the Denim Mine and told me to go and get anything I wanted and to meet her at the cash register in ten minutes. I don't remember what I chose. And they did throw me a party, at the cottage, in the garage, and nearly everybody in my grade came, even boys. We danced in pointy hats and ate a Mickey Mouse cake.

DAN

I HATED THE cottage. I had to sleep in a closet, on an army cot shoved in the back corner, leaving only six inches between me and Dad's suits and Mom's old furs. It reminded me of this summer school I went to for my dyslexia a few years before, when I was nine. I got the worst migraine ever. It was so bad that drugs couldn't help. I couldn't be touched. Light was excruciating. I just hid in the coat racks, lying down until the pain washed over me and was gone. The closet was like that; I could just lie there and disappear. It was my little cocoon, my musty incubator. And it was freezing in there, so I made this elaborate pulley system out of string so I wouldn't have to get out of bed at night to turn off the light. I stacked boxes so that I couldn't see the door from my cot, so I could hide. The only thing that kept me from feeling totally alone was Ralph. Ralph was a German shepherd–beagle mutt, born six months after Dad died. Mom said that he was a good omen, because she believed that animals were good energy.

One night, lying on my cot with Ralph, I wrote FUCK LIFE on the wall in pencil. When Mom found it, she freaked out. I felt so bad—the last thing I wanted to do was make her worry. She had enough to worry about. Ever since Dad died, she told me I was the man of the house. I wanted to pull my own weight, not add to her load. Like at the tag sale when we were moving out of the gray house, I ran around putting little colored stickers on things, pricing them. I wanted to chip in, so I sold my baseball card collection. I had the entire 1976 lineup, every single person in the league, 1,127 cards. I sold them for, like, forty bucks. I sold everything I owned and gave the money to Mom. I can't remember bringing anything to the cottage. Where would I have put it, anyway?

Mom sent me to a shrink after she found what I wrote. He had a beard and longish hair, the kind of guy who would put the Muppet on his hand to ask, "Where did he touch you?" I liked him, though. We talked for, like, twenty minutes and then played tiddlywinks for the rest. I talked about missing Dad and how hard it was being the only boy. That was the big thing for me, being the only boy.

DIANA

DANNY GOT GROUNDED because he wrote FUCK on the wall in his closet. Mom made him erase it when she found it. I know because I snuck in there when no one was home, parted the plastic-covered jackets, and saw its ghost on the white wall. Mom was mad, so was he. Everyone was grumpy since we moved to the cottage, even Liz.

I liked the cottage. Every afternoon after school, I came home to an empty house. Once inside, I'd drop my knapsack on the floor and drag a chair from the dining-room table up to the counter. Then I'd climb onto the creaking straw seat that was woven in the same pattern as the God's eyes we made in arts and crafts. With one knee on the yellow counter, I could reach the cupboard that held the graham crackers and the one that held the cups. My favorite was a tall glass with the purple Grimace on it that I got with a McDonald's Happy Meal.

It was nice to sit in front of the TV, right up in it so I could feel the hairs on my face talk to the electricity coming off the screen. I watched *Scooby-Doo* and ate graham crackers until my stomach hurt, generally half a package, soaking each rectangle in the milk past my fingertips, waving it back and forth until the cracker was soft enough to fall apart on my tongue.

One afternoon, Liz came home and broke the spell by telling me I'd ruin my eyesight sitting so close to the TV. Wiping my milky fingers on my pants, I backed up a little bit and rested my chin in my hands, splaying my legs out one on each side like a frog. Liz started talking on the phone as she unpacked the groceries, slamming cabinet doors with her shoulder and drawers with her hips. She was making so much noise I couldn't even hear the show, so I retreated into my and Mom's room, leaving my cup and cookies on the floor.

I didn't come out of the bedroom until much later, once the windows had gone dark and I had completely filled in my Barbie coloring book. I only came out because I wanted to go to Carvel, one of my and Mom's favorite places. In the commercials, an old guy named Tom Carvel always talked about his whale-shaped ice cream cake that said "Have a Whale of a Day!" on it in blue icing. I ate it once, at a friend's birthday party, and it was gross, all mushy and cold on my fork. I liked a vanilla cone with rainbow sprinkles, and Mom liked a vanilla cone dipped in a hard chocolate shell. We'd start licking before we were out of the shop, and by the time we got to the car, my face would be covered in ice cream and so would her hand. Mom would flip down my visor so I could see my reflection in the mirror, and we'd giggle about my ice cream lipstick while she licked her hand and mewed like a cat. Then she'd poke me in the side, making me twist in my seat. I'd laugh so hard I'd get a double chin and kick the dashboard, my cone held high in the air.

So I walked into the main room where Amanda and Liz and Dan were all hanging out. Mom wasn't there. "Can we go to Carvel?" I asked. Nobody answered. Dan was scrunched on the couch watching TV, his chin resting against his knees, his dirty white-socked feet sinking into the down cushion. Liz and Amanda were to my left in the kitchen, talking to each other. "Can we go to Carvel?" I asked them, a little louder this time. But nobody answered, not even Liz. She and Amanda just kept talking, and Amanda threw her head back and laughed loudly, baring her fanglike incisors to the harsh yellow track lights on the kitchen ceiling.

Being ignored was new, but I was getting used to it. Even gross old Mimsy, Mom's hundred-year-old cat, was ignoring me, sitting on the couch next to Dan with her eyes closed, purring. So I went back into my and Mom's bedroom and felt sorry for myself, really sorry. Like wondering why everyone hated me so much, why they all acted like I wasn't even alive, or like if they pretended that I wasn't there, I would go away. But I had nowhere to go besides this stupid bedroom, and I wanted to go to Carvel!

The tears came gushing out with so much wind behind them that my lungs couldn't keep up. I was heaving, my tongue flapping against my throat. I wanted Mom, but she wasn't there; and when she was, she was always tired or busy; and my sisters didn't have time for me; and my brother felt far away. Suddenly, Liz was at the door.

"What's wrong?" she asked me, weary. She had a dish towel hanging from her hand, which was on her hip. In my despair, I had flung myself on the bed and grabbed onto my right knee, and a perfect cover-up came to mind.

"I hit my knee," I sobbed. "And it hurts."

Liz frowned. "I think you're crying because you're spoiled," she said gently. "I think you want to go to Carvel, and you're crying because nobody will take you."

"Nuh-uh," I said weakly, rubbing my knee. Now, on top of everything else, I was caught. And I was mad, too, because if she knew I wanted to go to Carvel the whole time, she could have at least said something when I was out there asking over and over. It wasn't fair that she could just show up in the doorway and make me feel stupid. This was my room, where I went so nobody would see me. But when I looked back up to tell her so, Liz was gone.

AMANDA

I HARDLY SPENT any time at the cottage. I was living in a freshman dorm at NYU in Washington Square Park, but I took the train home most Friday nights. Still, I avoided the cottage as much as possible. I worked weekends at Heller's Shoe Store in Mount Kisco to pay for stuff, like food and books and going out, and I also had a job mucking stalls for a woman named Abbie. When I wasn't working at Heller's or at school, I would stay at Abbie's until eleven or twelve at night, listening to her talk about her kids or her horses.

On some weeknights, though, I would meet Mom at Sloan Kettering Hospital on the Upper East Side. Earlier that summer, right after she got her job on *Loving*, Mom found out her cancer was not completely gone. Apparently, they didn't remove all the infected lymph nodes when they took out her uterus, so she needed radiation treatments to get it once and for all. The cast of *Loving* was so supportive. The writers actually wrote Mom's story line several weeks ahead; then everyone would shoot her scenes in a row so Mom could take a week off to do her radiation and recover. It was so cool of them.

Mom would drive the Mercedes in for her appointments, but she never wanted to pay for parking, so I'd take the subway to the hospital to meet her. She'd go in for treatment, and I'd drive to a nearby playground and wait in the car. Which was fine by me—I didn't want to go into the hospital anyway. I'd do my homework for an hour, and then drive up to the hospital, where she'd always be waiting outside. Then we'd drive home. I did that every time she had radiation. I don't remember any conversations on those rides home. She was always too tired to talk.

DIANA

MOM'S SCAR WAS puffy, lips sewn shut. Her pale belly waited beneath the quivering water, a silent monster lurking. With my sneakered feet curled beneath me on the bath mat, I put my chin on the edge of our cool yellow tub and looked at her. She was relaxed, eyes closed, head on the tile behind her, mouth open, slack. I poked my finger into the warm water, just barely touching the swollen line that stretched below her belly button and above her dark, sparse pubic hair.

"What's that?" I gently moved my finger across it. It was purple in parts, and when the water's surface, frantic from my slight movements, settled down, I could see the little dots where there had been stitches.

"A scar," she said, not moving, eyes still closed. Her cheeks gently puffed with each breath, like she was sleeping.

"I know," I said, quickly. I had scars, too. I was born cross-eyed and had scars on my eyeballs, which had been taken out and stuck back in a couple of times. I also had one from an operation I had when I was four, because I woke up one morning and Mom said I looked like a bullfrog. She brought me to the hospital where they cut open my throat and took out a gland. Then they sewed it up again and put a big white bandage around my whole neck. I couldn't turn my head; the bandage was big enough to rest my chin on. I had to wear it to school until the cut healed, leaving pale pink train tracks jerking across my throat.

Mom's scar looked like it hurt, more raw than mine. "From what?" I asked, my whole hand still in the warm water. Mom sighed, the dough of her belly rising beneath my finger. She said nothing, and it hurt my feelings.

Usually, Mom was the only one who didn't ignore me. When she was home, I was the center of attention. She'd pick me up for hugs; I'd sit on her lap while she paid the bills. I liked to give her long kisses on the lips, staring into her eyes and breathing out of my nose. She never pushed me

away; even when she was talking to people, she'd just talk out of the corner of her mouth with my lips pressed against hers. At night, she'd tell me
I was precious, and we'd snuggle in bed until we both fell asleep. The only
time I didn't love her more than anything in the world was when she made
me take my asthma medication in yogurt instead of ice cream. And I loved
her the most when it was just the two of us in the Jeep, running errands.
Mom would drive through the streets of Mount Kisco, her eyes searching
in front of her before they turned to me. "Where *are* we?" she'd ask, in a
worried voice.

"We're lost!" I'd say, buckled into the passenger seat next to her, barely
able to see out the windshield.

She'd just look to me, eyes wide, and bite her lip. "Where should we go?"

"Left!" I'd shout, and she'd follow my directions even though all I could
see was the sky ahead, the traffic lights, the telephone lines. With my head
pressed against the blue leather of my seat, I'd let her take me anywhere.
We were together, safe.

The last stop on our route was always the car wash. As Mom paid, I
rolled up my window, sealing us in as the car slid forward. When blackness blocked out the afternoon, I unbuckled my seat belt and Mom pulled
off her sunglasses. Eyes wide, she raised both hands as if she were in a
holdup, staring at the steering wheel that jerked about on its own, possessed. I squealed in the darkness as a wicked thunderstorm crashed all
around us, gushing water onto the glass. After the windshield cleared, we
could both see the rag monster dancing in the distance. I stood, leaning my
butt against the back of my seat to get a better view of the sudsy tongues
about to slobber all over us.

"Here it comes!" I yelled and, preparing for the climb onto Mom's lap,
dug the heels of my sneakers into my seat as usual. But on this day, instead
of grabbing me by the waist and pulling me toward her, she grabbed onto
the back of my pants.

With her right hand hooked around my rainbow belt, she nudged
me toward the windshield with her fist, crying, "Into the belly of the
whale!" For a second I was confused, not understanding why she was pushing me away. Then I leaned onto the dashboard and pressed my nose to
the glass.

LIZ

I WAS IN love. His name was Paul Martino, and he was a senior, the captain of the lacrosse team, and the hottest guy in all of Fox Lane. He was more than six feet tall and had thick dark hair, piercing blue eyes, and a gap between his two front teeth. He was always joking around, always laughing and flashing that gapped-tooth smile. But Paul didn't know I existed, even though I walked out of my way to pass his locker every day to get to my social studies class. Paul's locker was next to Sean O'Hara's, the older brother of my new best friend, Maureen. Liz Subin had gone to private school that sophomore year, so I started spending as much time as possible at Maureen's house. Every day, Sean would say, "Hi, Liz," as I passed, but Paul never seemed to notice.

That December, Maureen and I decided to go to the Snowflake Ball even though we didn't have boyfriends to take us. I borrowed a dress from my neighbor Betsy, who had a closet full of party dresses and let me choose whichever one I wanted. I picked out a maroon velvet scoop-neck dress with short puffed sleeves and a scalloped edge and wore it with a pair of Mom's black high heels. Sean gasped when he came to pick me up with Maureen. "It's Christie Brinkley!" he teased as I climbed in the back of their brown Chevy Citation.

"Very funny," I said, secretly pleased. That was the look I was going for. My hair, long and wavy, was still warm from Mom's curlers.

At the dance, Maureen and I sat on the radiators that encircled the Commons sipping Sprite punch, people-watching. When a slow song came on, Jeff, a junior whom Maureen had a huge crush on, walked over and sheepishly asked her to dance. She turned a dark pink, looked at her hands in her lap, and bit her lip before nodding and following him to the dance floor. I watched, riveted, as Jeff tried to figure out where to put his hands. Maureen covered her mouth with her hand and laughed as Jeff settled for her waist. Then she put both hands on his shoulders and smiled big, pursing her lips so as not to expose her silver-laced teeth. I felt a tap on my shoulder and looked up. It was Paul, towering over me. I figured I was in his way, so I moved to one side. But then he reached for my hand.

"Wanna dance?" he asked.

Before I could respond, he pulled me out onto the dance floor. I'd never slow-danced before, but it didn't matter. "I'm Paul," he whispered into my ear, wrapping his arms around me.

"I know" was all I could muster back. He pulled me closer, and I placed my cheek on his shoulder and scanned the room for Maureen. Someone had to see what was happening to me so I knew it was real.

Paul grabbed my right hand and held it close to his heart and said, "I've had my eye on you." Silently, I thanked God he was holding me so tightly. Otherwise, I would have been pulsating and convulsing and sparking, a live wire, right there on the dance floor.

As we rocked back and forth, I caught sight of Maureen. I slowly peeled one arm from Paul's shoulder, pointed at his back, and mouthed the words "Oh my God!" Her eyes bulged when she saw me, and she flashed a huge silvery smile.

When the evening ended, Paul gave me a kiss on the cheek and asked for my number. He called the following day to invite me to a party. As soon as I saw his car lights beam up the driveway, I ran out the door and jumped into the passenger seat before he had a chance to even turn off the engine. "Doesn't your mom want to meet me?" he asked in response to my enthusiastic "Let's go!"

He was wearing his red Fox Lane lacrosse jacket and smiling at me. I wanted to smash my face into his, like some couples I spotted on the dance floor the night before.

"She's not home," I lied. "Another time?"

We arrived at the party, and I suddenly knew how it felt to be famous. Paul held my hand as the mob of people milling around the keg in the kitchen made a path for us.

"Mar-ti-no!" one lacrosse player shouted, giving him a high five. Maureen's brother Sean was at the keg. He poured Paul a beer and winked at me.

I saw Maureen in the corner and practically ran to her side. I grabbed her hand and squeezed all my excitement into it. "Ow!" she said, wrestling her hand from mine but smiling wide. "So how does it feel to be Paul Martino's girlfriend?"

I had no idea. But after my third plastic cup of lukewarm beer, I began to see.

"Let's wander," Paul said. He pulled me past the game of quarters in the dining room to a door leading to the basement. As we descended the stairs, it was pitch black. I held Paul's hand with both of mine. He stopped suddenly, and my whole body slammed into his. Then he kissed me. We stumbled back toward a couch and spent the rest of the night as just lips and tongues.

From that moment on, I knew what it felt like to be Paul Martino's girlfriend: It was bliss. When he smiled at me in the hallway, helium replaced blood in my veins. If he snuck a kiss, I was paralyzed. And everyone at school knew we were dating. At Fox Lane, I was Paul's girlfriend, not the daughter of a sick widow. I worked hard to keep those two identities separate. No one at home knew I was dating Paul. There was no point in telling anyone: Amanda thought Paul was an asshole—to her, all jocks were—and Mom had other things to think about. June, her character on *Loving*, was about to murder her husband, Garth Slater, who kept her drunk so he could sneak into their daughter Lily's room at night to molest her. In the script, she kills Garth to protect Lily. While that may have been good for Lily, it was not good for us. June was being sent to an insane asylum, which meant Mom would be out of a job that spring.

I'd been dating Paul for several months when one evening I was in the kitchen searing pork chops and felt two arms wrap around my waist. I jumped. It was Paul. Horrified, I frantically scanned the room. The white walls were scuffed from too many things stuffed into not enough space. Mail was piled up on the kitchen table. Boxes lined the living-room walls. The couch and two armchairs that once furnished our den in the gray house crowded the small living room, where Diana was doing her homework on the floor. She looked up at him, her eyes magnified four times their true size by her pink glasses.

"Hey," she said, then went back to her homework.

"Hey," Paul said back, then turned to me.

"What are you doing here?" I gasped, panicky.

"I thought I'd surprise you," he said, grinning.

He sure had. Here I was in Mom's apron to protect my clothes from the pork chop splatter, my hair messily twisted into a bun on top of my head. At school, I was a girl with golden curls who got good grades and scored a hot senior boyfriend. That girl had a mom who made sit-down dinners and took her back-to-school shopping. I desperately wanted to be that girl, not the girl whom Paul was, at this moment, holding by the waist, the one whose ill mother still had to work long days in the city to put food on the table, food that she didn't have time to cook. Not the girl who lied to Diana's teacher when she dropped off birthday cupcakes and said Mom made them. Not the girl who lied when Maureen called with a sleepover invitation, saying she'd have to check with her mom, then hung up and called back fifteen minutes later, pretending her mother said it was fine. Paul wasn't dating that girl. He was dating the other one. And the longer he stood in the kitchen, the sooner he would figure it out.

I suggested some fresh air and led Paul to the pool house, which technically belonged to the Chisolms but was closer to the cottage than to their house. We snuck in through the sliding glass door, and as we kissed in the darkness, I tried to pretend that the pool house still belonged to my family, that nothing had really changed. But soon I felt a pang of paranoia: What if the Chisolms walked in? What would they say? I knew Amanda was bringing Mom home from the city. What if they arrived, saw the pork chops in the pan, Diana all by herself, and Paul's car parked in the driveway? I sat up, startled, and said I had to get back home.

As Paul was getting into his car, Amanda pulled into the driveway with Mom in the passenger seat. Paul jumped back out, and I introduced him as my friend.

My mother smiled wide. "So nice to meet you," she said.

Once inside the cottage, Amanda exploded. "I cannot believe you're dating him!" she said. "He's a total jock! A cocky jock! What's wrong with you?"

"Now, Amanda," Mom interrupted, "he seems a perfect gentleman. Leave her alone. Besides, your father was a jock."

I turned the stove back on and finished frying the pork chops, glad for the task. It meant I could keep my back to my family so they couldn't see my face, flushed with anger and shame. Mom was being a dork, Amanda was being a bitch, and I was grinding my teeth to stop from screaming at them both to shut up and leave me alone. No one ever mentioned Paul again.

The following Friday night, Paul invited me to dinner at his house. Paul said his family ate fish every Friday night, something to do with being Catholic. We all had to bow our heads before dinner, and then everyone touched his or her forehead, belly, and each shoulder, eyes closed. I had mine squinted so I could mimic them, half a beat behind. After dinner, Paul's parents went to church, his youngest sister to her room, and the two oldest sisters out with their boyfriends, leaving us alone. Paul led me to the den in the basement of his family's split-level ranch house.

It started like any make-out session would. But soon Paul quickly slipped his hand beneath my shirt and bra. I knew this was second base. Maureen and I had talked about bases, and she had gotten to second with Jeff. It felt okay when he touched my breasts. Sort of scary when he started to knead them, but still okay. Then his hand worked its way quickly to my pants. He unbuttoned them with one hand while we kissed, as if he had done this many times before. He pulled my pants and underpants down with one hand too, and I thought, okay, this is third base. Maureen and I had talked about this, but she had not done this before. None of my friends had. I was starting to get nervous; this was totally new territory, a new frontier. Paul stopped kissing my mouth and began working his way down my neck with his lips, then my breasts and my stomach. I watched, frozen, wondering, "What the hell is he doing?"

DAN

CURTIS TOLD ME that Paul ate Liz out. One afternoon, when Liz and I were sitting on the grass in front of the cottage, I told her what I heard because I wanted to get a reaction out of her. But I didn't expect the reaction I got.

She got mad, and Liz never got mad. She turned to me and said, "Don't you ever let anybody talk about me like that again." Then she just walked away. I felt awful; I had betrayed her. Someone was talking shit about my sister, and I should have stopped him. Then I got mad, too, not at Curtis but at Paul for talking about her like that. From that point on, I wasn't going to let anyone say anything bad about my sisters. I was only in seventh grade, but I started giving the high school guys mean looks when I saw them on campus. Just thinking about them disrespecting my sisters made my blood boil.

I knew what they were thinking: Mom told me that if I was going to lose my virginity, to do it with someone I didn't respect. I guess her thinking was that if I didn't respect the girl, I wouldn't fall in love with her and so I wouldn't have my heart broken. I guess she thought it was something Dad might say to me. That was my birds-and-bees talk.

But it wasn't enough: I had a hard-on the entire time we lived in the cottage. I had no idea what was going on. It was awful. My penis would get hard for no reason, and I wouldn't know what to do with it. I'd try rubbing it, but nothing would come out and it wouldn't go away. I had no one to turn to. Once, Amanda walked in on me watching *Caligula*. She had rented it and told Mom it was for a Latin credit, but this movie was basically a porno. One afternoon when nobody was home, I decided to watch it. Of course, I got a hard-on, right there on the couch in the main room. I didn't hear the car pull up, but suddenly Amanda came in through the front door. So I jumped up off the couch and started break-dancing on the living-room floor, hoping she wouldn't be able to see my erection.

I wound up spending a lot of time hanging out at Curtis's. Once, I stayed there for four days straight. I told his mom that my mom said it was okay, but I never told anyone at home where I was or what I was doing. No one ever asked. The kids who lived near Curtis were a lot like me in that way. I mean, we were way different: Curtis only had two pairs of jeans and five T-shirts, but each one was perfectly folded in his closet, pressed and washed. He took such good care of his things because they were all he had. Meanwhile, I was sleeping in a closet filled with my parents' fancy, rotting clothes. But we were similar in that our dads were gone and our moms were preoccupied with putting food on the table. In Curtis's apartment complex, everybody was in the same situation: None of the kids had any money to do anything, so they were trapped. It was this weird kind of freedom. We played Uno and, when that got old, spin the bottle. Kids started having sex there really young because there really wasn't anything else to do.

One time, I was in Curtis's bedroom, fooling around with this girl who was ten, two years younger than me. Curtis was right next to us, fooling around with her friend. All of a sudden, the girl pulled my pants down and stuck my penis inside of her. It was really dry and it hurt, but I just sucked up the pain. I guess I lost my virginity that night. I thought that whole situation was ugly. It broke my heart in a different kind of way.

LIZ

I NEVER TOLD anyone about going to third base with Paul, but in my own head I decided to go all the way with him. I had no idea what that meant. The only thing Mom ever told me about sex was that she was twenty-eight and a virgin when she met Dad, and that it was worth waiting for the man you loved. Well, I loved Paul. But lately he had grown a bit distant. When I passed him in the hallway, he flicked his chin up in acknowledgment instead of grabbing my butt or giving me a big bear hug. He never stopped by the cottage again, and I hadn't been invited back to his parents' house for another Friday night dinner. I knew he was anxiously waiting to hear from colleges, that he was hoping to get into Duke even though his dad wanted him to go to West Point. But I also wondered if he was aloof because he had grown bored with me. If we had sex, I thought things would go back to the way they were. Giddy and fun.

The only thing I knew about sex was from the hairy sketches of various positions from *The Joy of Sex*, which I found in Mom and Dad's closet when I was little, and from watching *Caligula* with Amanda. But that was so violent and bloody, I had to close my eyes throughout most of it.

None of my friends had ever had sex. I was on my own. So I started plotting the perfect night. I babysat for Daisy and Montgomery Stewart several times a week, often on a Friday or Saturday night. They had two kids: Jonah, who was two, and Addison, a newborn. One weekend, they hired me to take care of their dog when they went away with the boys. I decided it was the perfect opportunity to have sex with Paul.

I invited him over and cooked a nice dinner, which I served on Daisy and Montgomery's good china in the dining room. I lit candles, played classical music, and even put on a sexy dress that I had bought with my babysitting money. After dinner, I led him upstairs to Daisy and Montgomery's room.

All I remember about that night was sharp pain, flesh tearing. It was dark; Paul was on top of me. After it was over, we did not lie in bed, bodies entangled like lovers in movies. I lay on my back frozen, stunned. Was that sex?

Paul had to get home. As I got out of bed to get dressed, I noticed a small bloodstain, a deformed butterfly, on the stark white sheets. I quickly covered it, embarrassed. It was proof of my pain; I wanted Paul to think I'd enjoyed it.

I spent three hours washing and bleaching the stains from the sheets and wound up sleeping there alone. After that weekend, Paul stopped calling me. He avoided me in the hallways. Clearly I had done something wrong, but I had no idea what.

It was near the end of school, and I was at a party, sitting on the lawn with a few friends, when I spotted Paul. I jumped up and grabbed the bottle of Dom Perignon I had stolen from the Stewarts to give him as a graduation present. I had to hold myself back from running. He was chatting with Jennifer, the prettier of the twins who were also the smartest senior girls at Fox Lane. I played volleyball with her. She was on the varsity team and always so nice to me. She even helped me with my overhead serve.

But before I emerged from the shadows, I saw Paul steer Jennifer down the driveway. He was whispering something in her ear, and she threw her head back and laughed. Then he put his arm around her and pulled her close, and they disappeared into the darkness.

The stabs I felt that night were in my throat and in my chest. But I did not cry out or bleed from them. I got drunk on Dom Perignon instead, convinced that Paul had lost interest in me because I sucked at sex.

DIANA

I WAS LYING on my back, concentrating on keeping my throat open and my lungs working by imagining a parachute, like the one we played with in gym, filling with air and slowly descending. It usually worked, but this time it wasn't doing anything. My asthma had gotten worse since moving to the cottage; tonight, the sound of my wheezing woke up Mom.

She drove fast through the night, her hand on my cheek. My breath was a creaking door, opening and closing. At the emergency room, I was given a shot. Mom said I was brave, the bravest little girl she knew, and kissed me where the needle had gone in.

When I awoke late the next morning, Mom was standing in the living room doing the Jane Fonda workout, legs spread in a wide V, her hands at her waist, as Jane instructed her to breathe. "Good morning, my darling," she said, coming toward me with her arms outstretched. I ran to her, the maroon velour of her tracksuit soft against my cheek. "How are you feeling?" she asked as she crouched down so that her face was level with mine. I nodded sleepily and put my face in her neck, my eyes pressed closed by her skin. "I have a surprise for you," she sang, twisting my body back and forth at the waist. "Today is a special day!" she said. "One that's for just you and me!"

She rubbed her nose against mine and told me to get dressed. We were going to spend the whole day together, no school, no work, just the two of us, having fun. For starters, we would have a picnic in Leonard Park, where we could feed the geese. Then we'd go ice-skating in the new indoor rink. She was going to teach me how to do figure eights.

Mom filled our red-and-white-gingham-lined wicker picnic basket with tuna sandwiches, cookies, and fruit, and we were off. As we passed the turnoff to the gray house, I saw Hugh and Laura playing in the pasture. Mom rolled down her window and asked if they'd like a ride to their house, and I slumped in my seat. The Chisolms must have had one of those extra holidays you get in private school.

"Oh, that would be lovely!" they answered cheerily, their noses pink from the crisp spring air. As they clambered into the backseat, shouting "Hullo!" and "Thanks ever so much!" like the kids in *Mary Poppins,* I started to feel grumpy. The day didn't seem as special as it had before, when I was the only kid not in school, when Mom and I were the only two people on earth.

As Mom pulled the gearshift down a couple notches and slowly eased the Jeep forward, my only thought was that the Chisolms better not try to weasel in on our holiday. Then suddenly Mom's head bobbled up and down as the Jeep went over a big bump.

Hugh yelled, "Maahrk!" Mom's face crumpled. She bit her lip, opened the door, and disappeared beneath the car. She reappeared clutching three-year-old Mark, his big square head bloodied at the scalp. She cradled him in her arms like a baby breast-feeding. His mouth was wide open, screaming, saliva bubbling on his tongue.

"Are your parents home?" Mom yelled over her shoulder, back at the kids, both crying.

"No!" Laura wailed. "Just Nanny!"

"Diana, take off your jacket and give me your shirt," Mom ordered. I hesitated. I was wearing my Hard Rock Cafe New York T-shirt, a gift from Amanda.

"Di-ana!" Mom yelled sharply.

The tone was unfamiliar. I lifted the shirt over my head. She grabbed it and wrapped it around the head of the screaming child. I quickly folded my arms across my chest, embarrassed that Hugh might have seen my naked boobies.

In her arms, Mark soon quieted down, and as we made our way back to the emergency room for the second time in twelve hours, the only sound other than the whir of the engine and the sniffling of the Chisolms was Mom's gentle shushings.

"It's okay," she sang softly as she patted Mark's hiccupping back with her free hand. The other was busy holding the steering wheel. "It's okay." And it was okay, for Mark at least. It turned out that the bottom of the Jeep just grazed his scalp. Mom and I never did get to go on our picnic, though.

AMANDA

THAT SPRING, I did mushrooms for the first time with my friends Anna and Sue. We ate them in the cottage and decided to go check out the new house. It was framed, but there was no Sheetrock or anything. Mom said we'd move in that summer, and I for one could not wait. The new house was huge, palatial compared to the cottage. That night, I showed Anna and Sue where the kitchen was going to be, and the dining area. Mom called the living room "the great room" because it had cathedral ceilings and French doors that opened out onto a deck. And that was just the first floor. I was so excited; we were going to have so much space! As I was leading them to Mom's bedroom wing, all of a sudden the floor disappeared. I stepped into nothing and then I landed with a thud on my back, still in a walking position. My breath was knocked out of me, and it took me a moment to realize I had fallen through the hole where stairs one day would lead to the basement. I landed on a pile of plastic-covered gravel. I couldn't breathe, let alone answer my friends, who were wandering around above me, calling my name. I'm just glad they hadn't poured the concrete yet.

LIZ

WE MOVED INTO the new house that summer, and it made everyone happy. Especially Mom. She was done with her radiation and finally looking ahead. The house represented our future, our family redefined. And even though it was still a work in progress, I loved every corner of it, including the mudroom, which had pegs installed for all our coats and a bench where we could sit to pull off our winter boots.

The kids' quarters were upstairs. Amanda and I still shared a room, but this one was as long as the whole house was wide, and Dan finally had his own real room. It was adjacent to Diana's, which Mom had furnished with a new bunk bed even though Diana still slept with her at night. Mom's bedroom was downstairs. She called it the "master suite." It had its own foyer, a walk-in closet, and a bathroom with a Jacuzzi and a bidet. Mom had gotten rid of the crushed-blue-velvet headboard and king-size bed she'd shared with Dad in the old house and was using the bed she shared with Diana in the cottage instead. It looked small and sad in this cavernous room, but it was temporary. We'd buy new furniture once she got another job, because money was especially tight since Mom had been written off *Loving.* She'd only done one commercial, for IBM's Selectric typewriter. Still, she was going to the Actors Studio every week and trying in earnest to lose weight. She was focused on finding work, not only for herself but for me and Dan and Diana as well.

That summer, Mom shuttled us back and forth from Bedford to the city for auditions, and in between trips, I juggled as many jobs as I could. I worked as a maid for the von Unwerths, a wealthy couple who paid me seven dollars an hour to serve them breakfast and hand-buff their marble bathroom floors. I learned how to iron—Madame von Unwerth liked her bed sheets crisp—and to set a proper table and poach a perfect egg. On the weekends, they paid me extra to serve lunches and dinners, for which I wore my best Laura Ashley dresses. I also continued to babysit for the Stewarts, and I got a new gig babysitting for the Chamberlains, who had two kids. Three-year-old Margaret had so many food allergies that the list of foods she could not eat was longer than the list of foods she could. William, her baby brother, had come home from the hospital that spring. I liked their mom, Nancy, a lot. She loved to shop and would buy me Indian-print shirts at the Banksville open market and stock the fridge with my favorite foods. Ted, her husband, was kind and always grilling me about my musical tastes. For his birthday that summer I gave him two cassettes: Echo and the Bunnymen and Talking Heads, and he always made a point of playing one or the other in his BMW as he drove me home. Like the Stewarts, the Chamberlains asked me to housesit as well, which I did one weekend while they went to Martha's Vineyard for their summer holiday.

The night before they left, I'd met a cute boy at a keg party who went to John Jay, Fox Lane's rival. His name was Bobby, and he was muscular with a hawkish nose and floppy hair. I decided that he was the perfect guy for my experiment. Still convinced Paul dumped me because I was bad in bed, I was looking for a guy to have sex with. If I got better, then maybe I could win Paul back. I fantasized about surprising him at West Point that fall and had even planned the outfit: oversized sweater, tight jeans, and my favorite ankle boots. I'd seduce him, we'd have sex, and we'd start going out again. I invited Bobby to the Chamberlains' the following night.

The family had left hours before he arrived. He was dressed in baggy shorts and a baseball cap and brought a six-pack of beer. We drank it all in the sitting room before we started to kiss.

Bobby had no idea I was using him, but as his kisses got more urgent and aggressive, I started to get nervous. Our teeth crashed and his tongue gagged me. He wasn't kissing me so much as devouring me, but my determination trumped my fear. I led him through the empty house to the downstairs guest room with its peach sheets and matching wallpaper.

I had sex again that night, and it was even worse than the first time. I lay there like a corpse, worried that if I moved it might hurt even more. When he finally fell on top of me, limp and heavy, I bit my lip to fight back tears. I wanted him off of me and out of the house. He tried to kiss me again, but I said, "I can't. You have to leave." I lied and said the

Chamberlains were coming home that night. He got dressed and said he'd call, and I hoped he never would. Sex, I decided then and there, sucked.

The next morning I woke up in the Chamberlains' guest room sore between my legs and around my neck. I saw the marks in the bathroom mirror—dark welts ringed my throat, a splotchy purple noose. I called my friend Rita, easily the coolest girl in my grade. She was outgoing and flirtatious and always had a boyfriend or two. She'd know how to get rid of hickeys. And I needed to get rid of mine fast. It was Saturday morning, and I was supposed to go to the city to meet modeling agents that Tuesday with Mom.

"Try combing them out," Rita suggested over the phone in a matter-of-fact way. I found a wide-tooth comb in Nancy Chamberlain's bathroom and followed her instructions, watching myself in the mirror as I scraped the plastic teeth against my throbbing neck. It didn't work. In fact, it seemed to electrify the pain in the bruises. I called Rita again.

"Try an ice pack," she said. "I read that cold-water compresses and combing works."

I asked her if she had ever had a hickey before.

"Are you kidding me?" she said. "My father would kill me."

Nancy Chamberlain had asked me to weed her garden for extra money, so I spent the entire day pulling crabgrass and dandelions from the beds that surrounded the pool, taking breaks every hour to ice and comb my neck. Miraculously, the hickeys started to fade by nightfall. By Tuesday morning, when Mom picked me up to take me to the city, my neck was back to normal, and I swore I'd never have sex with a stranger again. Or with Paul Martino. Or with anyone else for that matter. Of course I couldn't tell Mom any of this. She'd never understand. We talked about my modeling future instead.

"It put me through college, Bitsy," Mom said. I had seen her modeling photos from when she was young, and it was hard to imagine that the co-quettish woman in those shots was Mom. Now forty-eight, she was on another diet that summer; her goal was to lose twenty pounds as, she always said glumly, "the camera adds ten."

I was excited about the money I could make modeling. Dan had already booked two commercials that summer and banked close to ten thousand dollars. As we drove toward the city, I thought maybe I would get back into acting. Maybe I'd apply to drama school. Maybe I'd be an actress like Mom after all.

I met agents at Ford and Elite who told Mom I was cute but, at five-foot-seven-and-a-half, not tall enough. My height did not seem to bother the agent at Wilhelmina, who talked about me in the third person to his colleague. They wanted test shots, and Mom brought me back to New York the following week. I sat on a stool as someone curled my hair, another person applied my makeup, and more people talked about me in the third person. Then someone directed a fan at my head, and the photographer told me to smile. I had no idea modeling would be so hard: I didn't like the bright lights shining in my face, or the people tugging on my clothes or applying more lip-gloss, or the photographer barking at me to "Smile! Not that much! Open your eyes! Raise your chin!"

A week later, we went back to Wilhelmina. "She's a bit stiff in front of the camera," one agent said. "And see that tooth? That's a problem."

My right incisor did pop out of line, making my smile lopsided. I glowered at Mom—she should have gotten me braces, after all.

"Get that fixed," the other agent continued. "And have her lose about five pounds, and we'll do another test shoot."

Mom was pissed. "That's just ridiculous!" she said several times as we drove back home toward Bedford. "You're perfect the way you are!"

"My thighs are kind of fat," I offered. "Maybe I should start doing Jane Fonda with you."

"Your thighs are perfect, Bitsy!" Mom sounded exasperated. "I'm the one who needs to lose weight, not you."

"What if we diet together?" I suggested. Mom looked at me and smiled.

"I'll work on losing weight and getting work," she said. "You just concentrate on being fifteen."

AMANDA

MOM REALLY DID think Liz could model. Once, Mom was up in our room showing Liz how to pose, pointing one foot in front of her and twisting her leg with her hands on her hips. She was standing in front of a full-length mirror, leaning back and striking these weird poses wearing her horrible red robe, all puffy, her hair uncombed. Liz and I started laughing. We were like, "That's not modeling, Mom." And she burst into tears. I hadn't seen her cry much since Dad died. We were being so mean, she left the room crying. We kept on laughing. We couldn't stop.

LIZ

AS THE SUMMER was coming to an end, Rita asked to borrow my favorite pair of Guess overalls to take on her family vacation. These pants were really cool—dark brown denim with beige linen patches. I'd bought them at the Denim Mine with babysitting money and was hesitant to loan them out. But I really liked Rita and her big laugh and the mischief in her eyes. Plus, she had helped me get rid of my hickeys. I said yes.

But then several weeks passed, and I wanted my pants back. I called her house and got the machine. "Hey, Rita, it's Liz," I said into the tape. "Hope you had a nice vacation and, um, I was wondering if I could come get my overalls."

I waited a day or two and got no response. So I left another message.

No response. I was getting annoyed. School was starting soon, and I really wanted to wear them the first day. I called again and decided she was not calling me back on purpose. I swore to never let anyone borrow my clothes again and called for the last time, to tell Rita just that.

This time, her brother Eddie answered the phone. He was a few years older than Rita.

"Oh, hi, um, is Rita there?" I asked.

"Who's calling?" Eddie sounded drugged, as though it was hard to get the words out.

"It's her friend Liz," I said.

Silence for a few seconds, and then his voice grew heated and energetic and angry. "Are you calling about your fucking overalls?" he nearly shouted into the phone. "Well, guess what, our parents are fucking dead, so fuck you and fuck your fucking overalls!" He slammed down the phone.

I hung up, shaking, and ran to find Mom. She was doing the Jane Fonda workout in her room, where we had set up the VCR and TV.

"I need to go see Rita," I said breathlessly.

"What is it, Bitsy?" Mom asked, mid leg lift.

"Her parents died," I said and started to tremble.

Mom's whole body tensed, her left leg suspended in midair, and she looked at me with wide eyes.

"Both?" she said.

I nodded, and she dropped her leg.

Rita's house was filled with people dressed in black. There was food everywhere—nut-crusted cheese balls, platters of cold cuts and cookies. Her aunt was wearing a black lace veil and wailing, her brother Eddie sat in the living room surrounded by more aunts and uncles who were petting him, grabbing hold of his arm, patting his cheek and bellowing like wounded walruses. There were so many tears in that room, such an outpouring of pain. It was terrifying. I finally found Rita upstairs sitting on her bed, alone, floating above the grief boiling below. I understood why she looked more bewildered and shocked than sad. I sat next to her and gave her a huge hug, and she collapsed into my arms and began to sob. "You're going to be okay," I said. "You'll be okay." I said it again because I didn't know what else to say. Then, between sharp inhales, Rita told me what happened: On the way back from their family vacation, Rita decided to ride in her aunt's car. A drunk driver hit her parents' van head-on. They both died instantly.

"What's going to happen?" I asked.

She looked at me, shrugged, and said, "I have no idea."

At that moment, Rita and I became best friends. A month later, she moved in; Mom didn't hesitate when I asked if it was okay.

Rita was a mess for a while. I'd bump into her in the hallway at school, between classes, and she'd burst into tears. Instead of going to our next period, we'd sneak out of the building and drive Rita's car to the Brownstone Café in Mount Kisco, where we'd order cappuccinos and talk for hours. I was the only person who understood her grief, she said time and time again. But that was not entirely true; I only knew what it felt like to lose Dad.

AMANDA

WE COULDN'T AFFORD student housing, so I commuted back and forth from NYU my sophomore year. Still, I was rarely home. When I wasn't in school, I was partying. I had this great clique of friends whose lives were way more fucked up than my own. I loved going to gay clubs; I would lose myself in my own little world, dancing, drinking, and being batted about by buff gay guys as if I didn't even exist.

Sometimes, I would make enough whiskey sours to fill a gallon water jug, and Anna and I would drive to see David Johansen shows in New Jersey, Long Island, and Martha's Vineyard. I had just bought a Karmann Ghia convertible for nine hundred dollars with the money I'd saved up from working at Heller's shoe store and at Abbie's farm. It was the first thing I could call my own. To me, the Mercedes was always Dad's car. I'd drive the Karmann to shows, blaring Madonna, Depeche Mode, or "Ride of the Valkyries," wearing my mirrored Vuarnet sunglasses and rubber bracelets up and down both arms. I thought I was the shit. Anna and I would drive four hours to see a show, then turn around and head back home. I'd be so spent, I'd take cat naps at red lights and tell Anna to wake me when the light turned green.

At that time, Mom was done with radiation, and we thought the cancer was gone. But then Mom started complaining of lower back pain, which she at first thought was gas. It got so bad that on September 27, 1984, Mom drove herself to the emergency room in Mount Kisco. That's when they found a tumor in her bladder, the size of a grapefruit.

She underwent surgery the very next day. I took Liz, Dan, and Diana to visit her in the hospital, but she was pretty whacked out on Demerol. The medical records describe her as a "very cooperative, markedly pale lovely lady who verbalizes that she misses her children." She was discharged on October 1, the day after Diana's seventh birthday. Then on October 4 she was readmitted for her first chemo treatment. She never got a fucking break.

DIANA

STARING AT THE underside of my top bunk, I tried to fall asleep but couldn't. I hummed a Prince song to keep my mind away from all the scary things I kept thinking of, like Dan's snake, Herbie, for instance, slithering around in his glass cage right next door. I wasn't used to sleeping alone, but with Mom in the hospital, there wasn't anyone for me to sleep with.

DAN

MY ROOM WAS weird. I'm not sure why Mom designed it this way, but I had to walk through Diana's bedroom to get to mine, which didn't make any sense. There were skylights above my bed that I snuck out almost every night by crawling through them and onto the roof. Then I'd jump down to the yard behind the house and go meet friends in Mount Kisco to play army. I could have just walked through Diana's room, down the stairs, and out the front door. No one would have noticed.

By this point, I decided I didn't need a best friend. Or, rather, I realized I could go from one best friend to the next. I'd stopped hanging out with Curtis, which hurt him badly. And it hurt his mom. They didn't understand; I didn't understand, either. I just didn't want to be attached to anyone for too long. I went from Curtis to Carlos to Tim. It was kind of sad, because I didn't care about anyone's feelings.

But every Wednesday night, I stayed home. I'd lie in Mom's bed with her and Di and watch *Wonder Woman*. One night, we were lying there and I told Mom how much I missed Dad, and she said she did, too. She had started getting chemo because of the bladder tumor, and she was nauseous a lot and was starting to go bald. That's when she told me that she would have committed suicide if it wasn't for us kids. So I asked her which one was her favorite, and she said, "Well, you're my favorite son!" and laughed. Then we watched *Charlie's Angels*. Dad always really loved Jaclyn Smith.

AMANDA

WHEN THE CANCER came back, Mom was still dealing with Dad's debt. Her finances were a mess. The Bank of New York was now suing her for the money Dad owed from the oil-rig deal. She was trying to file for bankruptcy, but it wasn't working, and she was really worried that we would lose the house.

I'm sure Dad didn't mean to leave Mom with such a mess, but he did. And I don't remember her ever saying one bad word about him. Ever.

LIZ

THE WHOLE MODELING for money thing never really panned out. Mom got me a retainer for my tooth and then she got sick. Within two weeks, I lost the retainer and gained five pounds, so we never scheduled that appointment for the second round of test shots.

It didn't really matter. Mom stopped talking about my modeling and her dieting altogether now that the cancer was back. By Thanksgiving, she'd lost ten pounds and most of her hair. It fell out in clumps, and she started wearing a scarf. On the days she felt okay, she'd putter around the house and even run a few errands, but mostly she stayed in her room in bed. So every day after school, Rita and I would go tell her about our day. She loved hearing all the gossip. She'd grill Rita on any new boyfriends and ask me how French was going. I was in an AP class and that made her happy. She had only been to Europe once—she and Dad went to the Swiss Alps for their honeymoon—and she often talked about taking us kids back one day. Not just to Switzerland but to France and England too.

After the daily update, I'd make Mom a snack—she was often nauseous but could eat Branola bread, which she liked to dip in milk. Then we'd play backgammon or Scrabble. Mom loved board games. Diana always joined us, and Dan often popped his head in and sometimes climbed onto the bed next to Diana to watch TV. They'd argue over how to position Mom's new Craftmatic bed, which was like a hospital bed with a handheld panel that had buttons to elevate your feet or your head. It also had a vibrate and a massage button. Diana liked vibrate; Dan liked massage. If you pushed both at once, it made Mom even more nauseated than she already was.

We all spent a lot of time with Mom in that room. And I spent less time babysitting as I had so much going on: physics, trigonometry, Latin, Honors English, and AP French in addition to household chores. Plus, I was playing varsity volleyball, and Rita and I both were elected class representatives for student government. And so the only pocket cash I had was the extra money I added to the grocery bills each week—enough to buy snacks at school and chip in for gas for Rita's car since she drove me everywhere, but not enough for any new clothes. And I desperately wanted these acid-washed paisley Guess jeans I saw at the Denim Mine, and this thigh-length purple sweater I spotted at the Silo, my favorite store at the Bazaar Mall. One afternoon, I was complaining to Rita, and her eyes lit up.

"Why don't you charge them?" she said. She pronounced "charge" with a long dull *ah* and dropped the *r*.

I had no idea what she was talking about.

"It's like using a credit card only you never pay the bill," she said.

I was still confused.

"I'll show you." She told me to bring my bag, which was oversized and slouchy. I had bought it that summer on Eighth Street in Manhattan. Then we drove to the Mall. At the Silo, I watched as Rita browsed the racks and nonchalantly carried five items into the dressing room. There, she talked loudly about each as she pretended to try them on while using a letter opener that she had concealed in her bag to pry the metal security tag off the one item she intended to steal. I watched fascinated as she shoved a glittery gold sleeveless turtleneck into her bag and then brought the rest of the items out and told the saleslady they weren't quite right.

Back in the car, I felt giddy. I could do that!

The following day, we went back to the Silo and I chose two loose-knit sweaters, a pair of ribbed leggings, a plaid blazer, and a silk Nehru jacket. I then mimicked Rita from the day before: "These leggings make me look so fat!" I shouted over the dressing room door.

"How about the jacket?" Rita yelled back.

"It's cute," I said, "but I'm not sure it's the right color."

Meanwhile, I had tugged the tag off the gray and white sweater before folding and placing it in my bag. As I placed the other items on the reject rack, my blood cells were vibrating beneath my skin.

"Did anything work?" the saleslady said.

"I'm going to think about the Nehru jacket," I said.

In the safety of the parking lot, Rita high-fived me and said, "You're a natural!"

I was. Soon, we were driving to the Bloomingdale's in Stamford, Connecticut, and stealing four or five items at a time. I got the paisley Guess jeans during one haul, a Liz Claiborne thigh-length sweater during another, and leopard loafers during yet another. Quickly, I moved on from clothing: I stole a bottle of Cuervo tequila as Rita tried to convince the old man at the counter to sell her Jägermeister, insisting it was for her dad. We looked at each other, shrugged, and sauntered out the door, the tequila bottle banging against my leg.

Back in the car, Rita hollered. "What an idiot!"

He was not alone. Idiots surrounded us. I once stole an entire case of Amstel Light from ShopRite. I placed two six-packs side by side at the bottom of my bag, grabbed a box of tampons, and then went to a register manned by a pimply-faced boy. His embarrassment overpowered the sound of bottles clanging in my bag. When I came back for the other two six-packs, he looked perplexed. I placed a bottle of aspirin on the counter and said, "Cramps." His face went raspberry red, I paid for the pills, and the bottles clinked with every step I took out the automatic glass doors into the parking lot, where Rita waited for me in the Jeep, engine running.

I always said I'd stop if I ever got caught, but I never thought I would. I was too good at it. Rita taught me the basics, but I quickly turned it into an art form, and soon we were skipping school and heading to Manhattan. One day, we went to Macy's at Herald Square. As I walked out of the busy department store with more than five hundred dollars' worth of clothes in my bag, I looked right at the security guard and said, "Have a nice day!" Rita blanched then quickened her pace. Once outside, she seemed more concerned than triumphant when she asked, "Liz, do you want to get caught?"

She didn't understand that I was simply perfecting the facade. Just as I did not look like a fatherless daughter with a sick mother, I did not look like a school-skipping kleptomaniac. And my stealing added credence to my ruse: My closet was stuffed with all the latest fashions, and because everyone at school thought I was rich, no one questioned my of-the-moment wardrobe. Except Mom. Whenever she saw me in a new outfit, she'd ask, "Where did you get that, Bitsy?"

"It's Rita's," I'd say.

More than once Mom noticed the holes, too. In my haste to pry the security tag off items, I'd often rip the clothing in one spot. But I had an arsenal of explanations: "It got caught on my locker at school," or "I closed it in the car door," or "It got snagged on the cafeteria table." And every time Mom seemed to believe me. Once, though, I told her I tripped in the parking lot, and she looked at me, slightly suspicious, and said, "You should be more careful."

DAN

LIZ STOLE US a six-pack of beer from the ShopRite, and then she and Rita dropped Tim and me off at his girlfriend Beth's house one night while her parents were at the movies. Beth had a friend over named Holly, who liked me. So we showed up with the beer and went into separate rooms. Holly and I had the lights and our clothes off when we heard Beth's parents come into the house. Beth's mom opened the bedroom door and saw me pulling up my pants. Behind her, I saw Tim race by followed by Beth's dad. By the time I ran out the door, shouting "I'm sorry, I'm sorry!" to Beth's mom, Tim was already down the road with Beth's father running after him.

I knew that Larry Williams lived nearby. He had graduated from Fox Lane the year before, and had stuck around to be a lacrosse coach. Even though I was only thirteen, we got along great. When I got to Larry's house, a party was in full swing. All of the black football and lacrosse players were there, getting high, dancing, drinks raised up in the air. I knew everybody from hanging with Curtis, whose older brother Mike was the most popular guy in high school. Everybody was like, "Hey, little dude," clapping me on the back. Finally, I found Larry and was like, "Larry, you gotta help me find Tim." I told him the whole story: the crash, the dad, everything.

Larry was like, "But it's my party, man." He felt bad for me, I guess, because he left his party and drove around for a while looking for Tim before he finally drove me home. He was such a sweet guy.

When we pulled up to the house, I saw Mom through the dining-room window. She was so frail looking, bald and skinny in her robe, creeping toward the kitchen with a golf club raised above her head. Then I saw Tim crawling through an open window in the kitchen. Mom thought he was an intruder! Luckily, I beat him in and reassured Mom that everything was all right. I told her that I'd explain everything in the morning, and she was so relieved that she just said okay and went back to her room.

The next day, I told her what happened. She was quiet for a second, then said okay, and then turned to Tim and asked, "Do you want to tell your parents, or shall I?" Tim said he would tell his parents, but of course never did. He didn't have the honesty with his parents that I had with Mom. Then he started to blame me for things. One time, I invited him over, but he said he wasn't allowed. His parents thought I was a bad influence. I was like, "How's that even possible? You're a fucking nightmare!"

Then he told me that he had cut down a bunch of trees in his neighbor's yard, and that when his parents confronted him, he told them that I did it. I was shocked, like, "Dude, how could you do that?"

"Who's gonna get mad at you?" he asked.

It seemed like Tim and I were always competing for everything. I was team captain and most valuable player on my eighth-grade lacrosse team, but I was jealous because Tim played on the high school team. Even though he got the lead in school plays, he seemed pissed that I had done two commercials that summer. Meanwhile, the commercials were ridiculous. For Chemical Bank, I had to dress in knickers and an old-timey hat and leapfrog over five other guys. And for Long John Silver's, a fast-food joint, I had to eat flash-fried fish. Each piece was golden on the outside but frozen on the inside so it wouldn't fall apart. I had to take a bite and then say, "It's delicious!" After fifteen takes, I wanted to puke.

But our biggest competition was for the ladies. One time, Tim secretly taped me while I was telling him a sex story. I was bragging about being with a girl, being raunchy, laying it on thick. Then he played the tape for everybody at a party, so all the girls were like, "How could you?" I was really popular with the ladies, and Tim was sabotaging me in the worst way. I felt so betrayed. I started running down the road because I didn't want anybody to see me cry. All these girls were running after me, screaming. I was just crying and running. I had to get away from them, but I was in the middle of Pound Ridge, and I didn't know how to get home. I don't remember how I did.

AMANDA

BY CHRISTMAS, MOM was completely bald and thinner than I'd ever seen her. Liz and I got a tree and decorated it with all our old ornaments from the gray house. On Christmas morning, Mom acted as if she was happy, opening her presents all wide-eyed, but it was all so sad and depressing. Karen Kayser was there. We'd known her all our lives. One of Mom's best friends, she used to come from the city every weekend when we were little. Since Mom got sick, she started coming again. That Christmas, Karen gave Mom a Nikon camera. And Liz gave Mom a sequined, cobalt-blue V-neck sweater that she had stolen from Bloomingdale's. Mom oohed and ahhed, but I doubted she would ever wear it. She barely got out of bed. Where in hell was she going to wear a sequined sweater?

Even though the chemo just seemed to make her sicker, Mom went in for her fourth and final round on December 29, and I threw a party. Liz told everyone at school, and again I charged at the door. We had kegs and a band down in the basement. It wasn't the first time I did this: I called them chemo parties, and by then, I had perfected it. We kept the rowdies in the basement with the keg, and my friends and I partied in the kitchen with the liquor.

When Mom came back in early January, she was really weak and pretty much bedridden. She even had an IV. Ever since she'd driven herself to the emergency room in September, I was trying to stay home more. I'd even go and check on her, but I never actually set foot in her room. I always stayed in her doorway and talked to her from there. She had to turn her head to see me. Then I'd escape back to the kitchen, where there always seemed to be people, either Liz's friends or mine, hanging out.

One day, I was sitting at the kitchen island barefoot with some friends, smoking a cigarette, when I heard Mom coming, wheeling her IV beside her. I dropped my cigarette on the tile floor and put it out with my bare foot. Mom came around the corner, all frail and worried. She said she smelled smoke.

"Really?" I said, looking her right in the eye. "I don't smell anything."

She just shook her head and wandered back to her room.

LIZ

SEVERAL WEEKS AFTER my sixteenth birthday, Mom came back from the hospital with a plastic bag attached to her belly. It was her new bladder; her old one had been removed due to a "persistent tumor." The months of chemo were supposed to shrink the tumor that was causing her lower back pain. Instead, she lost her hair, her strength, her smile, the shine in her eye, and even her throaty laugh. But not the tumor. It was persistent.

Mom's first night home after her operation was in late February. She was weak from the operation and needed to take pills every few hours. Since we couldn't afford a night nurse, I volunteered. I decided to sleep downstairs in the guest room to be closer to her.

I had a physics test the next day. That class bored me to distraction; I'd stare out the window or write Rita notes or make ideal mix tape lists on the back of my notebook. For the first time in my life, I thought I might fail. Still, instead of studying that evening, I sat in Mom's room with her and went over the doctor's notes. Mom said the name of the medication, and I found it in the clutter of white plastic childproof bottles on her bedside table. Then she read the doctor's instructions:

"Two every four hours."

And I wrote "2/4hrs" on the cap with a black Sharpie.

"One every twelve hours" became "1/12" on the cap.

When she said, "As necessary," I paused.

"For pain," she explained, and I marked it "AN" on the white pill cap.

After we finished, we watched Amanda's most recent mixed videotape: MTV videos cut with TV concert footage. Instead of studying for physics, I watched Thomas Dolby sing "She Blinded Me with Science" with Mom. When Cyndi Lauper did "Girls Just Want to Have Fun," Mom shimmied her shoulders back and forth. Then Wham! sang "Wake Me Up Before You Go-Go," and Mom started bopping her head back and forth. Her neck was so scrawny, I was worried her head would snap off. But she seemed happy, listening to George Michael sing. She even started tapping her fingers on her thigh, thin and bony beneath the blue blanket. Fuck physics, I thought.

Around ten o'clock, I said good night, went next door to the guest room, and set my alarm for 2 a.m., when Mom was due to take her next pill. I crawled into the four-poster bed, which used to be in Auntie Eve's room in the gray house. The canopy was made of white eyelet and matched the bed skirt, which brushed the floor with its scalloped edge. I fell into a deep sleep and had a dream about Dad, which was similar to ones I'd had before.

In this one, Dad was wearing a white cable-knit fisherman's sweater and standing at the stern of a steamship, waving at me as the boat pulled away from the dock where I was standing, waving back. I was so thrilled to see him—he was alive after all! But then I realized that I had missed the boat, and panic set in as I watched him slowly disappear into the fog. My heart started pounding fast in my chest, and I woke with a jolt thinking, "He's still alive!" But when my eyes sprang open, I saw stop-light-red digital numbers blinking at me: 2:00 a.m., 2:00 a.m., 2:00 a.m. I fumbled for the button to silence the clock's screech and felt a panic similar to the panic in my dream as I was lying in a strange bed, cocooned in eyelet and pink. Then I remembered why I was there. I jumped up and walked quickly and quietly to Mom's room.

When I opened her door, she was sitting up, waiting. She looked tired and ghostly, and I wondered if she had slept at all.

"Did you hear my alarm?" I whispered in the dark.

"Yes," she whispered back. "But I was already up."

I started with the bottle closest to her bed, marked "AN," unscrewed the cap, and shook two bright pink pills into her outstretched hand.

"These will help," I said.

I poured a glass of water for her and watched as she threw the pills into her mouth and tilted her head back to drink. She was completely bald by then, and her veins looked like thin blue rivers, one breaking off to another and then another, etched all over her moon-white scalp. Her cheekbones jutted out like rocky outcrops over the deep canyons that were once full cheeks. And her lips were parched, cracked creeks. After she took all her pills, I asked if she'd like some Vaseline to soothe them.

"Thanks, Bitsy," she said, puckering up as if to give me a fat kiss.

I dabbed some on her lips, which sucked the gel up, water disappearing into sand.

"Anything else, Mom?" I asked, now sitting next to her on the bed. My weight sank the mattress beneath me and raised her up a few inches. "A snack, maybe?"

She shook her head no, then squeezed her eyes tight and shook her head again. When she opened her eyes, they were glassy with tears.

"There is something else," she whispered hoarsely and pointed beneath the covers. "I think it's full." Her eyes darted away from mine.

I pulled back her covers and saw the bag, the size of a sandwich, lying on her sunken belly. It was bloated taut with an amber brown liquid that strained at the plastic and connected to a pencil-size plastic tube that came out of a slit in her stomach, two inches northwest of her right hip bone. The tube had a nozzle that slipped into a slot on the bag, attached to a Velcro belt. I caught a glimpse, then, of her plastic panties and realized they were diapers. I was confused. I knew I had to change the bag—Mom needed to regain strength before she could do it on her own. But no one ever mentioned anything about diapers.

I concentrated on the bag. I unhooked it from the nozzle, which was attached to a long tube that emerged from Mom's belly. I handed Mom the tube, which she held up in the air so that the liquid drained back into her body, and then I carried the bag to the bathroom. Holding it gingerly, as if it were a grenade, I was careful not to slosh or spill its murky contents, which I dumped into the toilet. That's when I was hit by the smell, a fetid stench that forced me to use one hand to clamp my nostrils and lips shut as I rinsed the bag out in the sink.

I reattached the bag back to the tube that poked out of the small pink slit in Mom's stomach. The incision looked like a small mouth without teeth. It looked hungry, scary, and raw. As soon as it was connected, the mouth started spitting and drooling brownish gold liquid back into the bag. I wondered how long it would take to fill up again.

"I hate that you have to do this, Lizzie Bits," Mom whispered in the quiet darkness. She patted my hand with hers, which was all bony and webbed, like a creature, not my mother. "I hate that you have to see your mother this way."

My jaw was tense as I mumbled, "It's no big deal," quickly slipping my hand from beneath hers.

She pulled her own hand to her chest and winced. I wondered what hurt more, the sickness that was consuming her or the realization that she scared me.

I felt suddenly claustrophobic: I had to get out of the room and away from this frail and bald figure more terrifying than any nightmare.

"You're my rock, Lizzie Bits," she whispered as I slipped out her door. Only when I was in the dark hallway and could no longer see her was I able to say, "Good night, Mom."

But I was lying. That was not Mom.

DIANA

AFTER A WHILE, I started sleeping with Mom again, which was scary, too, but a different kind of scary. Now, I was the only danger in the room. Once my thrashing legs jostled her in the night and made her cry out in pain. "Sorry," I whispered and curled myself into a ball, holding on to my knees so I wouldn't kick in my sleep.

"It's okay," she whispered back, patting my hip. She had a tube that went into her belly, and in the daytime, I watched as dark yellow liquid traveled through the clear plastic and into a bag that made a crinkling sound as it filled.

"You're peeing!" I said to her, giggling. She tried to smile. Her head was fragile, with skin stretched over her skull. Her hair was newly sprouting in whispers. She stank. The veins in her hands were puffy and blue. They moved when I touched them, over her bones, beneath her skin.

At night, that sound of the bag filling made me nervous, but I hugged her anyway. I imagined the tube getting yanked out as we slept, catching on my kicking leg and leaking out all over the sheets. There would be pee all over us, seeping along the mattress beneath my belly, up to my face. But the tubes never came out; they stayed in wobbly place, attached with bits of white cotton tape.

LIZ

MOM MUST HAVE realized that it was too hard for me to change her bladder bag because she started doing it herself. I moved back to my room upstairs a week or so later, and then a few weeks after that I got my driver's license. That meant I didn't have to depend on Rita. She was staying less and less at my house, more at her own. I think Mom's illness scared her as much as it scared me.

One March afternoon, I was on my way into the grocery store when I passed a woman standing next to a large cardboard box full of wriggling, fluffy, black puppies.

"What are they?" I asked the woman, who was wearing an ASPCA T-shirt.

"Mixed," she replied. "Someone dropped them on our doorstep–just the puppies. No mom."

I knelt down to pet them, and one with a white blaze on her chest crawled into my hand. She flipped over on her back, exposing her pink belly, and then bit my index finger with her tiny teeth. I had to tear myself away from her and force myself to shop. I raced down the aisles, pulling things we needed from the shelves: soothing foods like Branola bread, tapioca, and rice pudding, the only things Mom could tolerate. Even though she tried hard to stay upbeat, I knew she was tired of being sick. Depressed even. I could see it in her eyes, which were more distant that they'd ever been. Her mouth would curve into a smile whenever I entered the room, as if on cue, but her eyes seemed far away. As I stood in line at the grocery store, I had an idea. Mom loved animals, especially puppies. We had to get rid of all the horses because they were too expensive and too much work, but a dog was easy. We still had Ralph and Max. What was one more?

I paid for the groceries and practically ran out of ShopRite pushing the full cart out the automatic doors and back to the puppy stand.

"How much for a puppy?" I asked the lady, breathless.

"Free," she said, "though we're happy to take donations."

I handed her my twenty-five-dollar pocket money and pointed to the puppy with the white blaze.

I raced home and ran past Amanda, who was sitting in the kitchen, and into Mom's room. Auntie Eve was there, watching *The Merv Griffin Show* with Mom.

"What on earth?" Mom said as I plopped the puppy down on her bed. Auntie Eve shrieked. Mom looked stunned.

"Surprise!" I shouted. Mom's expression shifted from shock to sheer horror.

"Elizabeth," she said angrily. "What have you done?"

"I got you a puppy!" I shouted, jubilant. "Isn't she beautiful?"

By now, Amanda was standing in the doorway, and Auntie Eve had gotten up to turn the TV off. I was puffed up proud, until I registered the look on Mom's face.

"I can barely take care of you kids," she said sort of loud but still under her breath. Then her eyes grew wide and she shouted, "What the hell am I supposed to do with a damn puppy?"

I'd never been slapped in my life, but I imagined that was what it felt like: the sting in my face, the red hotness that followed, trickling like molten lava from my scalp to my toes. I grabbed the puppy, stormed out of the room, and heard Mom burst into tears. As I left, Amanda said, "Don't worry, Mom, I'll help take care of it."

I was lying on my bed staring at the ceiling and listening to my Alarm album, the volume set high, when Amanda walked into the room. The puppy was crawling all over me, pawing up my leg, falling down on her back, then scrambling up to my belly.

Still stunned, I said, "What the fuck is her problem?"

Amanda looked at me and shrugged, then looked at the puppy and smiled. We decided to name her Bentley. By May, she had chewed through three pairs of my shoes, Amanda's Vuarnet sunglasses, the corner of the gold brocade couch, and two family photo albums. But we loved her anyway. Even Mom came around. She apologized to me for getting angry and said that animals had good energy. That was all she needed to heal, she said.

DAN

MOM BELIEVED THAT Diana and I had special powers. Di might have had them, but I was pretty sure I didn't. Mom really believed in that stuff, though. Whenever I rolled doubles playing backgammon, she said I had ESP with the dice. One time, she actually got a spoon and said, "Let's bend it with our minds!" She literally thought we could bend that spoon. She also thought I could shrink her cancer.

For a while, it was just Mom and me doing it: I held my hands over her stomach and visualized the tumor. It looked like a sparkler in this dark vacuum, a radiating light that I was able to snuff out with my hands. I made it shrink and shrink and shrink until it totally disappeared. I tried as hard as I could.

Then these evangelical people came, one lady and four guys, all with perfect hair and big white teeth. I thought they were creepy, but I ignored the feeling because they encouraged me to help Mom. They told me that my hands had the healing power. We gathered around Mom's bed. She was very thin by then and had a scarf wrapped around her head. I slapped my hands and rubbed them together to get the heat going, then held my hands above Mom's stomach, closed my eyes, and imagined her tumor shrinking. But when I opened my eyes, I noticed that her glasses looked bigger on her face. And I realized that she was shrinking, not the tumor. And that I didn't have any power at all.

LIZ

HER DOCTORS WERE hopeful that they had gotten rid of most of the cancer when they removed her bladder, and that the chemo would kill the rest of it. But Mom didn't want to take any chances. She no longer trusted Western medicine, so in addition to weekly trips to Sloan-Kettering, she started going to healers, to church revivals, and to a macrobiotic nutritionist who designed a special diet for her. That meant I had to soak rye seeds in sauerkraut for Mom. That was her breakfast. Still, she insisted that "positive energy" would make her well. "That's all I need!" she'd say.

So I did my part, reporting to her room every afternoon with daily updates: No, I was not dating anyone. Yes, I was going to the junior prom. Rita was going to the dance with this guy Jake just as friends, so when Jake's friend Lance asked me to be his date, I said yes. Rita and I were more excited about dressing up than anything else. We spent over an hour getting ready—hair, makeup, the whole bit—and then walked into Mom's room to say good-bye.

"Elizabeth!" she cried. "What have you done to your hair?"

It was horizontal, brushed up and over as if a fan was blowing hard on one side of my head. To create this effect, I used Mom's curlers, half a jar of Dippity-do, and a blow dryer. I then sprayed the tabletop sculpture into place with Aqua Net.

"You could balance a bowl of soup on it!" Mom continued, aghast.

"It's totally hip," Rita said, sauntering in. Mom did not love Rita's hair, a side ponytail teased to look like a porcupine's tail, either.

"Are you two going to the circus or the prom?" Mom asked, aghast.

I rolled my eyes at her and said with a dramatic sigh for effect, "You're just jealous we have hair!"

Mom's face softened as she smiled big and said, "Have fun."

And we did—first guzzling beer in Lance's Saab before arriving at the

White Plains Hyatt, where we danced for four hours straight. It was fun until our principal, Mr. Lamonica, got on the microphone to announce Prom King and Queen. When Lance's name was called, he literally sprinted to the podium. When mine was called, I froze, then quickly slid beneath the table where I was sitting. I was on my hands and knees panicking when Mr. Lamonica called my name again. Rita's face suddenly appeared beneath the red polyester tablecloth.

"What are you doing down there?" she asked. "Get your ass up to the stage!"

"I lost my earring," I lied. The truth was, I didn't want to be Prom Queen. I just wanted to be a popular girl who wore fashionable clothes and went to New York City on weekends. Somehow, being Prom Queen was taking the fantasy too far. That meant everyone in that room beyond my tablecloth tent accepted my ruse, that I had tricked them all. And somehow that was a betrayal of Mom and my siblings.

"Elizabeth Welch!" I heard my name boomerang around the room and knew there was no escape. I crept out from under the table and walked to the podium, faking a big smile. Mr. Lamonica gave me a hug, put a tiara on my shellacked hair, and then handed me a trophy as tall as a toddler. The next morning, I gave it to Mom, who was so thrilled with my win that she placed the trophy on her dresser, next to her row of wigs. And that made me happy, to see her happy. She wanted me to be a normal teenager more than I did myself. So when I told her my AP French class was scheduling a special trip to Angers, France, that summer, she insisted I go. I was hesitant.

"Who's going to take care of Diana?" I asked one afternoon. "Who's going to take care of you?"

"Everything will be fine, Bitsy," Mom said. "I want you to do this."

And I wanted to do it too, badly. But I would not go without finding someone to replace me. Rita was too wild—plus, she had just started dating a twenty-two-year-old guy. Amanda had enough on her plate, chauffeuring Mom back and forth to the city for medical appointments. So I called Maureen, my best friend from tenth grade. Her dad had been transferred to Schenectady, New York, and I knew she missed Bedford as much as I missed her. So when I called her to see if she'd like to spend the summer at my house and take care of Diana in exchange for fifty dollars a week and a car, she didn't hesitate. She said yes.

Maureen arrived the week before I left for France, so I could show her the ropes—grocery shopping, laundry, keeping the house organized, making sure Diana was bathed and fed, and making Mom's macrobiotic meals. It took a few days for Maureen to get used to seeing Mom so frail. The chemo made her lose weight so fast her skin hung off her like loose clothing, and her hair had only just begun to grow in, a soft, see-through carpet covering her pale scalp. But with her hair, the spark in her eye was coming back. She had survived a brutal winter. She was going to be just fine. That was what I thought the day I left for Angers. I had to think that; otherwise, I couldn't have gone.

That morning, I popped my head into Mom's room to say "au revoir." She was sitting up in bed, having just finished her revolting breakfast.

"Eat many croissants for me, my darling," she said. I gave her a quick hug, promised I would do more than that, and shouted *"à bientôt!"* as I rushed up the stairs to finish packing.

Auntie Eve had come to see me off. She sat in my room as I sat on my suitcase to close it and placed my passport and traveler's checks in the money belt I had bought specifically for the trip. I was buzzing with excitement, but Auntie Eve seemed upset. Every time I looked at her, she shook her head from side to side as if something was wrong.

"What?" I finally asked. She was sitting on the edge of my bed, wearing one of her trademark polyester suits—pale green pants with a short-sleeved button-down top that had pale pink flowers, their stems picking up the green in the pants. Auntie Eve liked synthetics because, as she always said, "You don't have to iron them and you still look neat and tidy." Her silver hair stood up on its ends, like cotton candy, sprayed into a soft helmet.

"It's just that I'm getting old," she said. "This might be the last time I ever see you."

Then her eyes brimmed with tears. She would say that to me every time I left for anywhere over the next twenty years.

"You're not going anywhere!" I said as I wrapped my arms around her. "Who would take care of us?"

AMANDA

AUNTIE EVE STAYED with us for a couple weeks while Liz was gone that summer, to help Maureen around the house. It was a good thing she was there, too, because otherwise I would have killed Dan. He wouldn't listen to anything anyone said; he was so confrontational, like, don't tell me what to do, I'm going to do whatever the fuck I want. So I was like, well, then I'm going to kill you.

It escalated one afternoon when we were all in the kitchen. I said, "My friends saw you out at three o'clock in the morning. What were you doing running around Mount Kisco at three o'clock in the morning?" And Dan was like, fuck off, I don't care. Then he grabbed his crotch at me. I lost it. It was just so offensive, and he was giving me that I-don't-give-a-fuck face to go along with it. It made me so angry I tackled him. It was just all my rage at everything that I couldn't control coming out. I was on top of Dan, strangling him, and Auntie Eve was hitting me on my back with a wooden spoon, screaming, "You're killing Dan! You're going to kill him!"

DAN

MY CHOICES WERE: Do what I say, or die. Amanda outweighed me by at least fifty pounds. I was scared to death. My arms were trapped underneath her, and she was smacking my head against the tile floor over and over again. She was crying and her face was all red. She didn't talk to me for two days after that.

Amanda was a classic bully. In order to subdue her, I had to beat her. So I decided to challenge her to a game of Mercy. Amanda was great at it; I once saw her beat my friend Joe Knezevic, who at fourteen was six-foot-two and two hundred eighty pounds. Amanda turned his wrists upside down and twisted, literally lifting him up off the ground. It was insane. As we stood facing each other, I knew I couldn't lose this time. We clasped each other's hands by interlocking our fingers, my palms pressed against hers. The whole idea was to bend your opponent's fingers back until they're about to snap off. The first person to shout "Mercy!" loses. I clenched my jaw, dug in, and won. That was it. We were buddies from then on.

Amanda and I were the ones who went with Mom to the revival. Mom was doing everything in her power to get well, even going to charlatans in tents. When it was our turn, Amanda hung back and I pushed Mom up on the stage. She got out of her chair, and the preacher did his whole thing, pressing his palm against her forehead and banishing the cancer from her body. She fell backwards into her wheelchair, really dramatic, like "I'm saved!" When I wheeled her off the stage, she was smiling.

AMANDA

THOSE FUCKING REVIVALS didn't work. None of it worked—not the healers, or the macrobiotics, or any of that shit. Mom always had faith in the power of the mind. Just like she thought that Dan had magical powers in his hands and that Diana could communicate with the dead, she thought that she could beat her cancer if she tried really hard, if she had the right attitude. She never gave up, even after everyone else did. Including us.

Mom went back into the hospital that July because she had blood in her stool. The cancer had spread to her colon, which they removed on July 18. She weighed one hundred seventeen pounds. Medical records dated July 31, 1985, say that she "weighed one hundred ten pounds, was alert and oriented, spoke openly about illness and terminal prognosis, and voiced concern regarding her children."

DIANA

I DON'T REALLY remember how it started. All of a sudden, people were driving up our driveway, opening their car doors, telling me to hop in and buckle up, then taking me places I didn't want to go.

A lady called Dagne drove me to visit Mom in the hospital. She wore her hair in two long blond braids like a little girl, even though she was Mom's age. Sitting in the passenger seat of her car, I felt weird and resentful. As we passed the Finast where Mom used to take me grocery shopping, a song by Bruce Springsteen came on the radio.

"In the wink of a young girl's eye, glory days," Dagne sang in a clear falsetto like Mom's. She smiled and twitched her head from side to side in keeping with the beat, tapping the steering wheel and, eventually, my knee, walking her fingers up my leg, an itsy-bitsy spider.

"It's 'golden days,'" I said. Stupid, I added silently.

"Huh, sweetie?" she asked, turning her beautiful, smiling face to me for a moment before returning her gaze to the road in front of us.

"He says 'golden days,' not 'glory days,'" I said in my snottiest voice. I knew I was being a brat, but I didn't know why. Auntie Eve called Dagne an angel on this earth. She looked like one, too: Fair-haired and blue-eyed, she was the original Ivory Soap Girl, an actor friend of Mom's. I knew that it wasn't Dagne's fault that she was driving me around; I knew it wasn't her fault that Mom was trapped in that smelly hospital room full of beeping machines. But she was in Mom's spot, at the wheel. And I hated her for it.

"Oh," she laughed sweetly, crinkling her nose. "And here I thought, all along, that it was 'glory days.'"

The song ended, and the deejay announced in his deep, cheerful radio voice, "That was the Boss, coming at you with 'Glory Days.'"

I looked at Dagne, stunned that I was mistaken. I waited for her to laugh at me, to say I told you so. But she just continued to drive, humming a new song. Everything was all wrong. I shrank into the seat, digging the frayed seat belt into the soft skin beneath my chin.

LIZ

THROUGHOUT THE MONTH, I called home weekly from Angers to check in and share my latest news. "French people don't wear shorts!" was an early discovery I shared with Auntie Eve. I saved "There's no drinking age!" and "Heineken only costs a dollar!" for when Amanda answered the phone. Every time I called, either Auntie Eve, Maureen, or Amanda would pick up. Never Mom. And when I'd ask to speak with her, they'd say "She's out to lunch with a friend" or "She's getting her nails done." And I'd hang up even happier. That meant she really was getting better! Maybe the toasted rye seeds soaked in sauerkraut was working! Maybe we were finally home free.

As my entire AP French class flew back to New York, I took a Hovercraft from France to England to visit Janie Rayne, one of Mom's old acting friends. She lived with her husband, Robbie, and their son, Damian, in a four-story town house called Brunswick Gardens. One morning, Janie and I walked her two dogs through Kensington Park, and she told me how she and Mom had met in the sixties, while studying with Lee Strasberg at the Actors Studio. Mom had asked Janie to be her scene partner. "I'd only been in New York for one week and did not know a soul," Janie said. "Your mum was my guardian angel." She went on and on about how famous Mom was, shouting, "She was Dr. Maggie Fielding in *The Doctors*, for Christ's sake!" She called Mom the most beautiful woman in all of New York.

I looked at her, startled. Janie was a former top model. Glamorous photos of her from French *Vogue* and British *Elle* lined the hallways at Brunswick Gardens. And she was calling Mom beautiful? But then I remembered how glamorous Mom looked in the photographs that hung on the wall in her office in the gray house. I had spent my life longing for the Mom that was in those pictures. Now, thousands of miles away from home, I desperately missed the Mom that I knew.

I didn't have much time to dwell on it, because Janie had my day planned out down to the hour. That afternoon, I went to Madame Tussaud's Wax Museum with Damian before meeting her and Robbie at the Hard Rock Cafe for dinner. The next morning, I woke to the whisper of a typed itinerary being slid beneath the door: 9:00 a.m. brekki at Harrods; 11:00 a.m. Buckingham Palace; 1:00 p.m. pub lunch; 4:00 p.m. Tate museum; 6:00 p.m. pub for pre-theater drinks; 8:00 p.m. *Starlight Express;* and 11:00 p.m. supper at Annabel's. As I brushed my teeth, I could not stop smiling. This was turning into the best summer of my life.

After checking out the Tate, I headed back to Brunswick Gardens to change for the theater. When I walked in the front door, I heard Janie in her office at the end of the landing say, "She just walked in." She sounded concerned. When I popped my head into her office, she looked up at me, tears in her eyes.

"What's wrong?" I asked.

She shook her head back and forth a few times, cradling the phone receiver with both hands.

"It's your mum," she said.

She handed me the phone, and I heard Nancy Chamberlain's voice on the other end. I felt like Alice falling through the rabbit hole. "Liz, we didn't want to ruin your summer," she said. "Your mom just got back from the hospital. It's not good."

I could hear Nancy's words—colon, operation, didn't get it all out—but none of them made sense. Then Maureen got on the phone, sobbing.

"I wanted to tell you!" she cried. "But your mom wouldn't let me. She made me promise."

"Is Amanda there?" I managed to ask.

"Hey." Amanda's voice sounded heavy and tired, laced with lead.

"What the hell is going on?" I asked. She was the only one who could make sense of this for me. The others were talking gibberish.

"The doctors say she's too weak for chemo," Amanda said, steely and straight. "They say the chemo would actually kill her. And that the cancer is now in her kidney." She trailed off.

"And?" I said.

"And you need to come home," Amanda said quietly. "So we can figure out where everyone is going to live."

DIANA

ANOTHER LADY WHO picked me up was Mrs. Chamberlain. In the car on the way to the Bedford Golf and Tennis Club, she told me that little girls were "germ factories," and that Mom was too "susceptible to disease." Mrs. Chamberlain had two kids, whom Liz used to babysit for. They were younger than me and no fun; they could barely even swim. So I made friends with the pool manager's daughter, and one time I went to her house for a spend-the-night, but I hated it there. Their only pet was a ferret, and they ate Count Chocula for breakfast. Another lady who picked me up often tried to get me to weed her giant garden. When I said I didn't feel like it, she said, "After all I've done for you?" I just ignored her and kept reading, but it made me feel bad.

The only people I liked picking me up were Auntie Eve and Uncle Harry. They always took me to Auntie Eve's house in Yorktown Heights, where she lived with her son and his family. It was fun there. They had MTV and an above-ground swimming pool in their backyard. Auntie Eve's granddaughters, Cara and Bridget, were both blond and tan, and Cara had braces and long fingernails she painted pink. Bridget was ten, three years older than me, and I copied every move she made.

One evening, Bridget and Cara sat me down for a talk in their bedroom. I thought for sure it was going to be a lecture about copying, and how annoying I was. That afternoon, Bridget and Cara were talking about how hot one of the guys in Tears for Fears was, and when I agreed, Bridget asked, "Which one?" I pointed to the one who looked as if he was wearing a little bit of lipstick.

Both girls groaned. "That guy's so gay!" Cara said.

"Oh, I know," I said quickly, sliding my finger across the television screen to the other guy, who kind of looked like McGruff, the crime-fighting dog.

"No, you already said that you think the gay one is cute. You can't change it now," Bridget said.

"Fine!" I yelled, then ran into the adjacent room and played with Bridget's Barbies, embarrassed.

Now, up in their bedroom, the girls were looking straight at me, their backs against the white slatted folding doors of their shared closet. "We heard that you're going to live with the Chamberlains," Cara said gently. "We heard your mom was really sick."

"Yeah," I said, plucking at the blue carpet with my fingers. I hadn't been thinking about Mom, and it felt good just playing, watching TV, and eating Twinkies. Mrs. Chamberlain was just a lady who came by the house a lot and drove me places. I didn't remember anybody saying anything about living with her.

"Do you think she's going to die?" Cara asked, her voice almost a whisper.

"I hear that they're really rich," Bridget said, hopefully. "That'll be cool."

"Yeah," I said. Then I turned toward them and, feigning happiness, clasped my hands together in front of me and said, "Pray that she dies."

They looked at each other in horror. Bridget's face turned grayish white as her mouth dropped open, and Cara's went hot pink as she smiled a slow, shocked smile.

I could not believe what I'd just said. It was terrible. I didn't want Mom to die, and I hadn't really thought that she would until right then. My whole body felt hot. I scrambled up from the carpet and, starting to cry, ran into the bathroom to sit on the fuzzy pink toilet lid behind the closed door. When I pulled on the toilet paper, it released a gross smell from the beads inside the roller knocking against each other. I pressed the paper against my eyes hard until my body stopped shaking before I wiped them off completely. Then I went into the kitchen and asked Auntie Eve to call Uncle Harry so he could take me home.

There, I spent a lot of time alone, entertaining myself on a big pile of dirt next to our driveway. Even though I wasn't allowed in Mom's room anymore, I snuck in there sometimes to lie on the bed next to her. With my hands pressed together between the pillow and my cheek, I stared at her, at the row of wigs on her dresser, out her window. I listened to her breath, slow and deep, and kissed her face as she slept. Sometimes she would wake up with a start, like I did when I dreamt of falling off the bed, and her eyes would be wide and wild, searching the ceiling until they found my face, and then she would close her eyes and smile.

Earlier that summer, before she went away to Angers, Liz had surprised me with a pair of Guess jeans that zipped at the ankle. There is a rare picture of Mom and me in her bedroom during that time of quarantine. I'm sitting in a rolling office chair next to Mom's bed, wearing those Guess jeans, a Canal Jeans sweatshirt, and a white baseball hat that says "Danny" on it in puffy paint. Mom is wearing just her nightgown and her big dip eyeglasses, and as thin as she is, she is stunningly beautiful, all pink lips and high cheekbones and sad brown eyes. She is completely bald and sitting up on one elbow, leaning in toward me, stick arm around my stiff shoulders. The look on my face makes me think I am trying to act cool, but beneath the white sheet and thin blue blanket, I can see I am clutching Mom's hand.

AMANDA

I TOLD MOM I wanted everybody to live with me: We could stay in the house; Liz could finish Fox Lane; Dan would be at boarding school in the fall; and I would defer my education so Diana could stay with us. We talked about it a lot. But every time, it was the same: I was too young; I had to finish college; I deserved to be nineteen.

Aunt Barbara, Dad's older sister, offered to take all four of us, even though she and Uncle John already had seven kids of their own in Massachusetts. But Liz and I both thought that everybody should stay in Bedford, to maintain some sort of continuity, some normalcy. And then Mom did ask Auntie Eve if she would consider being our guardian. It meant we'd have to move—Mom still owed the Bank of New York that money and had arranged to pay them as soon as we sold our house upon her death. But Auntie Eve said she was too old; well into her seventies, she was already worried about dying herself. Beyond that, I just think Mom couldn't deal. Actively seeking out homes for her kids meant she was actually going to die. And she couldn't admit that, not until the bitter end.

A few local families did come forward to say that they wanted to help out, people that Liz babysat for—the Stewarts and the Chamberlains. Both families said that they could take either Liz or Diana but not both. And neither offered to take Dan: He was way too wild for Mrs. Chamberlain, and Mrs. Stewart bizarrely told Liz that she didn't want all Dan's friends hitting on her. Then this random guy named Topher Scott, an old friend of Dad's from Johns Hopkins that none of us had ever met, came by to see Mom. He asked her if there was anything he could do, and Mom said that yes there was: Take Dan. And he said he would. It was totally out of the blue.

Mom asked Liz and me to figure out where Diana should live. She couldn't decide—it was too fucking painful. The Stewarts were a possibility, but Montgomery bragged about his gun collection and that really freaked Mom out. It seemed that they weren't raising their children in the way we were raised: We had softball games in our yard; the Stewarts had paintball wars.

The Chamberlains seemed more like our family. Mr. Chamberlain seemed warm and genuine and was sweet with his kids. Liz said that they had a really nice house and that they were always kind to her when she babysat. And Mrs. Chamberlain truly seemed to care about Diana. So we decided that Liz would move in with the Stewarts, since she had only a year left of school and she really liked Daisy. Diana would move in with the Chamberlains, pretty much right away, so that she'd be living there when she started third grade that September. Mom had said more than once that she didn't want Diana to watch her die. But Diana's going to the Chamberlains could also have had something to do with Mrs. Chamberlain coming home with Diana one afternoon that summer and finding my friends and me hanging out in our living room, stoned out of our minds. Mrs. Chamberlain narrowed her eyes and stormed off to Mom's bedroom, shielding my little sister with her body. Diana moved out soon after that.

DIANA

WHILE EVERYTHING CHANGED, some things stayed strangely the
same. I went to the same school and lived in the same town. It was a big
house with a big yard with a pool and a pool house. There was one brother
and only one sister but they were both younger than me. There was a mom
and a dad. No horses, no cats, just one big, greasy standard poodle named
Thurman. No Auntie Eve to scratch my back or threaten me with a
wooden spoon, but there was a lady called Rhonda, who flashed a gold
tooth when she smiled and kept the kids in line with the threat she'd "box
their ears" if they didn't do what she said.

I felt most comfortable around Rhonda. She called the mom "Mrs.
Chamberlain," same as I did. Sometimes I slept in the sister's room, but most
nights I slept across from Rhonda in a gable above the kitchen. The two
rooms were practically mirror images of each other: two twin beds, a closet,
and a desk. While her room was cramped, both beds piled with laundry and
the walls lined with the yellow handles of brooms and mops, mine felt
empty. So I hung out in her room a lot as she ironed between the buttons
of Mr. Chamberlain's oxford shirts, only going into my room when it was
time to go to sleep. In there, strawberry wallpaper covered the slanted
walls, which came together in a point at the ceiling. Outside the window
were treetops that I watched sway in the dark as I fell asleep. But sometimes I would cry, my face smashed into the pillow to muffle the sound.

One night, Mrs. Chamberlain came up to say good night and found
me with my face in the pillow. "What are you doing?" she asked me from
the doorway.

"Sleeping," I told her, raising my head just enough to get the words
out. I wasn't crying anymore, but I was worried that my face would be
puffy and that she'd be able to tell.

"People don't sleep with their faces in pillows," she said to me, not
moving from the doorway.

I said nothing and she closed the door.

Another night that August, I got to go home. Mrs. Chamberlain dropped me off for Dan's going-away party before boarding school started. She came in to check and make sure that there was a grown-up around, and there was, a nurse. The house was dark. It felt good to be invited, but it was strange to be there, back in my home, which seemed to be doing fine without me. I wanted to go see Mom, but the nurse told me I wasn't allowed to. I wandered into the kitchen, and Liz and Amanda were there, putting the finishing touches on Dan's cake. They brought it out to him, and it was time to open presents.

Dan was sitting in the living room, surrounded by friends. His red hair was cut shorter and cleaner on the sides than it had been a couple of weeks ago when I last saw him. His face was extra freckled from the summer, and his skinny fingers seemed to be longer than ever before. People were laughing, listening to music, and smoking cigarettes. He opened a present from his girlfriend Dana, who had braces and wore a headband. It was a big painting of people lying around in fancy clothes. When Dan flipped it over, they were naked. Then he opened his other present; it was a carton of cigarettes. I got a present too; Amanda gave me the WHAM! *Make It Big!* videotape that we had all watched together in Mom's room before I had to move out. Mom loved "Last Christmas" the most. I liked "Wake Me Up Before You Go-Go."

I don't remember if I ever got to see Mom that night. I do remember that I ate six bowls of whipped cream that Amanda and Liz made from scratch. When I went into the kitchen for my fifth, a teenager I didn't know asked, "How much whipped cream have you eaten?"

"Four bowls," I said and shrugged. The teenager held her can of beer up and said, "Well, it is a party." She took a swig and smiled. I smiled back and went into the living room to sit next to Dan and eat my treat by the spoonful.

DAN

WHEN I ARRIVED at Trinity Pawling, I was intimidated. I mean, it was my freshman year, and I was leaving all my friends behind at Fox Lane, where I would have had it made. It really helped having a hot older sister; Liz was popular, and I was psyched to ride on her coattails. But Mom really wanted me to have some structure. She said I needed guidance. So she got me a scholarship to come to TP, where they said they specialized in kids with learning disabilities and behavioral problems. Mom thought I was getting lost in the public system. Because of my dyslexia, I needed extra attention.

To be honest, I didn't feel that we had the money or the prestige to be there. We had to wear jackets and ties every day, so Liz and Amanda dropped me off with a trunk full of Dad's old suits. But Dad was stocky and five-foot-eight. At fourteen, I was almost six feet tall and skinny, so all his suits were too wide and too short.

I knew I'd do all right, though, because I was a chameleon. I'd been changing my personality from year to year, from group of friends to group of friends. I remember going to Tim's house after spending a summer with Curtis. We were riding our BMX bikes around when Tim said, "You're talking black. You know that, right?"

"Really?" I said. I had been saying "yo" a lot, and "dag," and sometimes "homeboy."

And he was like, "Yeah. Stop it." And then he rode off.

That's when I realized that I had to be a different person for different groups of friends. So I became this surfer–Gator board–Tony Hawk–skater kid, and everything I owned suddenly had to have checkers on it. But at boarding school, everyone was into messy preppy clothes and the Grateful Dead. The big thing here was to wear your khaki pants down just low enough to expose the elastic waistband of your plaid boxer shorts.

My roommate was a real kook, this hick from the South who was really into eighteen-wheeler trucks. He had pictures of Peterbilts all over
the walls. He never shaved because he wanted a beard, so there were, like,
three pubic hairs coming out of his chin, and he never did his laundry,
ever. He had this piss-stained laundry bag with a Trinity Pawling crest on
it, and it had been sitting there ever since we arrived, just stinking up the
room.

Luckily, Liz helped me get some hot-sister cred at Trinity Pawling, too.
She and Rita came to visit me once, and my whole dorm started freaking
out about how there were these two cute girls on campus. When I brought
them up to show them my room, this one kid came out of the bathroom
wearing only a towel. "Oh, excuse me," he said, making his voice deep on
purpose. "I was just about to shave." And, like an idiot, he'd smeared shaving cream all over his face, around his nose and all the way to his eyes. He
didn't even know how to *pretend* how to shave.

I knew how to shave because, when I was little, I used to hang out with
Dad a lot in his bathroom. One time, he was taking a piss in front of me,
and I was staring at his penis, like, how come his is so big? He winked at
me and said, "Don't worry, it'll grow." He told me to wear boxers, not
briefs. He also taught me how to shave, right then. He lifted me up and
put me on the toilet and put shaving cream on my face. As he started shaving, he told me where to go against the grain for a smoother shave and
how to get against your nose. Then he took the blade out for me so I could
practice with his razor.

LIZ

I WAS OFTEN the only one home during the day, besides Mom and one of the nurses who were now with her around the clock. Amanda was at NYU, Dan was at Trinity Pawling, and Diana had already moved to the Chamberlains'. Still, I had to force myself to go visit Mom in her bedroom.

I understood what was happening to Mom. I could see her decline almost daily: The Craftmatic bed got bigger and bigger as her body grew thinner and smaller. And even though it hurt my heart to walk down the hallway that led to her room, I knew it was important to Mom. She wanted all the gossip. Rita had moved in with her twenty-two-year-old boyfriend. Mom wanted to know what he was like. Was Rita happy? And was my French better after my summer abroad? Mom also wanted to know about volleyball. I had started playing in the seventh grade, went to the Junior Olympics in eighth grade, and played varsity throughout high school. Tryouts had just finished, one week into my senior year.

There were twenty or so girls vying for twelve positions, and I thought I'd make it—no sweat. It was an intense tryout. By the end, my arms and legs felt weighted down with bowling balls. I fantasized I could snap them off, like a Barbie doll, and trade them in for new ones. But it felt good to be playing volleyball with my friends, to be part of this team. It felt good to feel something other than the all-consuming dread of what waited for me at home.

But right before the coach gathered everyone together to make his picks, he called me over. He looked disappointed.

"Welch, how are you supposed to spike the ball if you can only do twenty-five situps in a minute?" he asked. "Your spike is stomach muscle. What were you doing all summer?"

He was not being an asshole on purpose. No one at school except my closest friends knew Mom was ill, let alone dying. Still, I was shocked when

I didn't make the team that year. Then I went home and told Mom the whole story, pretending that it was no big deal. Mom shook her head. She was upset.

"I have a lot going on this semester anyway," I assured her. It was true. I had to retake my SATs and apply to colleges. And I had to decide where I was going to live once Mom died.

I had several offers. Liz Subin said I could come live with them. And the Stewarts had offered too. Then Alison McGovern, a senior at Fox Lane who lived in a mansion on Hook Road, invited me to go shopping with her and her mom in Manhattan. While Alison was trying on back-to-school clothes at Bendel's, her mother told me that Alison had always wanted a sister and asked me if I would live with them. I was dumbstruck. I hardly knew Alison, so I thanked Mrs. McGovern for the "generous" offer and said that it was not necessary. Mrs. McGovern looked alarmed. "I don't think you understand what I'm saying," she explained. "Alison really wants a sister."

In many ways, it didn't matter where I wound up. I was planning on leaving Bedford as soon as I graduated. I just needed a place to stay until I finished school. I didn't need a new family or new siblings, and I didn't want them either. At least I had options. Mom had to coerce Topher Scott into taking Dan. No one else seemed to want him. And even though we all thought the Chamberlains were the best choice for Diana, Mom told me one afternoon that she was nervous about that choice, too.

"Nancy Chamberlain came by today," Mom said.

We hadn't seen much of Nancy ever since Diana moved there. She said it was because she was protecting Diana, which sounded like a good answer—and a terrible one, too. Yes, an eight-year-old should not have to see her own mother near death. But, still, it was her mother.

"What did she want?" I asked.

"She wants to adopt Diana." Mom blurted the words out.

"Isn't that what a legal guardian does?" I asked.

"She wants Diana to change her name to Chamberlain," Mom said.

"Well that's ridiculous!" I laughed. "Diana's a Welch! She'll always be a Welch!"

"I know," Mom laughed, nodding her head, "I told her, 'Over my dead body!'"

DAN

I KNEW I was going to have to go off and live with a new family, just like Diana, but I had no idea who this Topher Scott was. Liz claims that the first time I met him was at parents' weekend at Trinity Pawling in late October, but I don't remember that at all. He was a friend of Dad's from college. That's all I really knew.

LIZ

AND ALL I knew was that Topher Scott was a big mistake. I figured that out on the drive up to Trinity Pawling for Dan's parents' weekend. After picking me up in his Mercedes-Benz sedan, he spent the entire ninety-minute trip talking about his daughter's engagement to a Kennedy. He did not ask one question about Dan, or about Dan's school, although he did mention that he knew someone whose kid went to Trinity Pawling as well. When we arrived at the campus, Topher saw his friend and spent the entire afternoon with him.

The whole thing really pissed me off. I was mad at Mom for making such a bad choice. I was mad at Mom for being sick. I was mad. Period. So mad that my afternoon visits with her became torturous. I kept forcing myself down that hallway every afternoon. I knew she lived for my bits and pieces of gossip, for my silly school news. I couldn't tell her the truth—that I was cheating in Latin and was failing pre-calculus. That I only read Cliffs Notes in English. So instead I lied when she asked me about college applications. I told her I had finished them all. I hadn't requested any.

I was still interested in acting and told her so, but she wanted me to get a liberal arts education. "An actor's life is hard, Bitsy," she said more than once.

I knew that was true. Mom had started script-doctoring for soap operas. She needed a certain amount of paid hours to be eligible for insurance through the actor's union she belonged to. Some afternoons, I'd come home and find Courtney Simon, an acting friend of Mom's, reading scripts aloud. The two would talk about the plot and the characters, and Courtney would take notes. Many years later, Courtney told me that the soap community loved Mom so much that they made up work for her just to make sure she had enough paid hours to cover her medical bills. On the afternoons Courtney was there, I'd simply pop my head in to say hello and then turn and race down the hallway. But never quickly enough. Mom would always shout out after me, "I love you, Bitsy." I would quicken my pace in a useless attempt to outrun those words. They chased me down the hallway. My skin would tense up like armor, my shoulders would scrunch up to my ears to block out the sound, yet those words would pierce my flesh every time, like darts. They stung. Those words hurt, and I had to swallow the response that came most naturally, "Fuck you."

Then one day at school, I was at a "Children Who Lost Their Parents" meeting with Rita and another new friend, Susy Flanagan. The odd little club was formed by the school's social worker, who had sought each of us out. I was describing my anger at Mom, and Susy started to cry. She had lost her father the year before to liver cancer. "I never told my dad I loved him," she said. "He died in a hospital bed before I got the chance to say good-bye." Susy's story snapped me out of my fog.

That afternoon, I came home from school and walked down that hallway. Nurse Patti was there, sitting in a chair knitting a sweater for her friend's new baby and chatting with Mom, who was sitting upright in bed, two pillows wedged behind her bony back, playing solitaire. Her face lit up, as always, when she saw me at the bedroom door.

"Hello, my darling," she said. "How was your day?" Every afternoon session started off this way. Mom was remarkably cheerful and upbeat despite her haggard scarecrow frame, her veins a murky blue beneath jaundiced skin.

"Fine," I said and went to sit next to her on her bed. Before she could say anything else, I grabbed her hand. It felt small, like a child's, and so fragile I worried if I squeezed too hard it might break. Before she could say another word, I said, "Mom, I just want you to know that I'm sorry I've been so grumpy lately."

Her big brown eyes grew glassy.

"And I just want you to know that I love you." The words came rushing out, a torrent. I squeezed her hand to repress my urge to give her a big bear hug. She weighed less than one hundred pounds. My weight could crush her.

"It's okay," she said, tears now streaming down her chiseled cheeks. "Just know that I love you more."

And with that, I wrapped my arms around her, and she let out a deep cry, a mix of joy and despair wrapped in relief. That moment was proof that her kids would one day forgive her for dying. One just had.

From that day on, I spent every afternoon with Mom. Fuck college applications and Latin class. By mid-November, Mom started to talk about Thanksgiving. "We'll use the good china," she said. She was determined to celebrate, excited about Dan coming home from TP. Diana would be there, too. The Chamberlains had agreed to drop her off.

The day before Thanksgiving, Amanda and I went grocery shopping: Mom ordered a twenty-two-pound turkey and gave us a list. We bought sweet potatoes and string beans, plus celery, apples, raisins, and onions for Mom's famous stuffing, canned pumpkin for pie, and a bag of fresh cranberries for homemade sauce. Once we were done shopping, Amanda and I decided to drive into New York City to visit Amanda's friend Patrick, who was working at Carumba, a Mexican place on Broadway. We drank two pitchers of extra-strength sangria and stumbled back to the Karmann Ghia at midnight. Somewhere on the Saw Mill Parkway, I frantically began to roll down the passenger window, but not soon enough. Vomit splashed against the dashboard and half-open window and all over my favorite acid-washed Guess jeans. Amanda was furious. As we pulled into the driveway, she said only, "This better be cleaned up by breakfast." Then she slammed the door and stomped into the house.

The next morning, I woke up Dan, who'd got home the day before. "I'll give you twenty bucks to clean Amanda's car, no questions asked," I said. He jumped at the offer and spent the morning chipping frozen puke from the Karmann Ghia's seats and floor and door while Amanda and I started Thanksgiving supper.

Auntie Eve arrived with homemade muffins and quickly started bossing us around the kitchen. There were potatoes to peel, cranberries to boil, silver to polish. I ironed the linen tablecloth before laying it on the dining-room table. Karen Kayser arrived from New York City with champagne and chardonnay and began chopping onions for the stuffing as I rolled out a piecrust and Amanda peeled apples. When Diana arrived, everyone cheered and clapped. She ran around giving everyone hugs.

Diana helped me set the table with Mom and Dad's gold-rimmed wedding china and crystal wine goblets. I went back to Mom's room to let her know dinner was ready and gasped when I saw her. She was dressed in the blue mohair sweater I'd given her for Christmas the year before. A long black velvet skirt hid the tubes and bags, and she had wrapped her head with a brilliant blue and black scarf. She even applied makeup for the first time in well over a year. Her cheeks were blushed pink, and a soft silvery blue highlighted her deep brown eyes. She painted her lips a dark ruby red.

"Mom!" I exclaimed. "You look beautiful!"

She beamed a smile and said, "I'm hungry!" When Patti pushed the wheelchair into the dining room, everyone erupted into applause. Mom sat at the head of the table, Diana to her right, Dan to her left, and proceeded to eat a bit of everything and even asked for a glass of champagne to make a toast.

"I want to raise my glass to my children," she said. "You each make me so very proud." We all raised our glasses and took a sip of champagne, then dished out the pie. Diana ate a plate of whipped cream, Dan ate three servings of pumpkin pie, his favorite, and Mom finished her glass of champagne before excusing herself to go back to her room. Everyone got up to give her a hug and a kiss.

The Chamberlains came to get Diana soon thereafter. Saying good-bye was not as painful as I expected. Somehow the success of dinner made everything feel temporary. Mom's cancer, Diana's absence—maybe they weren't forever after all. Even Amanda seemed giddy as we washed the dishes together. "She really rallied!" Amanda said as she hand-dried the silverware.

"I know," I said. "She ate everything on her plate!"

And while we didn't say it out loud, I know we both felt the same tiny spark of hope. Maybe, just maybe, Mom would pull through after all.

AMANDA

THEN THE MOANING started. Liz and I heard it first thing the next morning, these ghostly noises coming from Mom's room and floating through the rest of the house.

Thanksgiving had been more than Mom could take. The nurse told me that after dinner, Mom went back to her room, got wretchedly sick, then slipped into a state of semiconsciousness. She had started having seizures a couple months ago, but after Thanksgiving they got so bad that the nurses had to keep her doped up. Still, she moaned in her sleep. I'd come home from school and hear her all the way in the kitchen. It was awful.

Liz and I escaped to Manhattan as often as we could. We'd go to clubs, drinking and dancing—anything to get away from the misery that was our house then. In the city, we could forget about everything. We were wild. One night at Danceteria, we were drinking margaritas. Liz went off to find some lifeguard from the Bedford Golf and Tennis Club she had a crush on. But after a while, she was nowhere to be seen, so I went looking for her. It was late and we needed to go home. I found her slumped in the men's room, wasted. My friend and I had to carry her out of the club because her legs were like Jell-O. As we were stumbling toward the car, we passed a group of guys. Liz looked up and slurred, "Hey, guys, wanna party?" I wanted to kill her! She couldn't even fucking walk! I threw her into the back of the Jeep.

It was 4:30 a.m. when we got home. Liz managed to stumble upstairs. Then, suddenly, a shoe came flying over the banister. I looked up to see Liz's swollen face peering over the balcony that overlooked the great room. She was spitting onto the floor below. I was furious and whispered loudly, "What, are you going to puke, now? Go into the fucking bathroom!" Her face disappeared, and I heard this huge crash. The night nurse came running out to see what was going on, and I told her everything was under control. I went upstairs to see what happened, but the bathroom door was locked. I could hear Liz crying on the other side. When I finally got her to open the door, I saw that she had somehow managed to smash the full-length mirror into smithereens. She was barefoot, standing in a pile of broken glass, whimpering.

LIZ

I DON'T REMEMBER any of that. I do remember waking up because my feet felt like they were on fire. And I remember the morning. From time to time, I'd hear Mom shout "Da!" and was never sure if she was calling for my father or hers.

By late November, Mom no longer recognized me. The only noises she made were guttural, deep sounds that racked and rattled her ninety-pound frame. They sounded so big they might shatter her bones, tear through her flesh. They sounded as though they hurt.

Then one day, I arrived to a quiet house. I started walking toward Mom's room, but Patti stopped me from coming in.

"Mom's not feeling well," she said through the closed door.

"What's new?" I called back, thinking this was weird.

Then I heard a shallow cry, thick and mumbled, as if Mom had cotton in her mouth.

"Is there anything I can do?" I asked, leaning my head against the door.

"No, love, it's fine, all under control," Patti chirped back.

"What happened?" I asked.

"She had another seizure," Patti explained as she cracked the door open a sliver. I could see one eye and a freckled slice of her cheek. "This was a toughie."

I insisted on coming in, and Patti was right. It was a toughie. To begin, the cadaver lying in the bed was no longer my mother but a skeletal outline, paper-thin flesh pulled over jutting bones. Her extended belly made her look pregnant and anorexic at once.

She was asleep—Patti had knocked her out. The seizures had been bad—starting with leg twitching in September, which led to full-body tremors by October and crazy muscle spasms in November. It had gotten so bad that Mom's leg would jump from the bed as if electrocuted while the rest of her body stayed perfectly still. It made playing Scrabble and backgammon hard. But this one trumped all. This one was so bad that she clamped down her jaw and bit so hard that she shattered her top and bottom teeth, as if the cancer really was tearing her apart from the inside and her only recourse was to chomp down. If she kept her mouth closed, she might contain the cancer, for to scream her body might fragment into a million little pieces and scatter, scatter, scatter.

After that, Mom and I stopped having our after-school talks. I'd come home to moaning and go to sleep to it as well. When I forced myself to go into her room, it smelled like urine and formaldehyde and rot. It smelled like death and because she was close to it, there was no point in fixing her teeth, which looked, when she smiled in her semicatatonic state, like shark teeth, like broken bottles. Her mouth was saying "Keep out" without making a sound. I understood. It was no longer Mom. The monster within had won, and now it was only a matter of time.

DIANA

I WOKE UP in the middle of the night, wanting desperately to see Mom. It was a yearning that I can't explain, a pain almost, in my stomach, my lungs, my heart. Like ripping. I knew that I needed to go to her, as though she were in the room beckoning me, extending her arms toward me. But when I sat up to look for her, there was no one there; the room was empty except for a little girl sleeping in her bed next to mine. I swung my feet off the bed and sat for a little while, waiting. Nothing. No one. I walked down the stairs and stood in the doorway to the Chamberlains' bedroom. Mrs. Chamberlain sat up in her bed; she must have seen my silhouette against the amber hallway light.

"What is it?" she whispered. Her bed was far away from the door.

"Can we go see my mom?" I whispered back, still hovering in the doorway.

She had taken me home once before, in the night. I had woken up with a willful desire to see Mom and went downstairs to ask Mrs. Chamberlain to take me to her. She had said nothing, just got out of bed and told me to put on my coat and then drove me through the dark and to Mom. I thought we could do that again.

Instead she whispered, "Go back to sleep." I turned silently and walked back up the stairs to her daughter's room. I got back under the covers and stared out the window on the far wall, but there were no trees waving, only sky. Eventually, I slept.

The next morning, I woke up alone. I walked downstairs, and everyone was getting ready for school. When I stood in the doorway to Mrs. Chamberlain's walk-in closet, she stopped swimming through her hanging sweaters and turned to me. Her face was serious. "How did you sleep?" she might have asked. I don't remember. All I remember is her telling me that Mom died early that morning and that I didn't have to go to school that day. So I turned around and went upstairs and got back into bed. I don't remember if I cried. I do remember that I felt like cotton, floating apart from the stem.

LIZ

I WOKE UP to Daisy Stewart standing over me. I'd gone to sleep alone the night before—I think I was the only person in the house other than Mom and the night nurse. I'd been listening to the Alarm's "We Are the Light," my favorite song, over and over again. The album was still spinning on the turntable. It was 8:30 a.m., and my first thought was that I was late for school. Then my second thought was "Why's Daisy here?" But she answered before I could ask.

"Your mom died this morning," she whispered.

"Why didn't you wake me up earlier?" I asked.

She shook her head, her eyes watery, and said, "I wanted to let you sleep a little longer."

AMANDA

LIZ WASN'T ALONE the night Mom died. I slept next to her, in the same bed even. But I showed up late, after she was asleep. And Uncle Buzz was sitting like a useless lump in the kitchen when I came home. He arrived that night; it was as though Mom had been waiting for him. I couldn't understand how Mom could love this guy so much. But this was before I realized how important my siblings are to me, before I knew what it was like for us to be apart. Mom died the next morning—at 6:13 a.m. on Friday, December 13, 1985.

DAN

I WAS IN detention when my dorm master came in and whispered to the teacher in charge, and I just knew, that was it. As we walked through the quad, he put his arm around me, kind of like, "Sorry, buddy."

I kept it together but felt all this shit swirling inside of me. I broke down the second I saw Liz and Amanda waiting for me in his office. Liz came up and hugged me, and then Amanda put her arms around both of us and Liz said, "Mom died at 6:13 this morning." We stood there for a while, hugging and crying.

Back at home, Liz and Amanda asked if I wanted anyone to come to the funeral, and I thought of Parker Sweeney. He was a good kid. He looked like a blond albino bird with the palest skin you could imagine. He was the only friend I asked to come.

We stayed in Mom's house alone for a couple days after she died: Liz, Amanda, her friend Rasheeda, and me. We all got high together and were like, "Well, this is it. We're fucked."

It was the first time that my sisters really welcomed me into the whole getting wasted thing. And I was like, "This is what it takes?"

part three

· · · · · · · · · · · · · · · · · · ·

WINTER 1985 – WINTER 1991

*Together on Fire Island (l–r: Karen, Diana, Dan,
Liz, Amanda)*

DIANA

THE FUNERAL HOME was warm, filled with golden light, food, and flowers. A wake, they called it, although by then I knew it was just a send-off for the big sleep, gone forever. There had been one for Dad, but I didn't remember going and wasn't sure if I had been invited. But here I was, waiting my turn to go up and kneel in front of Mom's closed coffin, to say good-bye. Everybody was there—Dan, Liz, Amanda, Auntie Eve and Uncle Harry, people from school and from the Bedford Golf and Tennis Club. Actor people. Most were crying; I could hear them sniffling. But not me; I wasn't going to cry in front of everybody. I focused on the floor, which was carpeted, and on feet, which were all stuffed into dress-up shoes.

When it was my turn to kneel in front of Mom's coffin, Auntie Eve's granddaughter Bridget came with me. As we knelt, we whispered to each other, not knowing what to do. Eventually, we both put our hands in prayer position and giggled nervously. Then I closed my eyes and breathed deeply, because I thought maybe we were being disrespectful. I was supposed to be saying good-bye to Mom, so I tried to picture her sleeping inside the shiny wooden box, her face made up and her hair curled as though she was going to work, but I couldn't.

The last time I had seen Mom was when Mrs. Chamberlain drove me to her in the middle of the night. She had been sleeping with her head flung back, her mouth open, while her forgotten-about wigs stared at me from the dresser. That night, I had tried to superimpose Mom's smiling face on the white Styrofoam ovals that held the wigs up in head shapes, but I couldn't do it. Then, as now, I couldn't conjure Mom alive on command. I figured it was up to her to come to me. She always did love it when I saw ghosts.

So I got up and walked over to a clump of empty metal folding chairs and sat there by myself as people came up and apologized to me about my life. Even my math teacher, this mean old lady with bad breath and a wart on her chin, leaned into my face and told me how deeply sorry she was. All I could think about was how she made me go up to the blackboard to sort out impossible problems that I didn't understand. She should be sorry about that, I thought.

The next day, at the funeral, I sat between Mrs. Chamberlain and Liz in a hard wooden pew. I spent most of my time focused on widening the gap between Mrs. Chamberlain and me as much as I could without kicking her away. As I pressed into Liz with my shoulder and hip, Mrs. Chamberlain leaned away from me, too, her left leg crossed over her right. Though her head faced the altar, I could see that she was looking at me from the corner of her eyes. This satisfied me somehow. I was supposed to be thinking of Mom, up there, in the box, but all I wanted at that moment was for Mrs. Chamberlain to see me clinging to my sister, whose right arm was wrapped around my body, protecting me. I wanted Mrs. Chamberlain to see that it was my sister I wanted, that this was where I belonged. I wanted to hurt her with this knowledge so that she would get up and walk out of the church and leave us alone. She didn't.

Then, suddenly, as everybody sang "Amazing Grace," one of Mom's favorite songs, I started to cry. I couldn't help it. I saw her thin, fluffy hair that liked to hide under her silk scarf, and I saw her big worried eyes that closed when I kissed her on her soft warm lips that would smile just for me. My tears were hot and steamed up my glasses, which were smashed crooked between my nose and my sister's body. Liz was shaking slightly; I could feel it against my head as she ran her hand up and down my arm, steadily, over and over again.

LIZ

THE FUNERAL TOOK place at Saint Luke's church in Katonah, the same place we had Dad's funeral. I still get the two confused. I do know that Mom's coffin was pine because I went with Daisy Stewart to pick it out while Mom was still alive. But this time, when the funeral director tried to get me to look at fancier wooden boxes, I was prepared. I said, "No, she wants something simple."

Other than that, I don't remember the service or where I sat in the church. I don't remember people coming back to our house afterward for cold cuts and coffee, although I'm certain they did. I do remember Daisy Stewart and Nancy Chamberlain telling me to take Dan to the movies. We went to see *Weird Science*. It felt good to be in the dark, distracted. I think we may have even laughed.

AMANDA

ON THE WAY out of Saint Luke's, I was a sobbing mess, all puffy from crying. The Chamberlains had just put me in the back of their car to drive me home when the fucking funeral director came running out of the church waving the bill. He actually tried to shove the bill through the window. Ted Chamberlain confronted the guy and said, "This will get taken care of, but not now." He and Nancy stood up for me; I really appreciated that.

And it wasn't the first time. The day before the funeral, Uncle Buzz came back to our house with a U-Haul truck. He wanted to take all his family furniture back to Texas with him. Everyone was furious, including Nancy. She greeted him at the door, saying, "What do you think you are doing?" In the end, he took a Victorian settee, two paintings that our great-aunt did, and a brass throne that our cat Mimsy used to sleep on. Nancy stood watching him, her arms crossed, giving him the evil eye as he skulked out the door.

DAN

BACK HOME, AFTER the funeral, Topher Scott walked up to me with a tennis racket. There, in the living room in front of all these people, he told me that he couldn't be my guardian and handed me the racket. There was a note on it that said "To a good game!"

Like I said, I had no idea who this guy was. I don't even remember his face; all I saw was a headless suit handing me a tennis racket. Liz and I went to the movies that afternoon, and when we got back to the house, Karen Kayser said she would take me in. She lived in Manhattan and used to come visit on the weekends and make me garden at the gray house. I never really liked her. She'd bark orders at me even when my parents were around. My parents never barked at me. But at least I knew her.

LIZ

AMANDA, DAN, AND I drove six hours south to Falls Church, Virginia, to bury Mom next to her father. It was more than four hundred miles away from Quincy, Massachusetts, where we had buried Dad, three and a half-years before, next to his mother. He and Mom had never talked about where they wanted to be buried, just as they had not talked about who would take care of us kids after they were dead.

We drove through the wrought-iron cemetery gates and parked. As soon as we stepped out of the car, I saw Uncle Buzz rushing toward us, his silver pageboy bobbing with each step. For a moment, I was glad to see him, a familiar human face floating above the field of cold marble slabs. Then I noticed the frantic look in his eyes.

"Did you bring your checkbook?" he asked Amanda sternly as he approached.

"Excuse me?" she said.

"Your checkbook?" he repeated. "People are gathered around the gravesite, and we need to pay for the burial before they start digging." Amanda said nothing as Dan and I each took a step closer, flanking her.

"Well, who did you expect to pay for it?" he snapped. "Me?" He sounded angry, but not more so than I. My fury at that moment scared me more than my own grief. I put my hand on Amanda's lower back and looked hard at Buzz, funneling all of my rage into a beam that I hoped would zap him.

"I'll pay you back," Amanda said, coolly.

"Fucking asshole," I added, under my breath so only my siblings could hear.

He hurried off and we followed him slowly, a united front, toward Mom's gravesite. As we approached, the small backhoe parked nearby began to move, gnawing at the cold December earth.

AMANDA

THE DAY MOM died, her lawyer gave me a checkbook with "The Estate of Ann Williams" written on it and then started sending me all these bills. As executor of Mom's will and trust, it was my responsibility to pay for her funeral, her burial, everything. I also had to deal with the rest of Dad's debt, the sale of the house, the lawyers, all that. It was like I had no time to just miss Mom.

I wound up spending that Christmas at a riding school in Ireland with Dr. Tudor, one of Mom's good friends. He was a teacher at West Patent Elementary School who spoke as if he were reading lines from a play. They used to ride together, before Mom got sick. After she was bedridden, he'd visit often and they'd spend afternoons together in her bedroom talking about theater and horses.

It was Mom's idea that I go with him to Ireland; she set the whole thing up because she knew how much I loved to ride. Under any other circumstances, I would have enjoyed the experience, but not the week after Mom died. I should have been with my family. I don't even know why I went.

DIANA

DOWNSTAIRS, A WOMAN'S voice was shouting, "Come on, lazy-bones!"

I opened my eye to the rumpled sheets of an empty twin bed, the white cotton blankets thrown off in a hurry. I was in an identical bed, same sheets, same blankets, separated by a small night table with a lamp on it and a clock that read 7 a.m. I had no idea where I was. Then it came to me slowly, the panic in my stomach fading but not disappearing: I was at my new house, where I'd been living for four months or so, having moved in shortly before my eighth birthday. I was in my new little sister's room, where I'd spent the night. Her name was Margaret and she was five. She had a younger brother, William, who was two. They were downstairs with their mom and their dad. Their mom was calling me "lazybones." My mom was dead. I didn't know where my sisters were, or my brother. I had just seen them ten days ago, at the funeral, but I had no idea where they were now. I figured they were all off together somewhere, sleeping in. I closed my eyes and scooted my body down the mattress, pulling the blanket up over my head to block out the noise. I could have stayed there all day. "Come on, lazybones!" the lady called from the bottom of the stairs. "What's wrong with you? It's Christmas!"

The night before, I got to stay up late planting evidence in the living room after Margaret and William had gone to sleep. It had taken them a while to drift off because they were listening for the sounds of hooves on the roof. Their mom told me to take a bite out of the chocolate chip cookies and to drink a big swig from the glass of milk as proof to the younger ones that Santa had shoved his chubby body down the chimney. It felt special to be in on the grown-up side of things for a change. Afterward, instead of having to walk all the way to the other side of the house where I usually slept near the maid, Rhonda, I walked upstairs to Margaret's room with Mrs. Chamberlain and she tucked me in. She stood at the bottom of the bed and flapped the covers over me, letting the cool air puff up my nightgown before the heaviness of the sheets and blankets settled around me. It was nice.

"What are you waiting for?" She was still shouting from the bottom of the stairs. Margaret and William echoed their mother, tired of waiting for me to come down so they could open their gifts. I got out of bed and put a strange bathrobe on over a strange nightgown and walked downstairs. They were all hopping and waving and clapping in the living room in front of a Christmas tree propped up by piles of presents wrapped with bows and ribbons. Rhonda wasn't there; she was in the Bronx celebrating with her family, I guessed. Mrs. Chamberlain waved her hands in the air like an overeager cheerleader twirling invisible batons as Alvin, Simon, and Theodore screeched "All I want for Christmas is my two front teeth" in their high-pitched Chipmunk voices. Her kids hopped around and around in circles, one diapered, one pigtailed. Their dad stood in the corner of the blue living room, smiling and bending his knees, up, down, up, down, clapping slowly, in a trance. They looked happy, all of them.

Earlier that week, Mrs. Chamberlain had taken me home for the last time. There was no one there in the big sunny living room. Last Christmas, there had been a big tree covered in silver tinsel. Amanda and Liz had rolled their eyes and said that tinsel was cheesy, but I liked how it floated around, making our living room a sparkly mess while we all played Trivial Pursuit and listened to Placido Domingo, Mom's favorite. But there was nothing Christmas-y in the living room this year, just our saggy couches and stained Oriental rug. As I stood there, in that big, cavernous room, someone gave me an unwrapped rag doll Mom had bought me for Christmas before she died. The doll had frizzy silvery blond hair framing its pale, painted-on face, and it wore a blue Laura Ingalls Wilder dress. It was ugly and I hated it. But in my room at the Chamberlains', I kept it hidden in my closet, underneath my clothes, next to my shoes and a picture of Mom squinting in the sunlight.

"She's finally awake!" Mr. Chamberlain said when he saw me hovering in the living-room doorway. Still smiling and clapping, he looked like Lady Elaine Fairchilde from *Mr. Rogers' Neighborhood,* crescent-moon-faced and red-nosed. I sat down on the couch, looked at my lap for a while, and noticed that my hands matched the tiny pink flowers on my white flannel nightgown almost perfectly. The lace collar itched. I could hear Margaret ripping through presents and squealing—Pound Puppies and My Little Ponies to add to her collection—but I couldn't watch. All of my toys back home were drawn on or broken or gone. I never really cared for my toys, though I did have one bunny named Shoe that I loved enough to put a Band-Aid on his ear, pretending to fix a wound. I had no idea where he was now. I wished he were like Corduroy, that teddy bear from the books who found his way back into his little girl's arms after she left him at the mall. But I knew Shoe wasn't crawling out of a moving box and getting lost on West Patent Road trying to find me. How could he? I didn't even know where I was.

A red-wrapped present appeared on my lap. I was stuck. I couldn't move my arms, and my feet were bare and cold. I looked behind me, out the window at the stone walls and the bare trees.

Days ago, William, Margaret, and I were at the breakfast-room table writing letters to Santa, colored pencils and construction paper scattered before us on the tabletop. Mrs. Chamberlain was helping Margaret form letters and words, pointing to the paper. I was supposed to write a letter to Santa along with them, but I didn't know what to ask for. I didn't want any stupid toys. I wanted to go home. But after drawing some hearts on my piece of paper, I wrote "Brown leather pants," handed the paper to Mrs. Chamberlain, and left the table to go up to my room.

I was sitting on one of the twin beds when Mrs. Chamberlain appeared in my doorway, wearing a white button-down shirt large enough to cover her hips, which were wide, with black pants and black flats. She described her look as French chic. She had a habit of scooping her unpainted fingers behind her ears, expertly tucking the hair so that it curled around the lobe just so, keeping her blond, chin-length hair out of her pale face. She wore small diamond earrings and no makeup. The natural position of her lips was a slight frown. She was pretty but plain. Not beautiful like Mom. She held my letter to Santa by her hip.

"You'll have to ask for something else," she said. "Eight-year-old girls do not wear leather pants." I rolled over on the bed, away from her, and slid down into the crack between my bed and the wall. From there, in a funny, compressed voice that I wasn't sure she could even hear, I told this lady that Amanda had leather pants and that so did Jim Morrison. I told her they were what I wanted. I told her that I needed them for school. I couldn't see, or hear her; my shoulders covered my ears, and the bed protected me from the room.

I wasn't expecting to find any leather pants in the shiny red box on my lap that Christmas morning. "Come on, come on!" the mom shouted in her living room, waving her arms in the air.

"Yay, yay!" the kids shouted, and the father clapped.

So I unwrapped the present, and thanked them, and smiled, I think, I hope. Everyone was happy, and Margaret's face was reddening from all the yelling, turning almost purple as she ran around in circles, while William stood in a pile of shiny paper and ribbons, bending his knees like his father, his diaper crinkling with each awkward squat. I'm not sure what they gave me, but I seem to remember more wool nightgowns that crawled up to strangle me in the night.

LIZ

I WOKE UP on Christmas morning in the Stewarts' former guest room, my new room. It was painted pale orange that picked up on the peach in the Laura Ashley floral linens covering two twin beds. There was a small closet into which I had crammed all of my clothes. I kept my records in a red milk crate in one corner. My posters stayed rolled up; the English Beat and the Psychedelic Furs didn't mix well with Laura Ashley.

Jonah was four and slept in the room across the hallway from me in a bunk bed that looked like an English double-decker bus, and Addison, only two, was in the room adjacent to mine, still in a crib but one he could climb out of as he pleased. The bathroom I shared with the boys had a naval theme, dark blue boats embroidered on the towels and a big anchor on the bathmat. A framed letter on White House stationery hung above the toilet: Montgomery's parents were big Republican donors, so Ronald Reagan sent a letter to Jonah, congratulating him for being born. Daisy and Montgomery's room was on the other side of the house.

Daisy had invited Karen and Dan to spend the holiday with us at Daisy's mother's house in Westport, Connecticut. En route, we stopped by the Chamberlains'. Diana was already dressed when we arrived, around ten, and though she looked adorable in her taffeta dress and tights, I couldn't help but think that it was wrong. This was not how we did Christmas. Everyone was supposed to stay in their pajamas and sit around the tree opening one present at a time, dragging the process out as long as possible, until it was time for turkey at two. Yet there we were, dropping by with Christmas presents well before noon and Diana was already dressed for church. We never went to church. And then Nancy Chamberlain offered us bagels, cream cheese, and lox, and my heart sank further. Mom made homemade pumpkin bread, dense with molasses, raisins, and walnuts. I'd eat four slices over the present-opening period, which lasted hours. That, to me, was Christmas. Not bagels, cream cheese, and lox.

Dan, Karen, and I sat stiffly in the living room and gave Diana and her new siblings their presents. I cannot remember what gift I had brought for Diana, only that she looked at me and said thank you in a rather formal way, not anything like the Diana I knew. It's not that she didn't like my present; it's that she knew this was all wrong, too. She looked back at me, and her brown eyes got wide beneath her pink-framed glasses as if she were trying to say something via ESP. She didn't say it out loud, because she could not voice it there on Christmas morning in front of these strange people posing as her new parents, but her expression said, "Don't leave me here." So to soothe the gash that her look tore in my heart, I convinced myself, right then and there, that these strangers sitting on their silk couches in their church clothes were benevolent people who would take good care of Diana.

DAN

THAT CHRISTMAS SUCKED. After visiting Diana, we went to some house in Westport, Connecticut, filled with people I had never seen or even heard of before. Liz and I sat on the couch in the corner while Karen spent the entire day flirting with Daisy Stewart's father. She was literally etching circles on his thigh with her nail and giggling. It was embarrassing.

I kept thinking, "I'm going to live with this crazy woman with her leg up on some stranger?" But I knew she loved Mom. So at least we had that in common.

AMANDA

LOOK, KAREN WASN'T an ideal guardian. She was an old acting friend of Mom's, who would come up for weekends to garden and brush our dogs and skinny-dip in our pool. Auntie Eve would purse her lips and mutter about Karen flirting with Dad, but Mom didn't seem to mind. She took in people like Karen all the time. She took them in like she took in the owl with the broken wing or a stray dog.

To be honest, Karen could be cruel. I remember being eight years old and asking her to pass the potatoes because I wanted seconds. And she said to me, "You do not need more potatoes."

I just gave her a look like, "Bitch, pass the potatoes!" I never took any shit from her. Anyway, what's important is that she really stood up when we needed her.

DIANA

WHEN CHRISTMAS WAS over and we were done opening presents, Mrs. Chamberlain told me to make a list of each gift I'd been given and who gave it to me. I didn't know who many of the people were, and, like the letter to Santa, thank-you notes were something I had never done before. But, Mrs. Chamberlain explained, you had to write thank-you notes; otherwise, people wouldn't give you any more presents. Anyway, I didn't have a choice. I sat at the red Formica table in the breakfast room with a pile of white unlined paper. After folding one piece in half, I drew a sprig of holly with green and red colored pencils on the front flap. Inside, I wrote, "Dear (whoever they were), Thanks for the (whatever they gave me). Have a Happy New Year! From, Diana." After the eighth or ninth card, my hollies started to get sloppy, the spiky green leaves less filled in, the trio of red berries less bunched, trailing up like thought bubbles. But I finished them, left the stack on the table, and sat on the nearby couch to read.

"All finished?" Mrs. Chamberlain asked as she walked over to the breakfast table and picked up the pile. She moved each card to the back of the stack quickly, inspecting each one. When she finished, she squeezed the stack in one hand and asked sternly, "What is this?"

I just looked at her, not quite understanding the question. She began to shake slightly, just a quiver. The hand that clutched the thank-you notes was up next to her blond-bobbed head, a wadded fist. "You have got to try," she said, tears forming in her smallish brown eyes. Her nose started to run a little, and its tip turned pinkish like her husband's. As she wiped at it with her wrist, the thank-you notes hid her face for a second. "You have *got* . . . to *try*," she said again, shaking her head, and threw the cards on the breakfast table, scattering them, before she quickly left the room.

I wasn't sure what that meant or what I was supposed to do. All I knew was that I hated it there. I hated this lady who kept expecting things from me that I didn't understand. I thought that I was just staying there for a while, until things got settled, but it felt as if I had been there forever and I was sick of it. I had no idea where Dan, Liz, and Amanda were. For all I knew they were on another planet, with Mom and Dad, covered in tinsel, playing Trivial Pursuit.

LIZ

I'D BEEN AT the Stewarts' for about a week when Daisy asked, rather sheepishly, if I had finished my college applications. I had not. It was at the top of that all-important, life-determining checklist a high school senior was supposed to make, a list I had misplaced earlier that fall, somewhere between my mother's moans and the healers who failed at healing. I wanted to go to college, that much I knew, if only to get the hell out of Bedford. I figured I would live with the Stewarts until I graduated from high school that June. Then I'd go to college and get on with my life.

On December 27, I sat down to fill out the applications, which were due January 1. The first section—name, birth date, SAT scores—was relatively easy. "Address" was odd: After sixteen years of writing "West Patent Rd.," I wrote, "c/o Stewart, Succabone Rd." At least the town, state, and zip were still the same.

I chose six schools to apply to. Georgetown University was my first choice because I'd met a cute lacrosse player when I went to Key West with my friend Betsey and her mom over Christmas break the year before. He was a freshman at Georgetown who kissed me at midnight and cast a spell. If I got into Georgetown, I would find him and become his girlfriend. Then there was Middlebury, in Vermont, where Mom grew up. I heard the town was pretty and the school had a good creative writing program. I applied to Northwestern for their drama school and to NYU as my backup—I was still entertaining the idea of being an actress like Mom.

I also applied to Skidmore because they had an equestrian team and I thought I might like to start riding again. I chose Colgate as my safety school because it reminded me of Dad's favorite toothpaste.

Each college required I write an essay. From the selection of topics to choose from, I picked "Describe an event that has had the greatest impact on your life." Sitting at the Stewarts' breakfast-room table, I wrote "Liz

Welch" in the top right-hand corner of a piece of lined paper and put a horizontal line through the zag on the *z*, my signature style. Then I sat back and thought hard. We had discussed the college essay in my AP English class that fall. My teacher said it was important to think of ways to make yours stand out. I decided to write about my mother, the actress. That was different, I thought.

I skipped one line and wrote, "Ann Williams, actress: Known for her starring roles in *The Doctors,* as Maggie Fielding; in *Search for Tomorrow*, as Eunice Wyatt; in *The Edge of Night,* as Margo Huntington; and in *Loving,* as June Slater. She was widowed on April 21, 1982. She was my mother."

My teacher also said that the college essay was a good place to show off your vocabulary skills. I had scored higher on my verbal SAT than in math, though I wasn't sure if that was because I was good at vocabulary or sucked at math. Probably both. I used words like "laudatory," "debilitated," and "devastating" to describe how Mom was diagnosed with cancer a month after Dad died, how she beat it, then got cast on *Loving,* and got sick again. These, I thought, were impressive words.

I continued, scribbling in my pudgy print, upright letters with a bit of script thrown in for flair. "As my mother's physical strength progressively decreased, her inner emotional strength seemed to increase to the point where everyone perceived her as unconquerable." I used our last Thanksgiving together as proof. "She was vivacious, beautiful, and proud. The only signs of her illness were the wheelchair in which she was placed, her newly grown layer of hair, and the nurse by her side."

"She left us elated," I wrote, "convinced that her strength knew no bounds and that she, in fact, was unconquerable." As I wrote this line, hot tears welled up in my eyes, and I thought of Rita coming to my house the day Mom died, hugging me so hard I thought I might bruise, and saying over and over again, "I can't believe it. I can't believe it." Before she left, she whispered in my ear in what was more of a noiseless shout, "I'm not coming to the funeral. It's too hard." And I understood. It was the reason my tears were now spilling down my cheeks and splattering onto the page. It was too hard. I had thought Mom was unconquerable and I was wrong. I took a deep breath. I had to finish.

New paragraph.

"Her greatest and final role performed before her family and friends was done with such excellence and poise that her subsequent rate of deterioration and frequent bouts of unconsciousness were received by all with incredible shock and disbelief . . . on December 13, 1985, she died."

I paused. "Died" seemed the wrong word. I tried "expired," then crossed it out and wrote "ceased to live." And then I went back to "died." It was the wrong word, but it was the best of the bunch.

I continued: "She was a brilliant actress, able to convince her toughest critics, her children, that she was unconquerable. My mother was only human, yet she possessed one characteristic above all others that radiated throughout her bout with cancer: an inner emotional strength that I find both fascinating and bewildering."

The essay was supposed to be one thousand words, and I wondered how many more I needed to write. I decided to count. One, two, three, four . . . I counted each word and wrote the number at the bottom of each page, in the right corner. So far I had nine hundred forty-two words. I had sixty-eight to go.

"The greatest and most positive impact that I have felt from this dismal experience is that I realize the strength she possessed is equally evident in each of her four children. Her magnificent performance on Thanksgiving Day has inspired me to develop this quality to its utmost degree and realize that though I have lost this parent, this inherent quality will support me throughout my life." That was only sixty-six, but I figured it was close enough.

AMANDA

WHEN I CAME back from Ireland, everything had turned to shit. When I left, Dan was going to live with Karen. When I came back, only one week later, he was suddenly living with some family called the Hayeses. I was like, "Who the fuck are the Hayeses?" I wasn't involved in the discussion and had no idea how the whole thing happened. That was the whole reason Mom had set up the trust and organized the guardianships before she died. If Topher Scott wasn't up to it, why didn't he tell Mom then, when she could have had some control over the situation? Now these total strangers were making all these decisions even though I was executor of the trust. I knew what was best for my family, but nobody was going to listen to me. In their minds, I was just a fucked-up kid.

I finally met Mrs. Hayes a couple days before New Year's. She said, "All Dan needs is love," and I thought, "Lady, you are so fucked." It was as if she was walking through the pound and saw this cute puppy that needed a home; she hadn't thought it through. I just knew it was not going to work.

DAN

THE HAYESES TOLD me that "the town" decided I couldn't live with Karen because she was a single woman in Manhattan. It was probably Child Protective Services, or maybe it was just everyone talking. Anyway "they" said that I needed to be with a family, and that's when the Hayeses stepped in. They lived in Mount Kisco, and their son Brad was in my grade at Fox Lane, but we weren't friends or anything. Mrs. Hayes was tiny, less than five feet tall. She was also a chain smoker, and sort of jaundiced. Mr. Hayes was a gentle giant, this six-foot-four Vietnam vet.

I had to go back to Trinity Pawling the first week in January, and the plan was that I'd spend weekends and holidays with the Hayeses. Honestly, I couldn't have cared less about where I lived, as long as it was close to my sisters. I didn't really want to be with anybody but them.

LIZ

AMANDA DECIDED TO have a New Year's Eve party at our old house, where she was still living. I ate dinner with the Stewarts and then went to go see Amanda. I wanted to celebrate the start of 1986 with her, not them.

I hadn't been in the house since before Christmas. And even though it had already been sold to a preppy Bedford family I once babysat for—he owned the local real estate company; she wore headbands that matched her espadrilles—nothing had changed. Dan, Diana, and I were long gone, and with us all of our personal belongings. But the family furniture, artwork, photos, and books, all that stuff, was still there exactly as before.

Amanda was in the living room with a few friends getting high. There were several empty bottles of Korbel champagne lying by their feet and several more unopened ones in the fridge. I sat down next to my sister and did a bong hit. Then she passed me a bottle of Korbel. I took a swig and the fizzy liquid flooded my mouth, its rowdy bubbles sizzling up my sinuses, an intense burn. I took another swig.

At thirty seconds to midnight, Amanda put Prince on the stereo, opened another bottle of Korbel, and began the countdown: ten, nine, eight, seven. We all joined in, chanting together, and when we reached zero, we passed the bottle again. I gave Amanda a big hug and said loudly into her ear, "May this year be better than the last."

"It fucking better be!" she laughed, widening her eyes and flaring her nostrils before tipping the bottle into her mouth.

Then someone suggested going to a party nearby, but I couldn't go. I had a curfew, the first in my lifetime. "You go ahead," I said to Amanda. "I'll straighten up and then head back."

Once everyone left, I opened another bottle of champagne and sat in the living room alone, staring out the French doors that opened onto the deck. Mom was so excited about that deck. She'd even bought a picnic table and wooden lounge chairs for all the birthday parties and barbecues she planned on having there. But I couldn't recall one celebration, or even a meal out there. I switched off the overhead lights and sank back down into the couch. The bright moon and stars lit the fields an eerie silver. I lay my head back on the couch pillows and listened in the dead quiet for something.

I listened for Dan playing Run-DMC upstairs, for Mom watching *The Phil Donahue Show* down the hallway, for Diana's high-pitched Pillsbury Doughboy laugh that sounded like she was shouting "hey, hey, hey." I listened for Auntie Eve clanking pots in the kitchen or Bentley's nails clicking against the wood floors. I strained my ears in the dark for some familiar sound, but there was none. Then I realized, with an urgency that blocked my breath: I should have gone with Amanda to that party. I closed my eyes and imagined the purr of the Mercedes-Benz and the squeak and heavy thud of its driver's door opening then closing. I prayed that Amanda would receive my ESP S.O.S. and come back to insist that I go to the party with her. But there was nothing. The house was dead silent because it had become a coffin. The family I strained to hear no longer existed.

Then a double-picture frame sitting on the baby grand piano caught my eye. It displayed two school photos from 1978: Dan was seven years old in one, wearing a navy blue Shetland sweater, I was nine in the other, wearing a light blue ribbed turtleneck. We're both smiling.

I finished the bottle of Korbel in the dark silence then drifted off. I have no idea how long I was floating in that spooky outer space, but the next sound I heard was sobbing. I felt a sharp pain in my chest and a dull ache in my throat and realized those cries were coming from me. They started out soft but grew louder as I opened my eyes and realized that I was no longer in the living room staring out the French doors; I was curled up in a tight ball in Mom's Craftmatic bed. It was stripped bare, and I was in the fetal position clutching one of Mom's pillows, holding it tight against my body as if I were trying to will it into something more than cotton and feathers. I had no idea what time it was or how long I had been there or how long I had been crying, only that the pillow was moist as was the mattress beneath my head. I sat up in bed, my face heavy and swollen and shiny wet with tears. Then I stumbled out of the house, leaving the girl in the light blue turtleneck behind with her ghost family.

DAN

THE HAYESES DROVE me to Trinity Pawling the first week in January. I hated that school now more than ever. Every morning, I woke up and said to myself, "Okay, Dan, you just gotta make it through one more day." The whole thing sucked. I felt so far away from my sisters, so totally alone. I hated being around all those rich spoiled brats. I had to serve them their fucking food as part of my scholarship. I got a certain satisfaction knowing that the company that supplied the food also sold food to the local prison and insane asylum.

By early February, I was suffocating. Literally, I couldn't breathe. I was sitting in my dorm room one night and I felt this pressure clamping down on my lungs, and I realized that I needed to get out of there. I had to get out of that fucking room and off that fucking campus. There was this whole world out there, and I wanted to get out into it. So I decided to run away. This kid Clay came with me, because he was a total hippie who didn't like rules or structure.

This was how we did it: out my window and down this tree, with our laundry bags full of clothes. We ran around the perimeter of the campus and then through the woods so no one could see us, to get to Route 22. From there, we walked to town. By the time we arrived at the train station, it was nine o'clock and we had just missed the last train. Still, I wasn't about to turn back. I said, "Okay, we'll wait here until six in the morning, when the next train comes." Sitting there on the pavement in the freezing cold, I realized that I didn't know where I was headed. That I had nowhere to go. Nowhere.

So I just sat there shivering, until this van pulled into the station. Mr. Reed, the art teacher, got out. He was pissed. He told us to get in the van, and we did.

LIZ

DAN CALLED ME from Trinity Pawling one evening in tears.

"I fucking hate it here," he said. "It's like prison. You have to help get me out."

His desperation was all too familiar; I was miserable, too. I don't even remember turning seventeen that February, even though Adrianna, my best friend from seventh grade, threw me a surprise party and invited all my closest friends. Years later, she showed me photos taken that day. Those photos are painful to look at because I don't recognize myself in them: I'm puffy and pale, wearing a white shirt buttoned up to my neck and clasped with Mom's vintage ivory cameo. In one shot, I'm laughing, my mouth wide open—I can see my one crooked tooth and pink tongue, and my eyes are squinting almost shut. I can also see, through the slivers, that my eyes are as dull as tarnished silver. The laugh was a lie. My eyes told the truth.

It was that numb, faraway girl who drove up to see Dan one wintry February afternoon. I was going to try to cheer him up with some chocolate chip cookies I had baked for him. The gray skies were bloated with the threat of snow, so I took the Stewarts' four-wheel-drive Toyota Land Cruiser and headed north on Interstate 684. I stopped at Burger King to get Dan his favorite meal—a Whopper, Coke, and fries—and then kept driving until I saw Trinity Pawling's stone campus buildings sitting high up on a hilltop, the sloping front lawn freshly covered with a dusting of snow.

Dan was waiting for me in his dorm room, and though he seemed happy to see me, I sensed a familiar detachment. He smiled hard, his dimples piercing both cheeks, his lips clamped shut but stretching outward to connect the two deep dots. But his eyes were distant and so, so sad.

"Auntie Eve has been sending me care packages," he said when I handed him the Tupperware packed with chocolate chip cookies. "I sell her brownies for a buck a pop."

"Well, here's two dozen cookies," I said. "So that's enough for, like, three pizzas."

Dan stretched another fake smile and said, "That's good, because the food sucks here." His mouth began to twitch as his eyes darted from the ceiling to the floor. "Plus, I'm failing all my classes. People feel sorry for me because of Mom and everything, but I can't take it anymore. I hate it here." Then he looked right at me with wet eyes and said, "I want to go home."

Those words sucked the oxygen from my body. Amanda was packing up the house and moving to Brooklyn. I was stuck on Succabone Road, Dan in boarding school, and Diana in tights and tafetta. We all wanted to go home, but none of us could because there was no home to go to.

I spent an hour or so with Dan and then told him I had to get back before it got too late. He walked me to the car and stood there with his hands shoved deep in his pockets. I gave him a big hug, but he stayed still, like a statue. I could feel his body shaking.

"I'm always here for you, Dan," I whispered into his ear before getting into the car. From my rearview mirror I watched his gangly frame, dressed in Dad's old tweed coat, turn and tromp back to his dorm. As I pulled out of Trinity Pawling's driveway, I too began to tremble. As I drove south on Route 22, I thought, "What did any of us do to deserve this?"

My mind was racing and numb at once, my breath fast and faint. Then I passed the Goldens Bridge exit heading south on 684 and had an awful realization. Dad had been heading south, coming home from Boston, when his car veered off the highway, right there, between Goldens Bridge and Katonah. Somewhere along that dark stretch of highway, he'd crossed the median barrier and smashed into an abandoned car on the other side of the road. My headlights poked two hazy holes in the darkness.

"Did he fall asleep?" I wondered as I pushed hard on the accelerator and barreled into the thick blue black of night. "Or did he just turn the wheel once, hard?" The speedometer clocked eighty. As the Land Rover started to rattle, I thought of Dan trudging back to school alone and lifted my foot off the gas. I thought of Diana's eyes widening behind her glasses, and the way she clung to me whenever I hugged her hello or good-bye. I thought of Amanda's laugh and then of her packing up the house all alone. And I kept driving.

DIANA

THAT WINTER, I lost eight coats. One snowy evening, I walked right out of Heller's shoe store in Mount Kisco without my coat, the eighth. Back in the family's gray station wagon, Mrs. Chamberlain turned on the windshield wipers. The snow was really coming down. As she twisted her body to back the car out of its parking spot, her eyes fell on me. "Where's your coat?" she asked, startled.

"I don't know," I shrugged.

"How can you not know where your coat is?" she said, pressing her eyebrows together and jerking her head back in disbelief. I couldn't recall having a coat, and I didn't feel cold; I didn't really feel anything. But then I remembered—I had been wearing a coat, a new one. It was ankle-length, down-filled. Quilted. Mauve.

"I must have left it in the shoe store," I guessed. There was a Calvin and Hobbes sticker on the back of the driver's seat, its dirty edges peeling up from the red vinyl. I picked at it as William nodded off to sleep in his car seat next to me.

"Well?" Mrs. Chamberlain said, turning to face the front of the car. Her hands were on the steering wheel, her arms stiff and straight. "Are you going to go and get it?"

I opened the door to the cold. In the warm shoe store, I made a crack about how spacey I was to the sales guy, who laughed as the heavy glass door closed itself behind me. The car ride home was silent.

Around this time, Mrs. Chamberlain took me into New York City to see a psychologist. We played board games. I chose Chutes and Ladders because she didn't have Parcheesi.

I never went back. Mrs. Chamberlain told me that the doctor said I was well adjusted, which seemed right to me. I didn't feel there was anything wrong with me. But I did have lice a lot. They were a real epidemic at

West Patent Elementary. Maybe I shared combs with the wrong girls, or maybe I was the wrong girl. School had been weird ever since Mom died. My first day back after the funeral, people gave me presents like it was my birthday: a Cabbage Patch Kid and a paperweight in the shape of a dog. It wasn't so bad to be the girl who had lice, because I got to leave school early. And I liked it when the whole third grade lined up outside the nurse's office once a week to get checked. The sharp metal comb felt good scraping against my scalp, and the nurse's breath on my neck reminded me of nice things like Mom talking out of the corner of her mouth while I kissed her or Auntie Eve scratching my back while we watched her soaps on TV.

At the Chamberlains', Mrs. Chamberlain and Rhonda took turns scrubbing my head with RID while they made sour faces and raised their noses high in the air. It burned and it stank. Eventually, I just did it myself. It seemed like Mrs. Chamberlain thought I was disgusting, like she didn't want to touch me, like I had a disease. But one evening, when I was sad and missing Mom, I wandered into Mrs. Chamberlain's bathroom crying, my fist in my eye, just as she was getting out of the shower. When she saw me, and my tears, she sat down on the toilet, still naked and wet, and pulled me onto her lap. I hid my face in her neck and cried even harder. As my tears blended with the moisture on her skin, I thought, maybe, just maybe, this lady could love me.

AMANDA

I PARTIED SO hard that winter I barely remember any of it. I was living alone in Mom's house for three months before the new owners were ready to move in. Mom had sold the house to them before she died, for five hundred ninety-five thousand dollars. After the Bank of New York received the final two hundred fifty thousand that Mom owed them, the rest of the money went to the trust, which Mom had set up specifically to pay for our education and any medical emergencies. Thank God we had that money. It was our only security left in the world.

When it came time to get all our stuff out of the house that spring, not one adult helped us. It was just Liz, a few of her friends, and me. We spent several weekends loading up the Jeep with everything we could—the grandfather clocks, the sofa, the chairs, the Etruscan trunk. We had to leave a ton of stuff behind because there really wasn't anywhere for it to go. Some of it went to my friend Sue's mom's garage in Mount Kisco; some went into Anna's parents' attic down the road; and some went to Brooklyn, where I had found an apartment.

I furnished my new place with things from the house, and then, once I'd moved everything, I sold the Jeep. I couldn't get a title for it because it was in the name of one of Dad's bankrupt companies, so I sold it for a couple hundred dollars, cash, to a guy in Brooklyn who said he was going to use it as a hunting vehicle in upstate New York. And even though I still had my Karmann Ghia, I kept the Mercedes, and I drove that thing until the day it died.

DAN

I FINALLY TOLD the Hayeses how miserable I was at Trinity Pawling, and they said I could transfer back to Fox Lane. I was psyched. The Hayeses even let my dog Ralph, who had been staying with Amanda in Brooklyn, come live with me. At the Hayeses', Ralph and I watched a lot of TV together. I'd eat an Oreo and then he'd eat one, as I kneaded my toes into his back. Just like at the cottage and Mom's house, Ralph was still my best friend.

Of course, it was strange living with this new family so completely unlike my own. To start, they were religious kooks; they went to church every Sunday and prayed every night before dinner. Plus, they enforced a lot of rules, and a curfew, which was totally new to me. And though she was tiny, Mrs. Hayes was a tyrant. When she screamed, which was often, she would scare the crap out of everyone, including her giant husband.

They had two kids. Billy was twelve and already a hellion. He'd look at you wide-eyed and smiling like, "What window are we going to break? What tree are we going to cut down?" I shared a room upstairs with Brad, who was in my grade. He was popular and good-looking, and though we ran in the same crowd at school, we never became friends. Once, he said to me, "Between the two of us, we could get any girl we want at Fox Lane." But I had had such a weird experience with sex up to that point that I really didn't want to go out with anyone. The two girls I did wind up dating both wanted to have sex with me, but I couldn't do it.

I got to see Liz every day at Fox Lane, which was great, but otherwise I hated it at the Hayeses'. There were so many rules! Mrs. Hayes wouldn't let me go into the city on auditions, even though I had made ten thousand dollars doing commercials the summer before Mom died. She was messing with my livelihood! Plus, I wasn't allowed to hang out with older kids: I couldn't even get into a car driven by a teenager, including Liz. She said it was because teenagers were irresponsible. I was like, "Have you *met* my sister?"

LIZ

MAYBE IT WAS the spring or seeing my brother daily in school, but I came out of my winter depression, a snake shedding its skin. I started dating a guy from Horace Greeley, Fox Lane's rival school, and though I still had a curfew, the Stewarts would let me spend the night with Amanda in her Brooklyn apartment every so often. She and I would go to clubs like Pyramid and King Tut's Wa Wa Hut and dance until two in the morning, eat pancakes at a diner in the East Village, and head back to her place to crash. Dan was never allowed to come with me on those weekends. The Hayeses had him on a tight leash, but they did let me drop by whenever I pleased.

Seeing Diana was trickier. Whenever I called, the maid would answer "Chamberlain residence" in her clipped British accent before informing me that Diana was at ballroom dancing school, or at soccer practice, or playing at a friend's house. It made me feel good. As much as I missed my little sister, I thought that was exactly what an eight-year-old girl should be doing.

That was why Amanda and I had chosen the Chamberlains. They seemed normal, the opposite of the Stewarts, who were a funny mix of seventies hippies and Bedford preppies. Only fourteen years older than I, Daisy Stewart was more like an older sister or a young aunt than a mother, which was the reason I wanted to live with her. I didn't want a replacement for Mom. Daisy intuitively understood that. In fact, she couldn't have been more different from Mom.

One day after school, I found Daisy in the kitchen drinking herbal tea. She offered me a cup and then asked, out of the blue, "Have you ever dropped acid before?"

"No," I said, cautiously. "Why?"

"Well, if you ever want to, let me know. I know a doctor who can get us really good stuff."

I looked at her as if she *were* tripping.

"I'd rather you do it with me, here," she explained. "I think it's safer."

At the time, I was still attending weekly grief counseling sessions. One day, after session, Brenda, the social worker, told me that Daisy had come to see her.

"What did she want?" I asked.

"She's worried about you," Brenda told me. "She said you weren't having sex and that she didn't think that was normal for a seventeen-year-old girl. She wondered if it had something to do with losing your parents."

That explained why Daisy took me to the gynecologist to get fitted for a diaphragm, even before I started dating again. She was really trying, in her own way, to be cool. And she actually was. Later that spring, Daisy had a few errands to run in Stamford, Connecticut, and invited me along. When she turned down the street that led to Bloomingdale's, my heart-beat quickened. "Where are we going?" I blurted.

"I have to return a sweater. It'll only take a minute," she said.

"I can't," I said, my voice shaky.

She parked the car and turned to face me. "Why not?" she asked.

The only person who knew I had been banned from the Stamford Bloomingdale's was Maureen, who was with me the day I finally got caught shoplifting, two weeks before Mom died. Now, four months later, I told Daisy everything—that I had been stealing for over a year, that the security guards had my exploits on tape, that they threatened to have me arrested, and that the only reason they didn't call Mom was because Maureen had burst into tears and begged them not to, wailing, "Whatever you do, don't tell Liz's mother. It'll kill her!" The security men let me go with the warning that if I ever stepped foot in that Bloomingdale's again, I'd be arrested on the spot.

When I was finished, I waited for the disappointment to kick in. This was the moment of truth. I was not this good girl after all but a pathological liar and a raging kleptomaniac. I had duped her, and I waited for that realization to register on her face. Instead, Daisy smiled in a conspiratorial way.

"Well, let's see if that's true," she said, unclipping her seat belt. "If you get arrested, I promise to bail you out." I held my breath as I pushed through the heavy revolving doors. Instead of getting arrested, I got a free makeover, and Daisy bought me a bottle of Anaïs Anaïs perfume.

Even though Daisy was cool, I still couldn't wait to get the hell out of Bedford. Every day there was a reminder of the life I no longer lived. So I bounced an idea off Daisy and Montgomery. "I'm thinking about deferring a year from college," I said. "I want to go back to Europe, maybe work on my French . . ."

"I think it's a great idea," Daisy interjected. Montgomery agreed. They even knew a Norwegian family who wanted a nanny in Oslo. I wanted to go back to Paris, but I wasn't about to argue: I was simply stunned they supported my madcap plan.

As it turned out, I was accepted to Georgetown and everywhere else I had applied. Europe was, in my mind, as far away as I could get from Bedford. If I went to Norway, I could leave immediately after graduation. If I went to Georgetown, I was stuck in Bedford until the end of the summer, which felt like an eternity. I deferred for a year.

The Chamberlains brought Diana to my high school graduation barbecue. Amanda was there, and Dan, too. It was the first time we had all been together since Mom's funeral six months earlier. Diana had changed dramatically. I hardly recognized this quiet girl in her white silk dress and pale blue headband. She looked like Alice in Wonderland. I preferred Diana as a Muppet, all giggles and spunk. I knew her best as the girl who insisted on wearing pink and purple even though it clashed with her hair, and who would wear socks pulled up over her knobby knees with gym shorts to go play with friends. The girl who showed up at my graduation party was not the Diana I remembered, but I was still glad to see her. I was glad to see everyone. Auntie Eve came, too, wearing her best polyester pantsuit. Uncle Harry escorted her, wearing his one and only tie.

We spent a magical afternoon together by the Stewarts' pool, laughing and snapping photos. In one photo, Dan is squeezing Auntie Eve, his eyes are sparkling, and Amanda's head is thrown back and she's laughing. Even Diana loosened up. I saw the Muppet in her was still alive; it came out in that bubbly laugh and the sparkle in her eye.

Soon after, I went with Dan and Amanda on a road trip up to Maine to visit our Uncle Russ. I called the Chamberlains to see if Diana could come, too, but Nancy didn't think it was a good idea. She said that Diana was still settling in and that they already had plans for the summer.

It was too bad. Russ was everyone's favorite uncle, a softer, tubbier version of Dad. Perhaps that was why we loved him so, or maybe it was because of his infectious laugh, deep and hearty. He made a welcoming feast—steamers, lobster, corn on the cob, and blueberry pie—and throughout the meal regaled us with stories of Dad as a young man. "Did you know your old man was class president at Johns Hopkins University?" Russ asked. We did not. We knew Dad's mom died, but we didn't know it happened when he was sixteen, the same age Amanda was when Dad died. Nor did we know that Dad drove eighteen-wheel trucks every summer throughout college to help his dad pay for groceries and for school clothes for his younger siblings. "Your dad put me through art school," Russ said. "He bought me winter coats and boots throughout high school. He was a good man."

Hearing these stories made me realize that there was so much that I didn't know about our father. Yet looking around the table, I knew he was directly responsible for Dan's freckles and dimples, for Amanda's belly laugh, and for my squinty smile. And though Diana seemed subdued the last time I saw her, I knew in my gut that she inherited Dad's spunk and determination and certainly the up-for-anything glint in her brown eyes. We all inherited his sense of humor, too. So that night, Amanda, Dan, and I made a pact: Every summer, no matter what, we would spend a weekend with Russ. We all shook on it before heading off to bed.

DAN

I GOT KICKED out of the Hayeses' on the Fourth of July, two days after Liz left for Europe. I was so jealous—I wished more than anything I could have gotten on that plane with her. Instead, I was up in my room blasting the Violent Femmes' song "Add It Up" as loud as it would go. I was pissed. Before the Hayeses and Trinity Pawling, I had been free, walking around Mount Kisco in the middle of the night, hanging out with anyone I wanted. I never had to check in with anyone. Now, there were so many rules, I couldn't do anything. Curtis's mom had died of a heart attack earlier that spring, and Mrs. Hayes wouldn't let me go to the funeral because it was during a school day. I was devastated; even though Curtis and I had grown apart, his mother was like family to me. When I saw him in the hallway the next day, I told him I was sorry. I told him that I didn't know what to say.

"I thought you'd be the only one who would," he said, and I felt like such a coward. One of my biggest regrets is that I didn't just tell the Hayeses to fuck off. I should have been at that funeral.

But I had to watch myself, because I got in trouble for things I didn't even know were bad. Like the time I brought home the video of *A Clockwork Orange* for Mr. Hayes to watch. He told me that he had always wanted to see it but never had. It was my favorite book, the only one I ever finished in school. And the movie was a masterpiece; everybody knew that. Anyway, I was watching it with Mr. Hayes one evening as Mrs. Hayes was cooking in the kitchen. There's a scene where Billy's gang is raping this woman, and Malcolm McDowell's character comes in and stops the rape and then Malcolm's gang beats the other gang senseless. It was a pinnacle part, so I said, "Mrs. Hayes, you have to watch this scene." She came in to see five guys raping this woman, and she blew her top. She went wild. We had to turn the movie off, and I had to go up to my room.

I had borrowed the tape from the video store where I worked, but

Mrs. Hayes refused to believe that the manager would let me take an R-rated film home. She accused me of stealing it and made such a scene that I wound up getting fired. The whole thing was a mess.

Also, Mrs. Hayes thought I was a bad influence on Billy, her own crazy son. I got blamed for everything Billy did, like the time the whole house smelled like pot because he took apart some orange-spice tea bags and tried to smoke the leaves.

I was just sick of it, so I was up in my room, blaring "Add It Up," which goes, "Why can't I get just one fuck I guess it's something to do with luck." Mrs. Hayes had complained about the lyrics before—she hated swear words. So every time the word "fuck" came on, I turned the stereo way down, then turned it up again full blast. "Why can't I get just one." I kept doing it over and over, blasting it and turning it down, blasting it and turning it down. I was driving them nuts.

Finally, Mrs. Hayes screamed from the kitchen, "Dan! Your sister is on the phone! She wants to talk to you!" I picked up the phone and heard Mrs. Hayes going off on Amanda about me. I don't remember what she said, because when people yell at me, I just tune out. But I can picture her face all red and spitting. When she was done freaking out, she hung up, leaving Amanda and me on the line together.

And Amanda said, "Oh my God."

And I was like, "Yeah."

We were both quiet, until she said, "Well, pack your bags. I'm coming to get you."

AMANDA

MRS. HAYES WAS screaming, "I'm so sick of his shit! I can't deal with it anymore! It's ruining my family! He's not my problem! He's your problem!" Once she got all of her evil out, she was like, "Dan is no longer welcome in this house; he needs to be out. Tonight." So I went and got him.

Driving there from Brooklyn, I couldn't help but wish that Mom had let me be the guardian. If she had, then none of this would ever have happened. But I also knew there was no way a family judge would let Dan live with me now. I was about to turn twenty-one and was still partying hard that summer. I knew I needed to get an adult involved.

I called Karen, and she agreed to let him live with her immediately. She didn't hesitate. But this time around, I made sure my name was on any legal paperwork, so that if anything went wrong, I'd be able to step right in. There was no way I was going to let Dan be left like this again. Meanwhile, I couldn't get in touch with Liz in Norway. She was on some island taking care of those kids. I called the Stewarts to get her number, but they said she was unreachable for two weeks. So I wrote her a letter and forged ahead.

There was a lot to sort out. Like school. Karen lived in Manhattan, which meant Dan couldn't go to Fox Lane anymore. I was so pissed off that the Hayeses had pulled Dan out of Trinity Pawling without consulting me. Mom had worked really hard to get him in there. He had a full scholarship, and the Hayeses totally screwed that up. I was like, "Okay, yeah, don't follow the wishes of the woman who just died—just undo all that. That's just great." So now that I had some say, I decided to focus on getting him reaccepted.

Karen helped. We filled out all this paperwork and basically begged them to take him back. They were at maximum capacity, so they put him on a waiting list and it was pins and needles until late August. Karen started looking into public schools, but I didn't want Dan going to school in Brooklyn or Manhattan. Mom wanted him to go to Trinity Pawling. Then we got the call: They had a space for him, but we lost the scholarship; the Hayeses had fucked that. It was okay in the end because Mom specifically designed the trust to cover tuition for each of her kids.

So it was true, what I had thought all along: The Welches were better-off on our own, together.

DAN

RALPH AND I wound up crashing on Amanda's couch for a week or so before I moved into Karen's. It was fun while it lasted. Amanda was the coolest chick: She could blow perfect smoke rings out of the bowl of a bong. And one time, she brought me to a party where there were bowls of cocaine put out like peanuts. At fifteen, I thought that was very impressive.

But mostly, we just hung out in her apartment. Her friends would come over, and Amanda would be like, "Let's paint Dan!" So I'd lie on the kitchen floor in my underwear, and she and all her friends would paint my body while Grace Jones played in the background.

AMANDA

I WENT TO Tramps practically every night to see David Johansen test out his new persona, Buster Poindexter. And I was still hanging out with these three gay boys, Jim, Donny, and Rafael, plus my first boyfriend, Dennis. For my twenty-first birthday that August, Dennis took me out to his dad's place on Fire Island. When we got back, we had dinner with Karen and Dan. Liz sent me a long letter from Norway telling me about her adventures. She sounded like she was having fun. And Dan gave me a bunch of joke presents, like Silly Putty and a mini Slinky. The next day, Dennis, Dan, and all the boys came with me to see the Psychedelic Furs. Afterward, we went to Rafael's place and had cake.

A few days later, Dan, Dennis, and I went to see Diana at the Chamberlains'. They had invited me for my birthday, and I wanted to make a good impression. It was the first time I had seen Diana since Liz's graduation party three months earlier. I wore my best clothes, a paisley renaissance skirt with a black button-down shirt, new wave but conservative. Dennis wound up talking to Nancy and Ted while Diana gave me and Dan a tour of the property. It reminded me of our house growing up, with its pool and manicured lawns and gardens. I was happy that Diana was going to get that experience. But she seemed different, subdued—all buttoned up and belted down. Diana took us up to her room, but Nancy wouldn't leave me alone with her for too long because she thought I was a drug addict and a bad influence. And God knows what else.

DIANA

WHEN AMANDA AND Dan came to visit that August, my strongest
memory was of their leaving. I remember being with Dan on the lawn,
away from the Chamberlains, who were clumped together on the slate
patio, watching us while they talked to Amanda and her boyfriend, some
guy I'd never met. As they talked, Dan and I both pulled at green blades
of grass; I remember the sound of them ripping. Dan's face was the most
familiar thing I had seen in so long; I saw myself in his freckles and his
eyes, which looked worried, sad, and scared, despite the close-lipped grin
that covered his small, yellowish teeth. His teeth were like Dad's. My two
front teeth were big and rounded and white, brand-new and full-grown.
Margaret, who still had mostly baby teeth, described them as having ruf-
fles; the edges were scalloped, not yet ground down.

Amanda sat primly on the slate patio as the Chamberlains asked her
questions like "How is school?" and "What kind of work do you do?" I'd
never seen her act this way before. She wasn't laughing or dancing or being
mean. There was no music, no smoke. She was being so serious. Grown-
up. I wanted her to come over here on the grass with Dan and me. I
looked back at my brother. I thought about grabbing his neck, pulling
him down, and rolling around. We would laugh and have fun. But Mrs.
Chamberlain had dressed me in white pants and a white shirt with a blue
Indian print on it. It made her mad when I got things dirty or stained; she
would hold the soiled thing in one hand and say, "Who do you think you
are?" and I'd never know the answer.

Finally, Dan asked if I would show them around, and Amanda excused
herself from the Chamberlains, leaving her boyfriend on the patio. I jumped
up, took Dan's hand, and dragged him farther out onto the expanse of
grass and trees that fanned out toward the stone wall that lined the busy
road at the bottom of the hill. Thurman, the Chamberlains' dumb, friendly

dog, lurched alongside us, wearing a little box on his collar that zapped him if he crossed the property line. This was called an Invisible Fence, and it made him yelp. Once we were out of the Chamberlains' earshot, I told Amanda and Dan that I thought the Invisible Fence was awful, and they agreed. When I had moved in, one year ago, I had told Mrs. Chamberlain the same thing, and she'd looked at me as if I was a moron. She said it was better than getting hit by a car. I said nothing then but thought that maybe getting hit by a car wasn't so bad after all.

When we reached the stone wall at the bottom of the big green lawn, I thought of lyrics from the Tiffany song "I Think We're Alone Now": "Running just as fast we can / Holding on to one another's hand." I loved Tiffany. I thought that we could make a break for it. We weren't wearing any collars. But I didn't say anything; I just hopped up on the wall and walked on it as if it was a balance beam, testing. Then Dan asked if they could see my room, so I jumped down and led them back to the house. As we passed Dad's old, banged-up Mercedes, I wished that Amanda would get in and turn the key and Dan would push me into the backseat and that we would drive off, like a kidnapping. But she didn't and he didn't and we didn't. We just walked right past the Chamberlains, still talking to Amanda's boyfriend on the patio. Mrs. Chamberlain was drinking her favorite drink, Campari and tonic.

Amanda and Dan followed me up the narrow stairs single file to my room. It felt small. The strawberry wallpapered walls closed in on us. I didn't know what to say, so I showed them the Cabbage Patch Kid that I got for Mom dying. Amanda grabbed it from my hands and held it beneath its armpits, making it dance. She used to do this to me when I was a baby. She told me she used to pick me up and say to her friends, "Look at the demon baby!" And they'd all laugh as my crossed eyes rolled around in my head. Now, here she was in my room at the Chamberlains', laughing and making my doll dance and saying to Dan, "He looks like Buster Poindexter, doesn't he? He looks exactly like him!" And to me she said, "You have to call him Buster Poindexter!" I told her I would. I had no idea who Buster Poindexter was, but I knew this Amanda, the one who knew about cool stuff and who was loud and laughing.

I don't know how long we stayed up there in my room, but it wasn't long enough. They probably asked me questions, told me stories about their lives, and maybe even made me laugh. I don't recall. I just remember that they didn't stay and that they didn't take me with them.

I didn't leave my room for the rest of the night; I just took off my shirt and got into bed with my pants still on, pulled the covers up over my head, and started to cry, wondering how I could have made the visit go better. "Why didn't they take me with them, Buster?" I asked my stupid Cabbage Patch Kid. My tears made his hard plastic head slick. Maybe I was still too annoying to be around—maybe that was it. Maybe I wasn't fun enough. Maybe that's why they just walked down the stairs, got in that car, and drove away, leaving me alone with all those strangers.

DAN

WHEN I MOVED into Karen's apartment on the Upper West Side of Manhattan that summer, the first thing she said to me was "I've had five abortions."

I was still standing in the doorway, with all my bags. I was like, "So, you didn't want kids?" She said nothing, just continued to read the newspaper. Karen was a bitch; that was her way. I learned quickly that my survival there depended on my ability to be charming. As long as I told her she was smart and beautiful, crap like that, I'd be fine.

Looking back now, I realize how cool it was of Karen to take me in. I'll always be thankful for that. I had my own bedroom and bathroom in her apartment, though she made me sleep on the pullout couch whenever there was an est "Forum" workshop in town and a "Forum leader" needed a place to stay. Karen was this weird mix of eighties career woman and self-help hippie cult member: a commercial casting director who wore Donna Karan power suits but had framed sayings by Werner Erhard, est's leader, all over her apartment.

Also, I wasn't used to living with a grown woman who had boyfriends. I didn't think there was anything wrong with it; I mean, after she was sick, Mom went on a date with my friend's father. I thought that was the sweetest thing. But Karen's dating was gross, somehow. One time, I walked into her room and there was this old guy, bald but otherwise hairy, sleeping spread-eagled and nude on top of her bed.

Don't get me wrong: Living with Karen was way better than living with the Hayeses. I mean, Karen made it clear that it was her place. I wasn't allowed to smoke inside, and she'd yell at me about putting the dishes in the dishwasher a certain way, but besides that, she was cool. She treated me like a roommate, not like a kid. After all, my monthly Social Security checks went to her for room and board.

Plus, I got the place to myself a lot. Karen would always be at the theater or out on dates. So I would watch TV and eat cheese tortellini for
dinner, because that's all that was ever in the fridge. That and chardonnay.
I'd finish whatever bottle was open and then drink another one to the spot
at which the last one had been filled. The trick seemed to work; Karen
never noticed.

LIZ

I SPENT MY first two weeks in Norway on a small island off the western
coast called Vaskalven where the Ankers had a summer cottage. There was
no electricity or hot water, so the first morning, I followed the Ankers'
two young boys down to the sea for our morning bath. They dove in head-
first, so I did too. As soon as I hit the icy water, my heart stopped beating
and my breath froze in my lungs. I thrashed my way to the surface and let
out a howl, which set the boys off in a fit of giggles.

By then, their mom, Hege, had walked down to the end of the pier with
Elisabeth, her youngest at eight months. "Didn't the boys warn you the
water is cold?" she said in her sing-songy English. The boys continued to
laugh as I splashed my way to the ladder and clambered up on the dock,
where I lay in the sun to defrost. By the end of our stay, I was jumping in before the boys. On rainy days, Hege taught me how to knit, and we'd sit in
front of the fire drinking coffee and eating *bolle*, Norwegian hot cross buns.

Those two weeks were blissful—I wasn't homesick for a moment—
until we returned to Oslo, where a stack of letters awaited me. Amanda
sent me a care package with a mix tape that made me miss her in a visceral
way. I'd lie in my bed and listen to the first song, James Taylor's "You've
Got a Friend," over and over again. Amanda wrote that Dan was living
with Karen, which made the most sense to me. She was the closest thing
we had to family. She would never kick him out. Ever. I got letters from
Maureen, Rita, and Liz Subin, too. Daisy sent a sweet letter in which she
wondered if Norway's slow pace might be a tough transition for me. She
wrote, "I am sure it is a very difficult adjustment for you. Just bear in
mind that the long-term benefits are great. If you can't figure out how to
be by yourself, you will never be able to live with anyone else." Then she
joked, "So much for my motherly words of wisdom—or bullshit!" Auntie
Eve sent me care packages, too—a nail kit in one, a popularized version

of the Bible called *The Greatest Story Ever Told* in another. I read it, out of my love for her, but didn't think it was the "greatest" story.

Nancy Chamberlain's letters made me feel that we made the right decision for Diana. Poor Dan got screwed time and time again, but at least, I thought, Diana wound up with a stable family that seemed to love her. Nancy wrote in the first letter that she had taken Diana back-to-school shopping and that Diana had picked out a Guess jean skirt and Reebok sneakers. That sounded like the right outfit for a fourth grader. That sounded like the old Diana. In another letter, Nancy wrote that Dan and Amanda visited Diana in Bedford that August, and I wished more than anything that I had been there, too. She also wrote that Diana was getting yet another eye operation—she'd had two before she was two years old—to fix her lazy eye. I hoped this one would finally be a success.

DIANA

I STARTED FOURTH grade at West Patent with a flesh-colored patch covering my left eye. It looked disgusting beneath my pink glasses. I had wanted a black pirate patch to replace the thick gauze taped to my face after yet another eye operation to fix my lazy eye, but when I reached for one in the drugstore, Mrs. Chamberlain shook her head. "You'll just take it off," she said, scowling. She grabbed something that was higher up on the wall. "How about this one?" she seemed to ask herself. Before I could answer, she walked to the register and bought it.

Then, new gold wire-rimmed glasses replaced the eye patch. I didn't want to change from my pink frames, but Mrs. Chamberlain made me. And she made me cut my hair. She said I had to cut it short because my long red hair was unmanageable. I didn't argue. She told the lady to cut it like Dorothy Hamill, the ice skater. I didn't know who that was. Then the hairdresser whipped off the black plastic apron and handed me my new glasses. And when I looked at my reflection in the mirror, I wasn't sure who that was, either.

DAN

BACK AT TP, I became fully immersed in boarding-school hippie culture. I knew I was stuck—I hated TP but I had nowhere else to go. So I woke up in the morning and did a bong hit, then went to class and did another bong hit after lunch, then more bong hits at night. Every day, I slept, ate, and got high. My only real friend, Parker Sweeney, had gotten arrested the summer before for stealing car stereos. He didn't come back that year, so I just hung out with other people who got high. There were lots of them.

That first semester of my sophomore year, I'd go to Karen's on weekends and smoke cigarettes on the fire escape, get high in the bathroom, and drink her chardonnay. My new survival tactic was to be invisible. I never called Amanda when I was in town; I didn't want to burden anyone. I just wanted to get through it.

AMANDA

I DROPPED OUT of NYU that fall even though I was halfway through. Better than failing out, I figured. I didn't want to waste the trust money on school if I wasn't going to give it my all. So Karen helped me get a job at a payroll company for production companies. It was basically a bunch of math and typing. I was terrible at both, but I made nineteen thousand dollars a year, which seemed like a lot back then.

I spent most of it on drugs and Kamikaze mix drinks out at the boy bars, which were still amazing magical *Wizard of Oz* places for me. I could dance all night long, and no one bothered me. Everyone there was oblivious to my existence. No creeps, no expectations. I loved it. I was invisible.

LIZ

SITTING ON A train, reading Ayn Rand's *The Fountainhead*, I had barely used my voice in days except to say "Tusen takk," to shop clerks and waitresses and train conductors. After saving money from babysitting, I decided to set out in mid-October on a month-long tour of Scandinavia by myself. I left Oslo on a train bound west for Bergen, the colorful coastal city. I liked the anonymity and freedom of traveling alone. I continued north to Trondheim, where I spent two days wandering aimlessly around the city before heading south toward Sweden.

On the train, I watched the Norwegian countryside barrel by—houses with grass roofs, fields dotted with sheep, country roads, the occasional Peugeot, and gray skies forever. When I'd been on the road for over a week, for the first time I felt a pang of sadness, as if the loneliness and loss I had been running from suddenly plopped down next to me in the otherwise empty seat. I realized that I had no idea where I was other than south of Norway's third-largest city. And if I had no idea, that meant no one could find me if they wanted to. Not Amanda, or Auntie Eve, or even the Ankers. I wondered if anyone was worried, or even thinking about me.

Just then, the train entered a deep tunnel, and the cabin went dark, transforming the engine's steady, high-pitch scream into something dull and hollow. We emerged on the other side, and the sun's muted rays first hit a family of four sitting across the aisle from me before flooding the entire car. I'd noticed them before. The children were tow-headed elves, small and sweet with pointy noses and freckled faces. The parents, ruddy-cheeked and blond, were chattering back and forth as the mom pulled lunch out of her leather rucksack. The dad unwrapped the sandwiches while the mother poked straws into two boxes of juice before handing them to her children. The girl, who looked about eight years old, reminded me of Diana. While living in Oslo, I'd received a handful of letters from her. In wobbly, knock-kneed purple print, she wrote that she was on the soccer team, they had won their first game, and she was learning the clarinet. And she'd always sign the letters "love, Di," dotting the *i* with a tiny heart. And then, at the bottom of the page, she'd add another heart, this one pierced with an arrow and big enough to fit her name plus mine inside.

Seeing the Norwegian girl bouncing in her seat, drinking her juice, I felt a pang of jealousy. I wished I could go back in time to those precious moments when I'd mindlessly eaten the Dannon yogurt Mom handed me at horse shows, or munched on the popcorn Dad bought me at movie theaters. Now, anytime someone offered me a meal, I said "Tusen takk," a thousand thanks. I was acutely aware that if someone offered to buy me pancakes with blueberry sauce, as the Ankers had done the Sunday before I left for my trip, it was a very specific gesture and completely different from doing the same for their own children. I worked for my food. At least Diana wasn't working for hers. I imagined Nancy hiring a clown for Diana's birthday and Ted teaching her how to kick a soccer ball. I imagined sit-down chicken fricassee and beef Stroganoff dinners, served at 6 p.m. when Ted got home from work. I imagined salad forks and plates, and Diana waking up in the morning and coming down to a table already set with bowls and spoons and a variety of breakfast cereals. Her lunch would already be packed for her—a turkey sandwich with the crusts cut off, a piece of fruit, maybe a few Oreos or homemade cookies! And always a box of juice just like the one that little bouncing girl had. And just like that little girl, Diana would think nothing of it, because that was what being in a family meant. And as happy as I was that Diana had a family, it somehow made me feel all the more alone.

My eyes wandered from the happy Norwegian family across the way and farther down the train car to where a man sat, like me, by himself. He was middle-aged and had a slight double chin and thinning hair. His fat, hairy fingers grabbed hold of the hardback book he was reading. I could see the scaly red patches of skin on his face and neck. And I wondered, would he marry me? Would he want to take care of me?

DIANA

MRS. CHAMBERLAIN THREW ME a party for my ninth birthday, and a bunch of girls from my grade came. We played pin-the-tail-on-the-donkey and wrapped each other up in toilet paper so we looked like mummies. It was Mrs. Chamberlain's idea and it was really fun. Also, Mrs. Chamberlain made angel food cake with chocolate icing and strawberries, my favorite, and she gave me a magic set.

After all the kids had gone home, I decided to put on a magic performance for the whole family in the library, without having read the set's instructions. I was going to wing it! I put a cassette of *Cats! The Musical* on the stereo and fast-forwarded to "Mr. Mistoffelees" before calling everybody in. Once they settled on the couch, Margaret between her parents and William on his mother's lap, I felt nervous, shaky, and hot. But I decided to keep on. I took the cards out of the red plastic kit and attempted a trick. There was a top hat, which I wore, and a wand, which I waved in the air, but the magic just wasn't there. I think I was expecting clapping and laughter. Instead, my theatrics were faced with awkward silence. Finally, Mrs. Chamberlain's voice, which seemed to be growing more and more irritable the longer I lived in her house, suggested slowly, "Maybe you should practice first." I felt so stupid. I packed up the wand and the cards and the colored scarves and went up to my room and put it all under my bed. Then I glumly stared out the window until I heard Mrs. Chamberlain's heavy footsteps coming up the stairs.

"I have something for you," she said as she entered my room. She opened the hard blue box that was in her hand. Inside was a familiar-looking necklace, thin gold hearts connected by a delicate gold chain. I reached my hand out to touch it but stopped and looked up at Mrs. Chamberlain first, unsure. She smiled at me, her chin folding into her neck. "Go ahead," she said. "It was your mother's."

It was so strange to hear her say "your mother's." Mrs. Chamberlain never mentioned Mom, never talked about anyone in my family, as though they didn't exist. I took the box from her hand and stared at the necklace, trying desperately to remember it on Mom's neck. I couldn't. "Thank you," I said. I started to shake, so I sat down, right there on the carpet, at Mrs. Chamberlain's feet.

After she left the room, I took the necklace out of the box and put it on, the tiny clasp digging into my finger as I struggled to keep it open long enough to snap it on the other end. Once it was on, I swore never to take it off. This necklace around my neck was proof that there was something before this, that I hadn't just dreamt my old life. There had been something solid before I was so unsure.

Ecstatic, I wore the necklace to school the next day. I couldn't keep it out of my mouth. Throughout class, I sucked on the hearts, felt the chain straining against my chin and the back of my neck. I pulled it out of my mouth and looked at the iridescent sheets of spit that clung to the chain.

Then, out on the blacktop, playing foursquare, I felt something pop and slither down between my chest and my T-shirt. I stopped dead in my tracks, the ball bouncing away behind me. I frantically pulled at my shirt until I found it, shiny in the waistband of my pants.

Back in my room after school, I held Mom's necklace in my hands. I had broken it. I couldn't even remember it around her neck. I couldn't shake the feeling that I didn't deserve something so precious.

When Mrs. Chamberlain came up to ask me why I wasn't practicing my clarinet, she found me with the necklace in my mouth, crying. She got angry. "I told you to take care of it," she said, her face twisting with disgust. Then she took the necklace from my hands and walked down the stairs.

AMANDA

THAT NOVEMBER, I decided to have Thanksgiving at my apartment. I called the Chamberlains to invite Diana, and surprisingly, Nancy agreed to let her come. I was so excited! I don't remember why Dan and Karen didn't come, but all my friends were there—Dennis, Donny, Patrick and Rafa, this guy Mike, and this punk girl Christine.

When Ted dropped Diana off, she seemed in her element, totally comfortable. She and Rafa had the best time. He had a ball playing with her all night, riding her on his shoulders and dancing. Everyone knew how important it was that Diana was there, so that Thanksgiving was totally normal; no one was doing cocaine or anything like that. I made a turkey, stuffing, and an apple pie, and I set the table with Mom and Dad's wedding china. After dinner, Rafa and I pushed two armchairs together in the living room to make a little bed for Diana, and we tucked her in. It was very cute. I went to bed hoping these visits would continue.

I had no idea that it would be the last time I saw her for five years.

DIANA

I REMEMBER BEING on Rafa's shoulders and playing with his ponytail. And I loved falling asleep listening to the sound of Amanda's laugh, hearing the murmurs of conversation, and smelling the familiar, dusty scent of the down-filled armchair from our old living room. When I was little, I hated having to go to bed when a party was going on, so I would curl up in a chair, close my eyes, and fall asleep listening to the voices and the laughter. I didn't want to miss anything.

Back at the Chamberlains', I made the mistake of telling Mrs. Chamberlain about this cool thing I had learned from one of Amanda's friends: Christine told me she had pierced her ears when she was eleven by filing down her mother's favorite diamond earrings and then jamming one through each earlobe, numbing the area first with an ice cube and putting a potato behind her ear so she wouldn't stab herself in the neck. I thought it was awesome, but as soon as I said it, I realized it was a betrayal, as though I had tattled. When I saw the sour look on Mrs. Chamberlain's face, I wished I could take it back, but it was too late.

AMANDA

THEN I GET this letter from Nancy, on her fancy fucking mono-grammed stationery. She called Diana a child in need and said that they had sought professional help for her emotional problems. I had already heard from Nancy that Diana wasn't doing that well in school and that she was losing things. But what did she expect? A totally carefree kid who would just show up and be happy? The letter went on to say that, after consulting a child psychologist, they realized that Diana was a child in need of boundaries and security. I was like, uh, yeah, lady, that's why we wanted her to live with you and your perfect family in the first place.

Then the letter got weird. Nancy started talking about how Diana was asking for their permanent commitment of love and a guarantee that they wouldn't die. Since they couldn't guarantee the latter, she wrote, they needed time to prepare Diana for our visits, which were only going to happen at their house, supervised. In other words: no more Thanksgivings in Brooklyn. Fine, I thought. I get it. I'm a pothead fuckup. But then she went on to request that we not call the house asking to see Diana. She said that she'd call each of us individually and invite us over when she felt Diana could handle it. She ended the letter by telling me I needed to understand that she wasn't trying to break up our family.

This letter confused me at first. Diana had seemed so happy at Thanksgiving, so comfortable. I thought she had fun. The only conclusion I could draw was that the Chamberlains had gotten a retarded child psychologist. I definitely didn't think that they were going to cut us off from seeing Diana entirely. That just wasn't even a remote possibility, not in my mind. And, to be honest, the letter really hurt my feelings. I never gave the Chamberlains a hard time about anything. On the contrary, I treated them with total respect. But I also knew I had to go along with it.

More than anything, I wanted what was best for Diana.

LIZ

MY LETTER FROM Nancy was a little bit different. It was waiting for me in a stack of letters when I returned to Oslo in late November after traveling as far as Finland. The only reason I didn't get to St. Petersburg was that I didn't have enough money to stay in Helsinki and wait for a Russian visa. Otherwise, I would have kept traveling.

Nancy's letter said that Diana was having a hard time transitioning from her old family to her new one, and since the Welch kids were so scattered, we should be respectful of Diana's need to merge with her new family. That meant limiting our contact and always calling to make an appointment to see her when we were back in Bedford.

I thought this was odd, especially since Diana always seemed so happy to see me, Amanda, and Dan—we were her siblings after all. But then again, I saw no harm in having to call ahead before visits. I didn't think it was a big deal.

DIANA

SOON, I STARTED to get into trouble. One day, I came home from school and went into the kitchen and did something—I don't know exactly what—that set Mrs. Chamberlain off. I think I lied about something, or said something mean to Margaret. I can't remember. All I remember was Mrs. Chamberlain asking me "Who do you think you are?" real loud before ordering me to the sink, and that Margaret was standing in the corner, looking scared, with her fingers in her mouth.

My face was close to the empty silver sink as Mrs. Chamberlain grabbed the sponge. It had a clear plastic handle filled with bright green soap. She told me to open my mouth. I did. She squinted her eyes and the plastic handle knocked against my teeth. The soap released into my mouth, and I started to gag on the froth. When she was done, she threw the sponge into the sink where it dinged, plastic against metal. I had heard of people getting their mouths washed out with soap, and I think I had even been threatened with it, but this was new. I had never been touched in such an angry way.

One afternoon, that past summer, I'd stepped on a bee while playing in the yard by the pool. When I'd limped into the kitchen, Mrs. Chamberlain had been so nice to me, wiping some white paste on my swollen red foot and telling me that I was a tough little girl and that bee stings hurt. I thought of this as I wiped my mouth and spit soap into the sink. I turned away from her to go up to my room, where I was told to stay until dinner.

Dinner was usually something gross, like veal and spaghetti squash. I helped Rhonda make it sometimes, banging the gray meat with a wooden mallet before sprinkling it with lemon pepper. Mr. and Mrs. Chamberlain ate when it was dark, after Mr. Chamberlain got home from work, in the dining room, with candles and fancy plates.

Margaret and William and I usually ate in the breakfast room while it was still light outside. One time, we were lucky and got pizza. Margaret and I were laughing and stretching cheese out of our mouths when I noticed that William was silent in his high chair, his head a tethered balloon weaving back and forth. He was slowly turning blue. His pizza was on the white plastic tray in front of him, cut up in chunks that he had been eating one by one. Without thinking, I reached into William's mouth and felt around, my thumb and forefinger sinking into his wet throat. I pulled out a chunk of cheese, all gooey and hard at the same time, like worn-out chewing gum. William coughed and began to cry. Margaret had her piece of pizza in both hands, her tiny teeth clenched at the tip of her slice. Mrs. Chamberlain came in when she heard William crying, and she saw the chewed-up chunk in my hand. As she lifted William out of the high chair, I said, "I reached in there and pulled it out," somewhat mystified and proud.

Mrs. Chamberlain tucked her chin over one of William's shoulders, which were shaking with sobs, and closed her eyes as she hushed the scared little boy. Once William's screams had turned into little hiccups, Mrs. Chamberlain opened her eyes and looked at me and said, "You're good under pressure." She smiled her smile that looked more like a frown.

Another time, Margaret, William, and I were eating a dinner of chicken and rice. We were all three quiet, just eating. Suddenly, a hand smacked down on the tabletop next to my white plate. I froze, mouth open. The chicken on my fork quivered.

"How many times do I have to tell you not to shovel your food?" Mrs. Chamberlain said loudly, her body right behind mine. This had been a recurring issue: Mrs. Chamberlain thought my manners were atrocious, and she often told me so. On my behalf, she instituted Sunday-night manner parties, where she and Mr. Chamberlain graded us on our manners. We would all dress up and eat together in the dining room, the fancy plates lit up by candles. First things first, place your napkin in your lap, but only after Mr. Chamberlain had done so. Second, never put your elbows on the table. Third, always have one hand in your lap unless you are using both fork and knife, and so on. I didn't mind the manner parties; I thought they were fun. I remembered that, when I went out to dinner with my real family when I was little, the waitresses always said what good manners I had. That was when Dad was alive, when those things mattered. I'd had good manners once. I could get them again.

"Your face is *inches* away from the plate, Diana," Mrs. Chamberlain continued, her voice almost desperate. "Sit. Up. Straight," she said, shoving her hard fingers into my back. Her voice hurt my ear, so I lifted my shoulder up to protect it and rested my fork on the edge of my plate. "Remove it," she said sternly. I did. As my bite of chicken hung in the air between us, skewered by the pewter tines, Mrs. Chamberlain yanked the plate away, leaving nothing to block my view of the plastic placemat. It had a map of the world on it. I stared at Africa as I heard the door to the back patio creak open and slam shut. I heard Mrs. Chamberlain muttering. I checked to see what Margaret and William were doing. William's eyes were big as he chewed his precut chunks of chicken. Margaret stared at her plate, both her hands in her lap, her face reddening. Both were silent.

The patio door creaked and slammed again, and Mrs. Chamberlain was back, her body close again as she placed Thurman's dog bowl in front of me. There, inside the greasy brown plastic container chewed around the edges, was my uneaten chicken and rice. "If you're going to eat like a dog, I'll feed you like one," she said in my ear, quieter this time but meaner. Then, turning to the other kids, she said cheerfully, "Okay, guys, finish up."

I still had my fork in my hand, so I quieted the jiggling chicken by putting it into my mouth. The rest of my food glistened with a thick residue of dog spit. I could see it on the rice.

LIZ

DIANA WAS THE only reason I wanted to go back to Bedford that winter. I had knit her a sweater in Norway for Christmas and bought her new siblings gifts as well—a crystal polar bear for Margaret and a stuffed walrus for William. I got Nancy and Ted a box of Norwegian chocolates and, remembering Nancy's last letter, called that afternoon from the Stewarts', who were in London for the holidays, to make an appointment to see Diana.

Ted answered. "Welcome home, stranger!" he said, kind and gentle as always.

"Hello!" I answered, my nerves rattling my voice. "I just wanted to see when I could come for a visit."

"When do you want to come?" he asked.

"Would this afternoon be all right?" I ventured.

"I don't see why not," he said. His cheerful tone made me feel silly for even asking.

The drive took only ten minutes, yet it felt as if there were years between us. I was worried I wouldn't recognize Diana. I was going to see my little sister, and I had butterflies in my stomach as if I were going on a date with a crush. "This is silly," I thought. "She's my sister."

I turned into the Chamberlains' driveway, parked the car, and walked to the front door, painted a shiny red and decorated with a plump Christmas wreath. I rang the bell, and Nancy answered.

"Merry Christmas!" I shouted.

Diana was right behind her and almost tackled me. "Liz!" She was shouting, too. Margaret and William came running and were soon jumping around me like windup toys.

Ted came next. "The Viking returns," he said and reached out to give me a hug.

Nancy was silent, her face frozen into a frown. Her arms stayed crossed on her chest, but then she forced a smile and invited me in. We all sat down in the family room.

Diana was wearing tartan slacks, brown leather loafers, and a red mohair cardigan. Gone were the pink glasses Mom had let her pick out herself. Gone too were her ropy locks, now cut into a neat bob and held in place with a navy blue velvet headband. Margaret, in a wool dress and lacy white tights, was hopping on one foot, then the other, excited to open her gift. I sat on the couch, and Diana sat close next to me.

"How was Norway?" Nancy started the conversation after offering me cider and Christmas cookies. As I began telling everyone about my adventures, Diana grabbed hold of my arm and soon had smashed her freckled face against my shoulder. Margaret did the same on the other side, so I was the book between two sweet bookends.

"Diana," Nancy scolded. "Stop hanging all over your sister. You're suffocating her."

I could feel Diana's nine-year-old body tense up and begin to withdraw, the heat from her face bounced off my cheek.

"Oh no, it's fine!" I insisted, flinging my arm around her and pulling her in tight. I could feel the smile grow back across her face, the heat dissipating. "I don't mind at all. Actually, I like it."

"You're just saying that," Nancy continued. "Girls, leave Liz alone. She'll never want to come back."

Diana flinched. I wanted to look her in the eyes and say that it wasn't true, that it would never—could never—be true, but I just kept my eyes steady on Nancy and tightened my grip on Diana. "Really, it's fine," I said.

We talked a bit more, and the girls opened their presents. Diana gushed over her new sweater, asking Nancy if she could change into it.

Nancy said no. They were on their way to the city for mass. They were going to have to say good-bye.

I gave everyone a hug and held on to Diana the longest.

Back at the Stewarts', I started calling high school friends to see who was in town. I was planning to be in Bedford for only a night or two and wanted to make the most of it. The phone rang. It was Nancy.

"Who do you think you are?" she hissed.

"Excuse me?" I said, utterly confused.

"Didn't I tell you to call? Didn't I tell you to make an appointment? Don't you understand how devastating it is for Diana for you to float in and out of her life?" She railed on and on, not breathing between sentences.

My face grew hot as my whole body began to tremble.

"But I called," I said.

"You are so selfish," she continued. "Just whisk off to Norway for six months and come flitting back here as if it's no big deal and with no concern whatsoever for what a fucked-up little girl I have to deal with."

"I called," I said again.

That broke the rant for a moment. "What?" she said, annoyed.

"I called, I spoke to Ted. He told me to come," I explained, my heart racing from the outburst, the receiver warm in my hand.

More silence.

"Well, he never mentioned it," she said. I waited for the apology.

"Well, that doesn't matter. I still have to deal with this, and the effect that it's going to have on her. Diana is part of our family now, Liz. She's a Chamberlain, and she lives by my rules. You have to respect that."

Then she hung up.

I was shaking, whole-body tremors as though whatever was whirling deep inside me might bust me open. I called Amanda, but she wasn't home. The pressure building inside me was intense, straining at my lungs and throat. Then I thought of Brenda Leif-Johnson, the social worker from Fox Lane. I dialed her home number and told her the story in a fast whisper. When I was done, Brenda said, "Liz, that makes no sense. It sounds psychotic." And while it may have explained Nancy's behavior, it did not make me feel any relief. Diana was living with that psycho, and I had no idea what to do about it.

DIANA

WHEN I HEARD Liz's voice in the doorway, I couldn't believe it. Whenever I asked about my sisters or brother, Mrs. Chamberlain said they were living their own lives and didn't have time to visit me. But here Liz was, home from Norway with a shopping bag full of Christmas presents. We all sat in the breakfast room, and it felt as though Liz was talking to everybody but me. I pushed against her as I had at Mom's funeral, willing her to stay with me forever as she placed the brightly wrapped presents on the coffee table in front of us. There was one for me, and one for William, and one for Margaret. We each opened ours. Then I reached for the one that was left on the table, unopened, and held it in my lap. It said "ADD" on it in my sister's big, neat handwriting.

"Who's Add?" I asked her, interrupting a story about her travels.

"Oh," she said, taking it out of my hands and putting it back in her bag, still loaded with presents. "That's for Addison." My stomach jumped. Addison. That was one of the Stewart kids. They went to my school. Liz was probably going to leave me here to go hang out with them. Mrs. Chamberlain was right: Liz was too busy for me because, like me, she had new little brothers that she saw every day. Liz probably made Add snacks and hugged him and laughed at his jokes. She probably loved him as much as she loved me. Maybe even more. I was just another stop on her Christmas tour.

It was clear to me then: I was stuck at the Chamberlains' for good. There was to be no heroic kidnapping, no laughing, happy reunion. Things were settled and I was staying. Forgotten about, tossed.

Next thing I knew, we were at Gram's house. She was Mr. Chamberlain's mother. She lived all alone with her maid, a black lady who stayed in the kitchen and rarely spoke. Gram's brother was a cardinal who became a bishop, or maybe it was the other way around. Mrs. Chamberlain told me that when Mr. Chamberlain was little, his dad abandoned them all on

Mr. Chamberlain's birthday. She said he walked around the table, kissed all the kids on the head, and said good-bye. She said he was an alcoholic.

I thought of these things as I looked at Gram. She was a mannish lady, a smoker who wore her gray hair short. She was wearing pants and a sweater and leather slippers with no socks. As I looked at her—the lines in her face, her broad shoulders—I couldn't imagine her passing out cake slices on plates. She was kind to me but so formal. On our way there, in Mr. Chamberlain's car, Mrs. Chamberlain reminded us to sit with our ankles crossed and to mind our manners as she nervously fussed with her hair in the visor mirror. Once inside her mother-in-law's home, she laughed a lot and spoke in an exaggerated, drawn-out way. Her voice seemed louder, higher somehow.

We were all sitting around quietly eating nuts in the living room when Gram snuffed out her cigarette and told me to follow her into a large bedroom that felt like a set from an old movie with its dark wood and heavy drapes. We were far apart, and the light from the green table lamps was dim. I sat on the bed with my hands in my lap, my back straight. "You know what I think would be a nice thing?" she asked, standing above me, hands dangling, loosely clasped in front of her.

"What?" I said, looking long into her face. This private moment between us was exciting.

"If you would start calling them 'mom' and 'dad,'" she said, leaning down and putting both hands on my shoulders. "Do you think you could do that?" We were still far apart; her elbows did not bend.

I didn't know what to say. I stared at my hands for a while and hoped that maybe she'd give up. My wool skirt itched. I knew I should say no, but I also knew I had to say yes. "I guess" is what ended up coming out.

"Good," she said, smiling and taking her hand off my shoulder to light a cigarette. "Good." Then she walked me out into the living room, guiding me with her free hand still on my shoulder. "I think Diana has something to say to you all," Gram said proudly and squeezed my shoulder encouragingly. I turned my head and looked at her, stunned. Now? I had to call them that now?

So I said, "Um, can I have some nuts, Mom?" And Mrs. Chamberlain jumped up out of her chair and gave me a big hug, and her husband came, too, and he hugged me and I said, quietly, uncomfortably, "Thanks, Dad."

It was like walking off a cliff.

AMANDA

LIZ CALLED ME in tears to say Nancy Chamberlain had yelled at her. I was sad to hear it but not surprised. I figured she was simply an uptight Bedford lady who just didn't get us. I guessed she thought we were wild and a bad influence on Diana. And I thought she might be a little nutty, but I still thought Diana was going to have a stable life, like the one we'd had before Dad died. I wasn't worried about Diana. I was sad for me, Liz, and Dan. But I didn't let myself get too upset about it because I felt there was nothing I could do. In Nancy's eyes, we were bad kids. I really didn't think there was anything I could do to change that.

The whole experience made me realize how important my siblings were to me. That year, I had Christmas at Karen's apartment on the Upper West Side with all her weird est friends, which was fine, because Liz and Dan were there. Even Auntie Eve and Uncle Harry came for dinner. Karen made a goose because she was allergic to turkey, and we decorated the tree with the family ornaments I retrieved from storage.

Christmas morning, I made Mom's pumpkin bread, and we opened presents in Karen's living room. Dan gave me a Calvin Klein underwear poster that he had torn off some subway station wall. He'd stapled his own impish black and white head shot on Marky Mark's ripped body. He gave Karen a Tiffany box with brass earrings in it that he bought on Eighth Street, and he gave Liz a huge box, the size of a TV, with a Massengill douche inside. The kid had lost a lot, but he still had his sense of humor.

LIZ

THAT JANUARY, I moved back in with the Stewarts, and Montgomery got me a job working as the receptionist at his father's company, where he was vice president. It was only temporary; I was leaving for Paris at the end of the month. Daisy had a pregnant friend living there who needed a nanny. She wanted me to start a few weeks after she gave birth in mid-January. If all went according to plan, I'd be in Paris by February 3, my eighteenth birthday. I couldn't wait.

Montgomery was really getting on my nerves. I had gained weight in Norway, so he insisted on waking me up every morning at six to accompany him to the gym. I swam laps while he lifted weights. Then we drove to the Bedford Hills station to take the 7:47 a.m. train to Grand Central. Montgomery was not only bossy; he was also oddly possessive. Even when the train was full, he insisted that we find a seat together. It was so irritating.

Montgomery was not only annoying me; he was bugging Daisy as well. He was drinking a lot and often in a bad mood. Daisy said it was his early midlife crisis—he bought a Hummer and bragged that he and Arnold Schwarzenegger were the only two civilians to own the all-terrain Army vehicles. I thought it was pathetic. I was counting the days until I could go to Paris, but every time I mentioned it to Daisy, she said she had not heard from her friend. By late January, I was getting desperate.

At work, Montgomery often left his door open, which meant I could overhear his phone conversations. I usually tried to block them out, but when I heard him say "Hello, Peter!" one afternoon, my ears perked up. It was Peter Anker calling from Norway. When he said, louder than usual, "Oh, Liz is great," I was riveted. I was so not great, and it was so obvious. Then he said, "Well, actually, Paris didn't work out. She decided to stay in New York and work for me until Georgetown starts in the fall."

I began to tremble. All this time both Daisy and Montgomery were telling me everything was set: I was going to Paris; I was just waiting for Daisy's friend to give birth. And this was his pathetic way of letting me know it was not going to happen? I looked at the calendar. It was January 28. Georgetown didn't start until late August. There was no way in hell I was going to be a receptionist and live in Bedford for another eight months.

Then it dawned on me. In six days, I turned eighteen. I would be free to do whatever I wanted. Instead of confronting Montgomery, I took my lunch break early and got a *Village Voice*. There, in the back, I found an advertisement for cheap flights to Europe. Montgomery was gone for lunch when I made the first call, to my Swedish friend Kathy who was living in Paris as a nanny. I'd met her through the Stewarts—she was an au pair for one of their friends in New York the year before. I was not allowed to make personal calls from work, but I didn't care.

"Bonjour, je peux parler avec Kathy, s'il vous plaît?" I said when a French woman answered the phone. I told Kathy what had happened and asked if she thought I would be able to find work if I came to Paris on my own. She said yes and told me I could stay with her until I did. I hung up the phone feeling victorious. I was going to Paris after all.

AMANDA

WHEN LIZ TOLD me she was going to Paris, I thought it was pretty brave. I would never do that, just up and go traveling somewhere with no real plan. But I understood why she was so desperate to leave Bedford; everyone there was fucked up. Montgomery was never overtly inappropriate with Liz, but there were all these weird insinuations that were just gross. It was the classic suburban man drooling over the babysitter. And Nancy wasn't even speaking to us or letting us see Diana. Meanwhile, Dan had basically disappeared. There was no reason for her to stick around.

So Liz was right to leave. She could take care of herself, and she should do what she wanted. But I knew I was going to miss her.

LIZ

I BOUGHT A one-way ticket on an Air Pakistan flight to Paris that left JFK on February 10. My plan was to find an au pair job until June and save money to be able to buy a Eurail Pass to tour Europe with Liz Subin that summer. I was so excited. My year abroad was back on track. I could do it on my own.

I packed two duffel bags and was proud of traveling light, until my hands started to throb at Grand Central. By the time I met Amanda in Greenwich Village for my au revoir dinner at Pizzeria Uno, my arms felt as though they might fall off. Amanda was really proud of me for going. She kept saying, "Fuck them, Liz—do what you want!" I was so glad to have her on my side. When I had told the Stewarts I was going to Paris, they had said nothing. Daisy looked scared, shook her head a few times, and then left the room. Montgomery just sat there.

I said good-bye to Amanda and then took the subway to the plane and was at Orly airport the following morning, Paris time. It was a cold, gray day, but I didn't care—I was in Paris! Kathy and I had arranged to meet at a café on the Champs-Élysées, and I decided to splurge on a cab. I had five hundred dollars, more than enough to get me through until I found a job, I thought.

Kathy worked for a wealthy family. She had her own room in their sprawling apartment on Avenue Victor Hugo in the sixteenth arrondisement, and she also had a *chambre de bonne,* or maid's room, on the top floor of their building. She was not allowed to have guests stay there, but she said I could sneak in and out while I looked for work. Since the entrance was in the back of the building by the trash and was accessible only by stairs, she was sure it would be no problem.

After schlepping my bags up seven flights, I stacked them in the corner of Kathy's tiny room, which barely fit her double futon, and went in search of the bathroom. All I could find was a small closet with a seatless toilet and filthy metal sink that had only a cold-water spigot. The following day, desperate for a hot bath, I found a nearby indoor pool where I could swim and shower for ten francs. From there, I headed to the nearest café with a list of au pair agencies that Kathy had compiled for me and a stack of newspapers to look for help-wanted ads. I was eager to start working. I imagined the family that would hire me would be much like the Ankers: I'd have my own room. I'd make enough money to buy cool French clothes and splurge on steak frites at quaint cafés. Perhaps I would invest in a language class, unless I met a cute boy first who'd teach me for free. Then I'd spend my extra money on silky lingerie!

By February 17, I still had no job and had spent one hundred dollars, mostly on café crèmes. The au pair agency I registered with wanted a one-year commitment, and any waitress jobs I applied for wanted better French and at least some restaurant experience. Then the heat got cut off at Kathy's room. That February was the kind of cold that penetrates the bone to its marrow. I spent hours in cafés and museums and went to the pool on the days it was open—not to swim but simply to stand beneath the hot shower until my skin turned pink and my blood began to simmer. Back in the room, I put on two sweaters, leggings, and socks before getting into bed, where I curled up in the fetal position, trying to stay warm. It was there, in the dark quiet, that I began to wonder if coming to Paris was a mistake.

By February 23, I was down to three hundred bucks. That afternoon, I went to Notre Dame. For the first time ever, I wished I believed in God. I wanted to pray for a job, for heat, for a winning lottery ticket. For someone to save me. Instead, I lit one candle for Mom and one for Dad, knelt down before the burning flames, and thought: "Dear Mom and Dad, help! I don't want to go back to Bedford with my tail between my legs. No, I will not go back to Bedford. Period."

That night, I dreamt that Dad was still alive. He was driving the Mercedes-Benz, and I was sitting behind him, asking where he'd been all those years. Instead of answering, he looked at me through the rearview mirror and smiled wide. I asked again, and he let out a boisterous laugh. And then I woke up.

It was yet another gray cold day. I went to Sacré-Coeur and lit more candles. That night, I dreamt about Dad again. This time, I burst into tears in my dream. I was hugging him and kept saying, "Where have you been?" He just laughed and laughed.

I woke the next morning in Kathy's freezing room feeling worse than the day before. I had heard that families posted notices for au pairs at the American church, so I went there and wrote every name and number down. On March 4, I finally got a job taking care of a one-year-old girl called Emma. I had to sleep in her room—the family's apartment was small—but I didn't care. I had a warm bed and my own bathroom, with hot water. I was thrilled.

Kathy and I celebrated that night at a café on the Champs-Élysées. We were drinking champagne when a middle-aged man with slicked-back hair asked if we would join him and his friends. "Non, merci," I said, rolling my eyes at Kathy. This was a common occurrence. Men in Paris could be a nuisance. They hissed at you in the streets and aggressively flirted in cafés, and more than once, I had been touched in the subway, and not by accident. It infuriated me.

Things were not so great with my employers, either. The dad was in Alcoholics Anonymous and taking a pill that made him have an allergic reaction to alcohol. I learned this when he arrived at the apartment at noon one weekday swollen and splotchy red, gasping for air. This happened several times over the next few weeks. Plus, he and his wife expected me to babysit twelve hours a day, seven days a week, for a measly two hundred francs. One Friday night, they said they'd be home by eleven, so I made plans to meet Kathy at a club at midnight. When they did not show up by two in the morning, I went to bed writing my resignation speech in my head. The next morning, they were still gone. The mom called later that day to say they decided to go to Biarritz for the weekend.

So on Monday morning, I quit. I couldn't take it anymore. It was April 4. Since I had nowhere to go, I told Emma's mom that I would work until she found my replacement. I figured that would give me enough time to find something else. But when her husband heard the news, he was furious and said he wanted me gone before he got home from work. In a panic, I called the closest youth hostel to reserve a bed. Then I called Amanda.

AMANDA

THAT WAS THE most terrifying phone call, ever. Liz was freaking out. That drunk bastard refused to pay her the money he owed her and kicked her out of his house, with nowhere to go! And when she told me that she kept getting harassed by seedy men, I was a wreck. My worst fear was Liz getting sold into sexual slavery somewhere. So I told her to call Janie Rayne and get her ass to London, ASAP. I wanted her somewhere safe.

Around that time, Abbie, the woman I had mucked stalls for in high school, got in touch with me again. She was moving to Charlottesville, Virginia, and asked me to drive one of her cars down there for her. She also offered to sell me her old Saab, cheap. I had sold the Karmann Ghia and, since the Mercedes was on its last legs, I decided to buy the Saab.

Charlottesville was beautiful. It reminded me of Bedford with its wide-open fields. It was horse country. During that short visit, Abbie asked me to come work on her new farm. I thought it sounded like a good idea. Since Liz was in Europe and Dan was in boarding school, there wasn't anything keeping me in Manhattan anymore.

Back in New York, I spent hours wandering the city, imagining the life I really wanted, which was basically a place where we could all be together again. I wanted to bring back the feeling we'd had when we were little. I wanted there to be a place where everyone knew they could go, so Dan wouldn't be left stranded again, Liz wouldn't have to choose between being alone and vulnerable or dealing with Montgomery's bullshit. I wanted to get my life together, so that my house could be a place where Nancy might let Diana come, too. Eventually.

DIANA

A LITTLE MORE than two years after I moved in, the Chamberlains' house was invaded by a steady stream of men who knocked down walls to expose the entire eastern side of the house. They added on my new bedroom and a bathroom for William and me to share. They completely transformed the kitchen, swapping out the dark red tile for a gleaming, peachy pink. They scratched the wet black paint on the new library's walls with a comb, exposing the bright red paint beneath in a repeating shell pattern. Faux finish, my new mom called it.

My new room was in the same wing with the rest of the family, right next to William's bedroom and down the hall from Margaret's. It was all so permanent, so disappointing, with its peach carpet and white wicker furniture. The bedspreads were purple with big peach butterflies. They matched the headboards rising over the two twin beds in padded arcs.

Above the kitchen with the maid, I could pretend I was a mistreated heroine who would be saved any day by someone who truly loved me, like Sara in *A Little Princess*. It was my favorite book, a tale of a once-rich orphan who bore the humiliation and torture of living in the attic of her fancy school until her father, thought to be dead, came back from overseas to collect her. I read it over and over again, looking for clues as to how a dead father might come alive.

In my new room, I spent a lot of time hiding in my closet, where I tried to contact Mom by Ouija board. Sitting in the dark, with the little plastic triangle hovering beneath my fingers, I concentrated on opening myself up to ghosts. Mom always believed in them, and believed that I could channel spirits if I worked at it. It seemed only natural that she'd be there, on the other side, waiting for me. I thought maybe she could keep on being Mom, even though she was dead. Once, the board did spell out M-O-M, though I'm not positive I didn't do it on purpose. I kept a picture of her hidden in there, too, behind my shoes.

One afternoon, my new mom spotted it as she pawed through my closet, organizing. "I thought you didn't like that picture," she said. I had told her that I didn't like it in a cowardly moment, hoping to please her, to make her think that I didn't miss Mom, that I was happy where I was, that she, this new lady, was all I needed. I had thought maybe if I acted more grateful we could get along better.

"You can put it up, you know," she said.

"I know," I said. But seeing Mom's picture outside of the surreal darkness of the closet sent me into a state of confusion. Here I'd be calling another lady "mom," while my real mom smiled at me, testing my loyalties. I liked to keep it put away, so that I would only look at it in the dark of my closet, with no interruptions.

Things were changing all around me. I was going to go to a new school next fall, the same one my new siblings went to. Rippowam Cisqua wasn't new, not really. I had gone there when I was little, before West Patent, before Dad died. When I went to go visit Rippowam Cisqua with my new mom, it was as if I was loosened in time.

Mrs. Handlen, my junior pre-kindergarten teacher, stopped me in the hallway. "Look at you," she said, her body bent down so that her old, familiar face was level with mine. "Why, I remember you when you were four years old. Your daddy would pick you up every Friday to take you on a lunch date to Friendly's. Do you remember that?" She smiled. "I'll always remember you and your little white cowboy boots. Do you remember those?" I didn't and told her so. I couldn't remember anything anymore. My gloves were attached to the elastic wristband of my puffy blue coat by little metal teeth, because otherwise I'd forget them, too.

"Oh, your dad bought them for you on a trip to Dallas," Mrs. Handlen continued, straightening to her full height. "You were so proud of them. You were the cutest little girl I'd ever seen, and I've seen a lot." She laughed warmly. "You'd always hide your eyeglasses in your pocket and say that you'd lost them." She winked at me and smiled at Mrs. Chamberlain, who quickly smiled a smile that looked fake. Mrs. Handlen walked off, and we continued down the hallway and saw Waldo Jones, the headmistress. I remembered her because she looked exactly like the man on the Quaker Oats box.

"Well, hello there," she said, her voice kind. "We're so glad that you've come back for a visit, Diana." I felt shy and stuck my chin into my coat so that my smile was covered up to the nose by my zipped blue collar. She led us to a hallway lined with hooks for coats and backpacks, where my new mom left me. The girl named Kate waiting to show me around for the day was familiar to me, too; we had been in Mrs. Handlen's class together. She led me to her fourth grade homeroom. There, I sat, quietly looking at the blackboard, mystified. I had no idea what was going on even though I had already completed fourth grade. After class, I said so, and the teacher looked baffled. She took me to a third-grade classroom, where the chalk marks on the blackboard looked familiar. I was moving backwards at a pace quicker than I could comprehend.

Then, between classes, I passed a teacher with a bowl cut and a strong nose. She put her hands on my shoulders. "Diana Welch!" she said, smiling. "We know people in common!"

"Yeah?" I said, smiling, thinking she had another story about Dad or me when I was little.

"My daughter is dating Brad Hayes!" she said, triumphantly. The look on my face must have given away my confusion. "Brad Hayes?" she said, lightly. "Ring a bell?" I shook my head, and her smiling face changed. "Your brother lived with him," she said, her eyes searching my face for something I just didn't have to give her. I had never heard the name Brad Hayes before in my life.

LIZ

I ARRIVED IN London to an empty house. Janie and Robbie were in New York for Easter and asked if I would walk their two dogs and feed Damian's rabbits, which they kept in a hutch in the back garden, while they were gone.

Vera, the Italian housekeeper, let me in. Janie had filled the refrigerator with food and left a note that said, "Make yourself at home! And call Amanda, immediately." I knew Amanda would be at Karen's for Easter, so I called there first and got to speak to Dan for the first time since Christmas. He sounded great, as did Amanda and Karen. No one had seen or spoken to Diana. I decided to call the Chamberlains. She was my sister, after all, no matter what Nancy said. Ted answered the phone and sounded pleasantly surprised to hear my voice. Nancy got on next and peppered me with kind questions about my travels. Then I spoke to Diana, who sounded as enthusiastic and goofy as ever.

"Have you been getting my letters?" I asked. The phone went silent.

"I didn't know you sent me any," she said, quietly.

Then Nancy's voice was back on the line. "We have to run off to Easter mass!" she said, still chipper. "Keep us posted on your travels!" And with that, she hung up.

DAN

THAT SUMMER, I got in trouble for running up Karen's phone bill. I called some 900 numbers, and Karen said I ran up almost a thousand dollars in charges. I can't imagine that was true. I remember doing it only, like, five times, ten times tops, and most calls didn't last that long, if you know what I mean. But Karen made such a big deal out of it, she told everybody, even Liz and Amanda. It was uncomfortable, to say the least.

It wasn't like I was having an easy time finding a girlfriend—I went to an all-boys school, and New York City is a really lonely place. There are millions of people around you, but you can't walk up to just anyone and say, "Hey, can I be your friend?" So I got in trouble for making some phone calls. Big deal! Meanwhile, that same summer I also tried heroin and smoked crack.

I was spending a lot of time with Clarke, this druggie friend from Trinity Pawling. One weekend, he bought us a ton of coke and suggested that we go get prostitutes. He was paying, so I was like, Fuck it. Why not? That night, we met Wendy, a beautiful black girl who gave me a blow job on Ninety-third and West End Avenue, in a stairwell underneath an entrance to some apartment building. Her hair was a glistening Jheri curl, and I remember really wanting to put my hand on her hair, but every time I tried to touch her, she'd swat my hand away.

When we were through, Clarke and I still had tons of coke left, so we went back to Karen's and did more lines. It was, like, four in the morning, but we were so wired Clarke said we should both go get another blow job. Karen was away that weekend, so we decided to bring this well-weathered lady back to the apartment. She was a lot older than us, not beautiful like Wendy, but she was really nice. I was so wasted I couldn't get an erection; I couldn't even get the condom on. But, like I said, the lady was really nice.

DIANA

THAT SUMMER WAS my first at Camp Wyonegonic, an all-girls camp tucked in the shadow of Pleasant Mountain, near Bridgeport, Maine. There were soft, pine-needled paths and small wooden cabins where generations of girls had written their names on the walls. My new mom and I searched through these cabins until we found her name marked in bubble letters inside a door. Her mom went there, too, but we couldn't find her name etched anywhere in wood. The search was fun, like a treasure hunt. My new mom said Margaret would go here, too, eventually, and William would go to the brother camp Winona across Moose Pond. It felt good to be included in the family ritual, and even better to be the first.

In my cabin, my counselor, a wiry, athletic girl in her late twenties, smiled and told me I was the first girl there so I got first dibs on a bed. The beds were all the same, squeaky and covered in scratchy forest-green wool blankets, Wyonegonic's signature color. I dragged my black trunk over to a bed in the corner and changed into one of the uniforms that had been mailed to me a couple weeks before, an assortment of green and white shorts, shirts, and sweats. Then my counselor gave us a tour of the camp, past the bathrooms, called Greenies, and the Wiggie, a bigger cabin decorated with oars that was for junior-intermediate campers, and finally Cobb Lodge, the dining hall where we younger kids got to mingle with the teenagers who made up senior camp.

Then, out by the horses and cars, my new mom gave me a hug and got into her new Isuzu Trooper. Back at the cabin, I met my cabin mates. Hannah was skinny and tan with frosted hair. She tacked a picture of her bedroom in California on the rough wooden wall next to her bed. It was huge, with a recessed sitting room and fluffy white carpets that matched her fluffy white dog. Fay was blond and genteel and had an adult-sounding Texan drawl. There were other girls, identical blond twins named Honey and Allison, and a girl named Veronica who wore her hair in beads and braids. She peed in her bed a lot, and I would help her pull the thin striped mattress out behind the cabin where no one could see it drying.

I flourished at camp. I felt powerful, unchecked. I developed friendships with the counselors-in-training, girls close to Amanda's and Liz's age who smuggled me illicit stuff like candy and told me stories about their racy exploits with the male CITs from Camp Winona. I learned how to sail and how to properly right a tipped canoe. I got pretty good at tennis and won an award in archery. I learned camp songs that we sang every day at lunch, and every night I fell asleep to the sound of taps on the trumpet. When it rained, we all played jacks in the Wiggie, where we'd also perform the songs we made up on our overnight canoe trips down the Saco River. My name is still up there in the Wiggie today, painted on a plaque that hangs on the wall, because as captain of the Wampanoags, I led our team to victory against the Penobscots in the summer camp equivalent of Field Day.

When summer ended, I was chosen by the counselors to be one of the Candle Girls, which was a special honor. The last night of camp, I lined up with other Candle Girls out on the docks as the black waters of Moose Pond lapped at the floating wood beneath our feet. We all lit our candles and sang, as everybody sniffled and sobbed in the quiet dark.

The next morning, my new mom was waiting in the same spot where I had last seen her, seven weeks ago. After we said our hellos, she said to me, "You didn't miss us much, did you?" She smiled her frowning smile as she lifted up one end of my trunk by its handle.

"What do you mean?" I asked.

She raised her eyebrow and said, "Not one letter?" I realized that no, I had not missed her. I hadn't missed her looking at me like I was an idiot. I hadn't missed second-guessing myself. I hadn't missed getting put in my place. I hadn't missed William or Margaret, nor had I missed my new dad. I hadn't even missed Liz or Amanda or Dan. At camp, for the first time in too long a while, I had been myself. I had been happy.

LIZ

WHEN I RETURNED to Bedford that August to pack my things for Georgetown, I called the Chamberlains to see Diana before I left. The housekeeper said she was away at camp. That's good, I thought. I didn't ask where. Then Dan and Amanda and I went back up to Maine for a long weekend. Uncle Russ rented a log cabin for us on Moose Pond and we spent three days catching up. None of us knew it then, but that summer Diana was right across the pond, which was really a giant lake. As she sailed with her friends, we all went canoeing, and as she went to bed listening to taps on the trumpet, we heard more stories about Dad.

Russ said that Dad was the best running back North Quincy High had ever seen. The night before the state championships, Dad was at the movies with his girlfriend when a couple of thugs from the rival school crept up behind him and whacked him in the head with a crowbar. Dad couldn't play and North Quincy lost the big game, which the local papers blamed on the incident. "Your pop was a local hero," Russ said as Dan, Amanda, and I devoured yet another tidbit about this mythical man, our father.

Montgomery wound up driving me to Washington, D.C., and we spent the night with his friends Dick and Lisa Castle. Lisa had done her master's degree at Georgetown, and she and her husband were huge Hoya basketball fans. I liked Lisa a lot. She was this petite southern lady who wore her long blond hair curled off her face, like a country singer. She had big breasts, small ankles, and a mischievous smile. Dick was Montgomery's best friend and had a helmet of silver hair and a permanent, cheesy grin. He reminded me of the bald eagle from the Muppets. That night, at dinner, Dick told me that he and Lisa had written me a recommendation when they heard I was applying to Georgetown. I was touched. But then he said, "So please don't embarrass us." My stomach cramped.

My roommate was a skinny blond from Marblehead, Massachusetts.

Her name was Susanne. She was already unpacking when we arrived, and I could tell from her first smile that we'd be friends. Her brother Freddy was there, too, helping her. He unpacked an opened box of sanitary napkins from one of Susanne's trunks and started throwing them onto her bed, saying, "Extra pillows for you gals." He reminded me of Dan. I said good-bye and thanks to Montgomery and spent that first day exploring the campus and surrounding neighborhood with Susanne. That night, as we both lay in our twin beds in the dark, Susanne told me that I was the first person she had ever met who had lost one parent, let alone both.

I loved waking up in my dorm room, which Susanne and I had decorated with Indian print textiles, an enormous REM poster, and some plants. It was the most settled I had been since Mom died. I loved everything about being at the university, from my classes, to the fact that I had daily access to a hot shower, to the new friends I was making. The only thing I didn't like was the cafeteria food, so I called Amanda to see if the trust would give me the food-plan money so I could make my own meals. "Sure," she said without hesitation. I bought an electric wok, a small refrigerator, and a toaster oven and put the rest in a savings account for groceries. Soon I was making eggplant parmigiana, steamed sea bass with shiitake mushrooms, and spaghetti carbonara in my dorm room. It didn't take long for Susanne to go off the meal plan, too.

But as much as I loved school, I had this nagging feeling that I got in on a fluke, that I might fail out. And Dick's words, "Don't embarrass us," fueled that fear. I'd cheated my way through junior year at Fox Lane, reading Cliffs Notes and, on occasion, even using Mom's illness to get out of taking tests I was unprepared for. At Georgetown, I had no excuses. I had to apply myself. I signed up for extra help whenever it was offered, took fastidious notes, and read each assignment not once but twice. This was too good a deal for me to fuck up.

Amanda and I stayed in touch weekly now that I had a permanent address and a phone. She was growing tired of city life, and of partying, too. She was thinking about moving to Virginia. I hoped so. She'd be closer to me. I called Dan every so often, but he was harder to track down. Whenever I called his dorm pay phone at Trinity Pawling, he was nowhere to be found. Both Amanda and I were worried about him. I had hardly recognized him when I returned from Europe. He had grown his red hair long and shaggy and was wearing a beaded necklace. And he was bragging about how he planned to sell drugs at school that year. I knew if he got caught he'd be kicked out of Trinity Pawling once and for all. I decided to invite him down for a weekend in Washington, D.C., and finally got him on the phone one October evening. When I told him I'd pay for his train ticket, he said he'd come the next weekend.

His hair was even longer than I remembered it, and he was wearing a tie-dyed T-shirt. We went to a party the first night, and he flirted with all my girl friends and had my guy friends in stitches with his boarding-school stories. He crashed in my twin bed that night, his feet in my face and mine in his. The next morning, we went to Houston's, a restaurant on Wisconsin Avenue famous for its all-you-can-eat breakfast buffet. We piled our plates high with eggs, sausage, chocolate chip pancakes, and grits.

"Tell me everything," I said before digging in. "How are things? What have you been up to?"

Dan took a big bite of breakfast, and then he started to boast that he'd seen six Grateful Dead shows that summer, and how he had made tons of money selling pot to rich kids at TP. "I buy a dime bag in Harlem and sell it to these assholes for fifty bucks. And they pay it!" he said between bites. As I sat there, listening to this sixteen-year-old boy posing as Dan, I wondered what had happened to my brother. I was having visions of him in a juvenile delinquent home when he said, "Oh, and check this out: At the last Dead show, I dropped five and a half hits of acid."

He looked me right in the eye as he added, "In one sitting," as if it would impress me. I felt like he had just punched me in the face. Then he said, "I read if you do six hits, you're considered legally insane." I didn't break his gaze. As tears began to run down my face, Dan's cool composure crumbled.

"What's wrong?" he asked, leaning forward across the table.

"I already lost two parents," I said. "I can't deal with losing a brother, too."

Dan leaned back into his chair and looked at me, really looked at me, for the first time that weekend. He was quiet for a moment, as if he was trying to place his feelings. "I had no idea anyone cared."

I got out of my seat and threw my arms around my brother, in the middle of the breakfast rush at Houston's restaurant. "Your sisters love you more than anything in the world," I said into his ear, and he started to cry, too.

"Moron," I added.

And Dan let out a chuckle in the midst of his tears.

DAN

LIZ TOLD ME that morning at Houston's that I looked like the walking dead. I knew she was right. I felt that way, too. And when she said, "You're scaring the crap out of me. You're getting burnt," I knew what she was seeing. I was completely alien to her; I was alien to myself. Before Mom died, I was a happy, laugh-at-everything person. Even when Mom was sick, I was still a confident, popular kid. I could talk to anybody. Then something broke inside me. I lost that confidence. I wanted a drug that would change the way I felt about myself, and the way I was perceived. But, believe me, when you're feeling weird and introverted, acid doesn't help.

Right before junior year began, I booked a Combos Snacks commercial. It was a disaster. The night before, I went to buy acid with two friends. I was planning on selling it at a reggae concert that was coming up at school, so I bought one hundred hits in Central Park from three Puerto Rican guys. We were spending, like, three hundred bucks, so my friends and I each took a hit to make sure it was good before we paid the guys. It was good. Very good. We wound up cruising around the city until five in the morning, and when 6 a.m. rolled around, I realized I had ten minutes to run and catch a bus out to Coney Island for the shoot.

It was a nightmare. I showed up, still tripping, and was put in Chuck Taylor high-tops, suspenders, and a porkpie hat. I was supposed to throw the Combo up in the air, catch it in my mouth, and then eat it, which was torture. These were pizza-flavored-dehydrated-cheese-filled pretzels. They were disgusting! My line was supposed to be "They're great!" But all I could say was, "They're . . . they're so . . . dry!" Meanwhile, about twenty other actor kids were jumping and high-kicking all around me. It was like a fucking Lionel Richie video, all Technicolor and happy. And there I was, in the middle of them all, the guy on drugs with the gray face and the sunken eyes. The director finally gave up and kicked me off set.

Someone with a clipboard told me to wait on the bus, where I sat alone for hours, trying to remember how to spell "West End Avenue" so I could fill out paperwork and get paid.

So when Liz made me promise never to do acid again, it was easy to say okay. I meant it. I just got into coke and mushrooms instead.

DIANA

ONCE I GOT over the initial embarrassment of being held back, repeating fourth grade at Rippowam Cisqua was really fun. I made friends easily, and there was a big jungle gym that we crawled around on, swinging like monkeys. My new name at school was Diana Welch-Chamberlain, a compromise. My new mom had asked if I wanted to sign up at a new school as Diana Chamberlain, to deflect curious questions. I understood her point: I didn't feel like having to explain to everybody at school that my parents were dead; it was easier to just have the Chamberlains be my mom and dad and just be normal like everyone else. But dropping Welch altogether felt wrong. Like giving up. So Diana Welch-Chamberlain it was.

My best friend's real name was Abigail, but whenever she introduced herself, she said, "B with two quotes." She was on my bus route, and we always sat in the backseat, like cool girls. We liked to hang out in the library and read trashy young adult novels by Christopher Pike and Lois Duncan. From the backseat of the bus, we dared kids to eat chewing gum off the floor, and we told jokes about Frog Face, our mean and ugly bus driver. It was there that "B" quietly explained to me how her mom told her that clear stuff comes out of your vagina a couple weeks before you get your period and that's how you know you're going to get it. She didn't have it yet—none of the girls in my grade did—but everybody had read *Are You There, God? It's Me, Margaret* so we were all just waiting. None of us even had boobs yet.

My new mom wouldn't let me go over to "B's" house, ever, and didn't approve of our hanging out. She told me it was because "B" was a slut and her mother was a gossip. Her opinion didn't matter much to me; "B" and I hung out all the time at school, anyway. I was allowed to go to other people's houses and often went over to my friend Alicia's. She was the youngest of three, but her brothers were so much older that they were already out of the house and it felt like she was an only child. Her parents spoiled her, but not in a gross way. She rolled her eyes at them a lot, and once I watched in awe as she stamped her feet because her mother wouldn't buy her a Nintendo.

Alicia didn't know how good she had it. Her parents respected her opinion and told her they loved her. I liked to imagine what my life would have been like if Alicia's parents had taken me in. It'd be better, that's what. For one thing, Alicia's parents believed in privacy and never barged into Alicia's room without knocking. Meanwhile, it seemed that my new mom was always poking her head in my room, unannounced. Like the time I was cheating on my math homework by using a calculator that was hidden in my lap.

"Who do you think you are?" I stiffened. Her voice was like a string yanking at my spine. I turned from my desk, careful not to let my calculator show, and faced the figure in the doorway. "Margaret said that you *completely* ignored her at school today." She slapped her thigh to emphasize the word "completely."

"I don't know what you're talking about," I said, truly mystified. I didn't remember even seeing Margaret at school; she was in first grade. We had different recesses and everything.

"Don't give me that," she said. Her voice was almost a whine. "Don't give me any more of your lies, young lady."

"No, I'm serious, Mom," I said, pleading. "I don't remember ever seeing her at school today."

"She said she waved to you in the hallway, and that you just walked right by her with your little friends." Her eyes narrowed. "Do you think you're too good to say hello to my child?"

"I didn't see her, Mom. I swear; I did not ignore her on purpose."

It was as if she hadn't heard a word. She just nodded and smiled, as if she knew a dirty secret. Then she leaned forward and said, "You're just an ugly little girl," pausing between each word for emphasis.

I looked down at the carpet, and her voice carried on, no longer yanking my spine but curving it with its heaviness. It was the first time she had called me ugly. I was ugly; it was true. And she wasn't helping matters any, always dragging me to the hairdresser's for another ugly haircut. The one

I had now was the worst so far—a close-cropped, square helmet that made the conductor on the train to New York City mistake me for a boy. "The little fella rides for free," he had said, winking at me and clacking his hole-punch on the ticket.

The boys at school called me "Dino," as in Dino the Dinosaur, as in Fred Flintstone's prehistoric pet. And on the first day of school I got giddy as the cutest boy in the whole grade was walking toward me in the empty hallway. "Hey, ugly," he said, with a quick smile. It was just the two of us; there was no one else to laugh and make him feel cool for being mean. Further proof that my mom was right.

"You'll stay up here for the rest of the night," my new mom said, her tone final. "No one in this house wants to look at you right now." After she slammed my door, I took a deep breath and finished my math homework, with my calculator out on my desk in plain view.

AMANDA

I CAME HOME from work one night to find that my apartment had been broken into. Before I even walked through the door, I could tell something bad had happened. The dogs were agitated. Bentley was whining, and Ralph was pacing back and forth. As I made my way through the place, I saw that my VCR, TV, stereo, and camera were gone. The police came and were like, "Wow, they really tore up the place," because clothes and stuff were strewn everywhere. I didn't mention that it actually looked pretty much the same when I'd left that morning; I was never neat.

I think it was my upstairs neighbor's crack-addict brother. Whenever he hung around the stoop, he gave me the creeps. Anyway, I didn't want to live there after that, so I moved in with Karen. Then I got held up at gunpoint one night at work. I had gotten a second job working at Laser Video, a movie rental place in Greenwich Village, to help me save up for the possible move to Virginia. There were two guys, and the one with the gun was sweating and shaking. He looked terrified, which scared me even more. He kept yelling "Shut the fuck up! Shut the fuck up!" even though nobody was saying anything.

Shit like this was constant. My cars were always getting broken into. I had to replace windows on the Saab three times, and the Mercedes got to the point where the trunk wouldn't latch from being forced open so often. They even stole my mix tapes. Virginia was looking better and better.

I was hanging out with my friend Jim at Karen's when Dan called to say he had been kicked out of school because they found a bong or something in his room. I wanted to kill him. Jim and I drove upstate that afternoon to get him. By the time I arrived, I was no longer mad, just thinking a mile a minute as to how I could convince the school to take him back. But Dan was gone. I was literally walking around campus for three hours yelling "Dan? Dan!" while Jim played show tunes on the piano in the main hall. So

I called Karen's apartment to see if she had heard from him, and he picked up the phone. It turns out he got a ride with someone to New York. So I was pissed all over again.

DAN

EVERY YEAR, THERE was a well-known "surprise inspection" of our dorm rooms. One Thursday night, they announced one at dinner. That gave kids time to go back to their rooms and get rid of any evidence that would get them in trouble. At that point, I was making bongs and really elaborate hookahs out of chemistry equipment I stole from the lab. I stored them, along with some empty vodka bottles, in a padlocked plywood cabinet in my room. Getting rid of illicit material was difficult, because there was no way to get out of that building without running into a teacher. So I made an executive decision. I decided not to worry about it.

That night, the art teacher and assistant principal marched into my room and asked me to open up the cabinet. It was padlocked. Thinking I was clever, I said, "I lost the key." And they said, "That's fine." And, on cue, the science teacher entered my room with bolt cutters.

It took them forever to bust open the lock, and as they were doing that, I slowly backed out of my room and called Amanda on the pay phone in the hallway. She answered, and I said, "Amanda, any minute now, I am going to be kicked out of school." Just at that moment, Vice Principal Archibald Smith walked out. I said, "Mr. Smith, my sister wants to talk to you," and handed him the phone.

He took it and said, "We'll call you back," and then hung up. I couldn't believe it. I thought Amanda was going to handle this for sure.

AMANDA

I DID HANDLE it, somehow. With Karen's help, I got Dan back into Trinity Pawling that January. I think we played the orphan card. Then I packed all my furniture from my Brooklyn apartment into a U-Haul to move down to Virginia. I had accepted Abbie's offer of a job and a place to stay on her farm and was saying good-bye to New York. The night before I left, a bunch of friends came over to Karen's apartment for a farewell party. After we drank two cases of Karen's chardonnay, I invited everyone to drive down to Virginia with me. I thought it would be more fun that way.

So one crew drove the Saab. I don't remember how I got the Mercedes down there. I was in the U-Haul with the dogs when it started to blizzard. It was the worst winter storm in decades; I couldn't see the road in front of me. There were snowdrifts as tall as the U-Haul. It was horrible. And, unfortunately, so was my new apartment. It was in a barn, so dirty and crammed with boxes of Abbie's stuff that it was like living in a stall. The water was orange and smelled so bad I couldn't bathe in it, let alone drink it. But, I figured, at least I was only a two-hour drive from Liz.

LIZ

MY FRESHMAN YEAR at Georgetown was coming to an end, and I was in a panic. To start, my roommate Susanne and best friend Birgithe had given me a dwarf rabbit for my birthday. They were so proud of themselves, literally giggling and wide-eyed as they presented me with a box-shaped present the size of a microwave. It was wrapped in newspaper, and I could hear something scurry inside, little claws against metal. When I ripped open the package and saw this silvery gray bunny the size of a softball peering up at me, I froze. "Happy birthday!" my two friends shouted in unison.

"For the girl who has everything!" Susanne added, all boisterous and smiling.

"What's wrong with you?" I hurled the words at them. Tears were coming, fast, right behind. Their faces fell. "You don't give a fucking orphan a pet rabbit!" I was so angry, I practically spat the words at them. "I don't even know where I'm going to live this summer, and now I have to find a place for this fucking rabbit?"

My furious outburst startled Susanne and Birgithe as much as it did me. "It didn't occur to us . . ." Susanne said.

"Maybe we can return it," Birgithe offered, meekly.

Their gift was a kind gesture, and it took me years to figure out that their insensitivity was, in fact, my fault. I had set out to convince people at Georgetown that I was this outgoing, hardworking, fun-loving, up-for-anything, totally responsible nineteen-year-old girl and not some homeless and pitiful orphan. I worked hard on the facade. After being racked with worry I'd fail out my first semester, I made the dean's list with a 3.8 grade-point average. I did so well in my psychology class that my professor asked me to be his teaching assistant during my second semester, and then informed me I was the youngest TA he'd ever worked with. I was popular and had tons of great friends and a boyfriend named William who had gone to Exeter. And although he and my close friends knew that I had lost my parents, I never complained about it. In fact, I rarely talked about it. The last thing I wanted was people feeling sorry for me. I pretended that having no parents was no big deal—and tried to believe it myself. Getting a pet rabbit made me realize how lost I still was.

With summer fast approaching, I had to figure out not only what to do with this rabbit, whom I called Harold, but also what to do with myself. Susanne was going to Big Sur, where her parents had property; Birgithe was going back to Jakarta, where her parents lived; and William was going to spend his summer between Manhattan and his parents' summer home in Connecticut, seeing friends and having fun. So when my friend Kim mentioned she was going to summer school at Harvard, I asked if she wanted a roommate.

I signed up for a class in psychoanalytic theory, and Kim and I found an apartment through the university. When I called Amanda to tell her my plans, she offered me her Saab. "You'll need a car, Liz," she said. "Plus, the Benz is still kicking." She was being so kind and supportive. "The trust will totally pay for the schooling," she said without me even bringing it up. I felt bad asking her to bunny-sit.

"It will just be for the summer," I promised her.

"I take care of fifty horses and have two dogs," she said. "What's one more pet?"

But Harold wasn't just a pet. He was a nightmare. Within his first month, he had chewed through the telephone and stereo wire in our dorm room. He left BB-pellet-size poop everywhere, because Susanne thought keeping him in the cage was cruel, and his pee left smelly red-rimmed watermarks that looked like period stains. Thankfully he preferred Susanne's bed to mine. And God forbid you tried to touch him. If you could catch him, he'd fake an epileptic seizure, and if you held on, he'd puncture your hand with his two upper teeth. I didn't mention any of this to Amanda.

So I got the Saab, and Amanda got Harold.

AMANDA

LIZ CALLED ME that August in tears to say that the Saab was pouring smoke out from under the hood. She was headed back to Boston after a weekend away when the car began to overheat. "Did you check the oil?" I asked.

There was silence on her end of the line. "Is there any oil in the car, Liz?" I shouted. Then Liz started to bawl. I knew she didn't overheat my car on purpose, but, man, I was pissed. I gave her my car to borrow, not destroy. Meanwhile, Harold was the demon bunny from hell. He bit me every time I tried to change his water or feed him.

She finally wailed into the phone, "No one ever told me to check the oil!" She was crying hard now. It turned out she had a 102-degree fever; she was really sick. It broke my heart to think about her stranded on the side of I-95 in Bridgeport. So I told her to take my stereo and the license plates and just leave the car behind. She left everything behind, and I wound up getting tickets on those plates for years.

LIZ

TWO WEEKS AFTER the breakdown, I was still in Boston and back on my feet. Dan was heading into his senior year at Trinity Pawling, so he and Karen came up to look at colleges. Then we all headed up to Maine for a Welch family reunion that Aunt Gail, Dad's sister, had organized. Aunt Gail had moved from Oregon to Bailey's Island right outside of Portland where she ran a bed and breakfast called The Lady and the Loon. I was excited—more than forty people were coming, cousins I had never heard of, aunts and uncles I had not yet met, plus those I hadn't seen since Dad's funeral.

On her sun-drenched lawn, Aunt Gail had everyone gather around for a portrait. Dan, Amanda, and I stick out in that photo. One man, a distant cousin, wore a denim vest without a shirt, others had long beards and wore mirrored sunglasses, and many of the women had big, feathered hair. I had stopped using mousse and spray in high school and kept my hair long and straight, as did Amanda, who had driven up from Virginia to meet us there. We joked afterward how all our relatives said things like "wicked cool" and called horses "hosses." We didn't dress or sound like these people, our relatives, but if you looked closely, you saw that Dan and our cousin John could be twins, if only Dan wore carpenter pants and Red Wing work boots instead of baggy khaki shorts and tie-dyed T-shirts. And all seven of Aunt Barbara's kids had our sense of humor. "Black Irish" was how Aunt Gail described it. Our dad had it, too. It felt good to be surrounded by these people who had his big laugh and funny accent and freckled skin. Aunt Gail had long auburn hair, now silver-streaked with age but still thick and wavy. She wore it loose. "How's Diana," she asked me earlier that day. "Why isn't she here?"

The question stung like a slap because I didn't know the answer. As I looked into my aunt's face, it was like looking into a futuristic mirror. The

Diana I remembered had the same slanted brown eyes and slightly bulbous nose, that same mane of wild hair. Diana was the most Welch looking of all of Bob Welch's girls. Why wasn't she here? Here I was, surrounded by distant relatives, and I had no idea how my own sister was doing, or what she was doing, or where she was doing it. I was so caught up in being nineteen, in pretending that my life was just fine, that I hadn't thought much about her at all. Suddenly, I missed my little sister something fierce. Screw Nancy Chamberlain and her rules, I thought to myself. I was going to see Diana.

DAN

I CHERISHED THOSE weeks in Maine with my older sisters. I offered to take the smelly, weird-ass 1950s pullout couch in the den of the cabin Uncle Russ rented for us so that Liz and Amanda could each have their own room. I was so happy to be with my family, I would have slept on the floor.

Aunt Barbara, one of Dad and Russ's sisters, brought lobsters to the cabin for dinner one evening. It was idyllic until Russ and Barbara started bad-talking their sister, our Aunt Gail. I was shocked. I would never talk that way about any of my sisters. I worshipped them and the time we got to spend together. Those weekends were the basis of our relationships and the only time I was able to just be myself. Liz's self-confidence made me feel human, and Amanda always made me feel safe. To be honest, I never thought much about Diana. I just assumed she was happy and well. I don't think I could have handled imagining it any other way.

DIANA

CAMP WAS EVEN better the second time around. I was voted captain of the Wampanoags again, and I was in the intermediate camp so there were some teenagers to rub elbows with. I loved Maine and its cool breezes and the call of the loons from the lake. I loved the smell of the pine needles. This time, I brought my Goofy baseball hat that I got with the Chamberlains at Disneyland. It had two long ears hanging off the sides and two felt teeth hanging off the brim. Trying to roll with the ugly thing, I was hoping to get a new nickname going: Goofy. Thankfully, it didn't catch. Soon enough, I realized that there were no mean boys or moms to call me ugly, so I never had to put on my humor armor. Or my glasses. I could see fine without them. The only thing that happened was my eyes would cross when I got tired. And anyway, who was going to tell me I had to wear them? I soon forgot they ever existed.

Until my mom came to pick me up. "Where are your glasses?" she asked. I had no idea. I hadn't thought about them since the day I took them off.

"I lost them," I told her.

"You *lost* them?" she said, her voice high as she opened the car door.

"We were sailing," I said as I climbed into the passenger seat. "And we were going really fast. I was looking deep down into the water whizzing by, when the wind whipped my glasses off my face. I could only watch as they slipped down into the dark folds of the lake."

My mom looked at me suspiciously as she started the engine. "Why didn't you jump in and get them." It was more of a statement than a question.

"I couldn't abandon ship," I said, like, duh-uh. I smiled at her skepticism, before turning to look out the window.

The next day, back at home, Margaret and I were coming into the kitchen from an afternoon by the pool. Our mom was standing there with that look on her face that made me want to duck for cover. "So, I was unpacking your trunk," she said, her hands behind her back. "And guess what I found?"

My armpits began to sweat into my towel.

"Well?" she asked. "Any ideas? Come on, guess!" I looked at her and waited, silently. I wasn't going to say anything.

"Your glasses!" she said, smiling as if it was good news. She brought her hands around to the front of her body; in one hand were my glasses. She held them between us, waiting for me to say something.

"Wow," I said, quietly.

"Yeah, wow," she said sarcastically, still smiling. "Get up to your room, and stay there until we leave." I turned to walk through the door. "Hey," she called out. "Don't forget these!" I turned back to her and took the glasses from her without looking at her face.

That's when the Silent Treatment began. The Chamberlains had rented a house in Stonington, Connecticut, for a few weeks in August, so that afternoon we all piled into the Isuzu and drove there. I was quiet. I knew my lying drove my mom crazy, but I couldn't stop myself. I would lose something, and then I would lie about it. Every time I was about to get into trouble, I automatically scrambled for a story that might be the right one—the one that wouldn't make her flip out on me. She'd yell, ask what was wrong with me, call me ungrateful, send me to my room. But, still, I preferred the flipping-out to the Silent Treatment.

There was nothing I hated more than being ignored.

The whole time we were in Stonington, when I walked into a room, my mom would literally turn her head to avoid having to look at me. It was torturous. I avoided her as much as I could, riding my bicycle up and down the narrow streets of the town for hours, coming back to the house only to head straight up to my room to read *Catcher in the Rye.*

One afternoon, we went to the beach. The whole family was there, plus my mom's younger sister, Aunt Sandy, and her husband, Uncle Phil. We were all sitting on a blanket, and our mom was unpacking a picnic: sandwiches, fruit, potato chips, juice, and soda. She seemed to be in a good mood, laughing at Margaret and making monster noises at William. Then she took out some cookies and started to pass them around, and everyone was laughing and having fun. The sun was shining, and there was a nice cool breeze. William got some cookies, and Margaret. And, for the moment, I forgot that I was still being punished, so I asked, smiling, the sun on my face, "Can I have a cookie, Mom?"

She didn't turn her head an inch. She put the cookies back in her bag and leaned back in her beach chair, eyes closed. As everyone around me chewed cookies quietly, my face burned. I looked at the blanket, fighting back tears. There, in that perfect happy moment with her entire family around us, she made it clear: She'd prefer it if I wasn't around.

Embarrassed by the tears that were bubbling behind my eyes, I took a deep, ragged breath, stood up, and brushed the sand off my legs. I was going to go for a walk in the dunes, alone, so that I could cry. But before I could get away, Uncle Phil came running up behind me. "Hey," he said as he caught up. "Can we talk?"

"Sure," I said, kicking sand with my bare feet as I walked. Calmer now, I was glad that he had come. I had gone to visit him and Sandy once, at the all-boys boarding school where he taught. While I was there, I saw little of my new mom in Sandy. Though they looked a bit alike in the face, Sandy was smaller and way more relaxed. Mainly, she was nice to me. So was Phil, who was tall and blond and had a habit of looking down a lot.

As we walked out over the dune, Phil started to tell me a long story about some kid at his school that got in trouble for lying or cheating or something. I didn't see his point, and I told him so. "The point, Diana," he said, his glasses slipping down his nose a bit, "is that honesty is the best policy. He wouldn't have gotten in trouble if he had told the truth."

I looked at him then, and I wanted to tell him everything she had ever done, the way she made me feel every time she saw me getting too comfortable, too happy, too much myself. I wanted to tell him that I honestly didn't know how to stay out of trouble, that I was terrified of nearly every interaction I had with her, my mom, his wife's sister. "Okay" was all I said; I couldn't say anything more. I couldn't make him understand, because I didn't. I didn't know what it was about me that made her so angry. All I knew was that I couldn't help it.

LIZ

ON MY WAY back to Georgetown, I decided to stop in Bedford to visit Diana. I called Nancy to set it up, and to my surprise, she agreed. She invited me to come at 3 p.m. that Thursday afternoon and said I could stay for two hours.

When I arrived, Diana was waiting for me in the kitchen. Sharp-elbowed and gangly like a marionette, she had grown almost as tall as me. The Aunt Gail resemblance that I had seen so clearly in my mind's eye only days earlier was faint, just a shadow. This awkward eleven-year-old was nervous to see me; she barely spoke. She looked at me with suspicious eyes and then responded to my enthusiastic hug by stiffly patting my shoulders. Her hands were clammy against my skin.

Nancy suggested that Diana show me her new room, and I followed my little sister down the hallway and up the stairs. She didn't look back and wasn't saying much, and it seemed as if she was mad at me. I peppered her with questions—"How was your summer? Did you go to camp? Are you excited about school?"—but got only one-word answers: "Fine." "Yes." "Sure."

Diana sat on her bed, and I noticed she was wearing Bloochers, lace-up loafers from L.L.Bean. "I have a pair of those!" I said, and she suppressed the first smile. I scanned her room, decorated in peach and lavender hues. There were butterflies stitched onto her bedspread. Then I saw on her white wicker shelves the crystal polar bear I gave Margaret for Christmas. Beside it was the rag doll Mom bought for Diana right before she died. And then I saw the mix tape. It was vintage Amanda, marked up with black marker, a punk rock font. "Did Amanda send you that?" I asked.

Diana looked at me for the first time. "Yeah," she said and smiled again.

I picked it up and read the scrawled songs—Depeche Mode, the Psychedelic Furs, Madonna, the Go-Gos, David Johansen.

"She made me the same one!" I said.

"My favorite song is 'Borderline,'" Diana said. She was now walking toward me. "What's yours?"

That was a tough question. I liked them all. They represented the sound track of my teenage years. "Probably, 'We've Got to Get out of This Place,'" I said. Diana smiled again. She was starting to loosen up. I suggested taking a walk.

"I'll show you my favorite place," she said, and told Nancy we'd be back in an hour.

As I followed her down the driveway, Diana was still distant, walking faster than me, keeping five feet ahead. I had to jog to keep up. "What's the big hurry?" I asked, trying to catch up. Diana shot me a glance, and I could see the anger in her eyes. "Why don't you ever visit me?" she asked. "Or call me? Or anything?" The questions were like pointy javelins being hurled at me, sharp and fast. They explained her silence, her cold-shoulder treatment.

The problem was I did not have a good answer. "I did write for a while, Di," I said. "And I called, too. And I tried to visit. But Mrs. Chamberlain seemed to think it was better for you if we stayed away. She told us that you needed time to meld with your new family." As I said these words, I realized I was scrambling. They sounded ridiculous to me, a nineteen-year-old woman; I couldn't imagine what they sounded like to an eleven-year-old girl. "Diana, I know this is hard to believe, but if I wrote a letter for every time I thought about you, your room would be filled! There wouldn't be space for you or your things!"

And that made Diana soften. "Really?" she said.

"Really."

We started walking in stride, side by side. The farther we got from the Chamberlains' house, the more animated Diana became. When she mentioned she was taking golf lessons at the Bedford Golf and Tennis Club, I saw my chance. "Did you know Mom was club champion, like, three times?" I asked.

"Her name is engraved on one of the plaques in the clubhouse!" Diana exclaimed. She was bouncing instead of walking. I was even more excited. These were concrete things that linked her to me, to our family.

And each time we discovered another one, I saw the spark in her eye and the smile-induced dimples that were undeniable proof.

I told her about the family reunion, how I wished she could have been there with us. "Do you think Mrs. Chamberlain would have let you come?" I asked.

Instead of answering, she turned into a gravel driveway leading into one of Bedford's oldest cemeteries.

"Where are we going?" I asked.

"This is the place I was telling you about," she said.

I followed her, the sun casting intricate doily-lace patterns onto the grass beneath the centuries-old oaks. We sat on a stone bench that overlooked a few faceless graves. "Why here, Di?" I finally asked.

"It's the one place I can come and think," she said.

We sat there together listening to the multilayered chirps of birds and the occasional hollow and faraway *whoosh* of a car passing. I wondered if Diana thought of Mom and Dad as she sat her by herself, but before I could ask, she said, "How's Amanda?"

"She's fine!" I said. "She sends her love. She really misses you. Maybe we can see if Nancy will let her come next time?"

Diana's face tightened, and her head shook at the tail end of a full-body shudder. "She says Amanda's a drug addict." The words came rushing out as if she'd been holding them back this whole time. She was trembling as she said this, as if she were telling me a terrible secret.

"That's ridiculous!" I nearly shouted. My mind was racing faster than my heartbeat. Amanda stopped doing drugs entirely after she moved to Virginia. She was talking about applying to the University of Virginia to finish her undergraduate degree. She was talking about buying a house. I told Diana all of this, and I could see the muscles relax. She was breathing again.

"She also told me that Dan was a thief," Diana said.

I was boiling now. "This is insane!" My loud, angry words were incongruous with this peaceful place.

"Something about how he stole a movie from the video store?" Diana was trying to make sense of the story by giving me pieces of a puzzle she had been holding in her head for far too long. "Or a poster or something?"

"Diana, that was a misunderstanding," I said. "Dan is not a thief. He is still the goofiest, funniest, sweetest guy around. He'd throw himself in front of a Mack truck for you. We all would—me, Dan, and Amanda. We'd do anything for you, and I want you to know that."

I looked into Diana's eyes, shiny with relief, and hugged her close. "We love you more than anything in the world," I whispered into her ear. And that caused a tremor to set off in her long, skinny body. She let out a sigh that sounded as though it was too big for her esophagus, as though it hurt to cough up. I hugged her even harder. And as we sat on that stone bench in that cemetery, I said, "Don't believe a word Nancy says, okay?" She pulled away from me and smiled so hard her eyes disappeared. She let out another sigh, but this one sounded more like a laugh. This one sounded like it felt good.

DIANA

AMANDA NEVER SENT me a mix tape. At least, I don't remember getting it. Those songs Liz talks about don't resonate with my eleventh year, either. That summer, I was into the Grateful Dead and James Taylor. I do remember Liz coming to visit, though, and I remember feeling that she was just swinging by again, so I didn't let myself get too excited. I remember telling her what my mom was telling me about Amanda and Dan, and I remember her assurances that it wasn't true. But I wasn't sure whom to believe. What did it matter, anyway? I never saw those people. I was in a different world.

I was a Chamberlain now, officially. The trial period of being Diana Welch-Chamberlain came to an end when I started fifth grade as Diana Chamberlain, the eldest of three.

AMANDA

SOON, DENNIS AND I decided to buy a place together in Virginia. We had broken up when I moved down there, because he wasn't ready to leave New York, where he was born and raised. But when he came down to visit in July, he decided to stay. I was happy. I hadn't wanted to break up, but I also wasn't willing to structure my life around a guy. That's not my style.

We drove around the Virginia countryside checking out farms and old houses. Then we found it, a repossessed farmhouse on twenty acres. It was an old house with two bedrooms and a giant kitchen. It had a barn, a riding ring, and a garage. The grass was waist high, mice were living in the kitchen, and the house itself had been stripped of everything. There was no dishwasher, refrigerator, nothing; even the doorknobs were missing. Dennis thought it was disgusting, but I saw the potential: There was a living room where we would put the Christmas tree, a dining room big enough for Mom and Dad's dining-room table and hutch, and a huge kitchen, perfect for making big holiday meals. I borrowed sixty thousand dollars from the trust and bought it outright.

By then, I was fed up with Abbie. She pissed me off one too many times. I was mucking fifty stalls a day for her, and she'd criticize how I was doing it. One day, I put my pitchfork down and walked out. We had a contract on the house and it was vacant, so I squatted there for two months before the contract became finalized. Then Dennis and I tore out the nasty carpeting and redid the plumbing. We got a U-Haul and drove all of Mom and Dad's stuff down from Bedford—the grandfather clocks, Mom's portrait, the Etruscan trunk, the Oriental rugs, everything. This house was my dream, come true.

LIZ

AFTER SEEING DIANA, I kept the promise I made to myself and wrote to her more often. I pinned her photo above my desk at Georgetown. I made a point to try to talk to her on the phone, but I never got to actually speak with her. She was never home. Off doing whatever eleven-year-old girls do, I guessed. But I missed her now more than ever because, for the first time since Mom died, it felt as if the Welch kids had a home. It was called Morningside Farm, but it reminded me of the gray house of our childhood home. There were two large pastures out back and an old barn as well.

I borrowed my boyfriend's car to drive down several weekends that fall to help Amanda move in. We put the gold brocade couch in the living room, the trestle table in the dining room, and we hung Mom's portrait there as well. The hutch went in the corner, and I spent one whole weekend unpacking Mom's hunt-pattern china and arranging it so the horses looked as though they were galloping across the bone-white plates.

Dan and Karen came down for Thanksgiving, and we spent all day cooking. Amanda prepared the turkey; Karen made Mom's stuffing—lots of celery, raisins, and apples; I baked the pies. We set the table with Mom and Dad's wedding china—gold-rimmed white—and I polished the silver. Karen ironed a linen tablecloth and took lots of photos of the table laden with food before we dug in. We made a real feast, like the old days, and Karen brought a case of chardonnay.

Dan and Karen came down for Christmas, too. We spent an entire day decorating the squat cedar that we found in the woods behind the house. Amanda hung the four stockings Mom had made for us years ago—red and green patchwork booties with our names stitched in white rickrack letters: AMANDA, LIZ, DAN, and DIANA. As I unpacked all the ornaments, I discovered that the ceramic Mickey Mouse characters from our trip to

Disney World with Dad had survived. Sadly, the four fragile eggs Mom had hand blown before painting each with our portraits had not.

On Christmas morning, Amanda got up early and made Mom's pumpkin bread. Dan put on the Santa hat and handed out gifts, one at a time, from a pile so big it seemed to hold up the tree. We all stayed in our pajamas until well past noon.

That afternoon, Amanda and I made roast beef and Yorkshire pudding for dinner, and Karen made an apple pie for dessert. More photographs were taken, and in each Amanda and Dan and I are beaming. We were as happy as we'd ever been before things fell apart. But it still was not perfect; it was still not right. Diana should have been there too.

DIANA

THAT SPRING, WE all went up to Albany to see Mimi and Pop-Pop. They were my mom's parents, and they weren't rich like Gram, no maids or fancy cars. They still lived in the same house where their kids grew up. It seemed that my mom had good memories of growing up there; she was popular and roller-skated to school every morning. She even gave me roller skates for my first communion. I was particularly grateful for that gift because everybody else gave me religious stuff, like a white leather-bound Bible and a rosary made out of crystals.

Though I really tried, I couldn't imagine Nancy Chamberlain at my age, the eleven-year-old everybody called "Nance." I knew she was born somewhere in the middle of two sisters and a brother. They were all grown up now, living with their own families, but her brother lived just down the road. He smiled a lot and had a smiling wife and two little sons who smiled a lot, too. It seemed that everyone smiled in Albany.

Mimi was especially kind. When I accidentally farted in the bed one night and a little squirt came out, Mimi was the one I told. "It's not thyat byad," she said when she lifted the blankets to reveal the little brown stain. "It'll come right out in the wash." One afternoon, when it was just the two of us in the kitchen, I asked Mimi if I could have a donut. She opened the paper box that was on the counter and put two powdered-jelly ones on a plate. Winking at me, she cut another one in half, putting one half on my plate. I looked up at her, unsure if I could eat all of it, and she said to me, "There, now, go ahead," and nodded at the white mounds in front of me. "This is what grandmothers are for."

"Thanks," I said, picking up the powdery half circle. I licked the red jelly oozing out of the neat little hole. It was delicious. I finished it. As I reached for a whole one, I smiled, knowing that I had powdered sugar on my cheek. Mimi smiled back.

The front door slammed. It was my mom home from shopping with Margaret and William. As she came into the kitchen with two grocery bags in her hands, her eyes went from the plate in front of me, where one donut was left, to the powdered sugar on my face. I had the other donut in my hand. "You are so *selfish!*" she said to me loudly, before setting the grocery bags on the kitchen table. "Who do you think you are? Does it ever occur to you that there are two other children in this family who might want a donut?"

I looked at Mimi, who was at the sink, tidying up, to see if she would say anything. She didn't look up from the suds. "Go to your room," my mom yelled, pointing up the stairs behind her. "And stay there until you learn how to be a part of this family!" I put the uneaten donut down next to the other and shoved my chair back. Her arm was still pointing to the stairs. "Now," she said, firmly. I dragged myself away from the warm kitchen and the nice grandma and my plate of powdered jelly donuts, and I started up the stairs on my hands and knees, peeking through the banister at the women in the kitchen. "She's just so selfish," I heard my new mother saying as she started to unload the groceries. "To come upon a plate full of donuts and assume that they were all for her!"

Mimi, still scrubbing at things in the sink, said in a quiet voice, "She wasn't *told* that, Nancy." She shook her head and stopped washing, pausing for a moment to admonish her daughter. "She asked me for a donut and I gave her more than one. That's it."

My mom stopped for a second. "Oh!" she said, laughing and shaking her head as though getting rid of a fly. She seemed embarrassed by her mistake. Her mistake! I crept up the stairs, tingling. Mimi had just backed up my version of reality, one where I wasn't an ingrate, a lazy liar, too big for her britches. I was a normal kid. I didn't do anything wrong; it was my mom who was wrong, and somebody saw it! I was almost at the top of the stairs when I heard my mom's voice behind me.

"I am so sorry, Diana," she said. "I misunderstood." I turned to look at her, smiling sheepishly at the bottom of the stairs. "But when I came in to see you eating all those donuts . . ." Her voice trailed off and with it her smile. She looked worried, almost confused. And I, standing at the top of the stairs, felt victorious. I wanted to milk this moment for as long as I could. So I sat down and pouted, hoping that my sad face would make her walk up the stairs and hug me, rock me back and forth, and tell me she was sorry, so sorry. That she loved me. That she promised she would be nicer to me. That she realized that I was a great kid. That she was glad that I was a part of her family. That I wasn't a burden. Instead, she stared at my frowning face and downcast eyes for a moment before turning slowly to walk away.

DAN

LIZ SAID HER college essay got her into every school she applied to, so I told her I wanted to see it as an example. She sent it to me, and I changed a few words, so "Liz" became "Dan," and then I sent it to Curry College, because they have a special program for dyslexics, and to Rochester Institute of Technology, which had a really good photography department. I got into both..

That summer, I was seventeen years old. Liz and I lived together at Karen's apartment. I gave her my room and slept on the couch. I was happy to have her there. We worked together, too. She was a waitress and I was a busboy at this lame restaurant on the Upper East Side. Neither of us made much money, but it was fun to take the cross-town bus together back and forth. I bussed her tables and she was always really generous about sharing her tips with me. I was still booking commercials, and Karen got me a job working as a bike messenger for Don Giamatti, a head-shot photographer. That job made me want to become a photographer—Don was this cheesy balding guy with a ponytail, but he hooked up weekly with hot actresses. Basically, he got paid six hundred bucks to get laid. It seemed like the best job in the world.

Then I met Lisa while working at the restaurant. She was the most beautiful girl I'd ever seen. When I finally mustered up the courage to talk to her, I realized she was as sweet as she was beautiful. I fell in love that summer. I spent every minute I could with Lisa. I went to Staten Island, where she lived with her parents, almost daily. We'd play video games in the basement or go to the beach. And her parents always invited me to stay for dinner. It was the first time I had regular sit-down dinners in years.

That summer felt like a new start. It was a really exciting time. Lisa and I started to talk about making love, a new thing for both of us. Lisa was a virgin, and I had never been in love, never shared that experience with anybody. I was nervous, so I asked Liz about it one afternoon at Karen's. She told me to be gentle. She said it was a big deal. And I knew that.

When we finally did it, right before I left for college, it was worth the wait.

LIZ

THAT SUMMER WAS all about me making money. I chose to spend my
junior year abroad at Edinburgh University and couldn't wait to get back
to Europe. I chose Scotland because I was in the Honors English program
at Georgetown, which put me on a fast track for a master's degree. If I
continued taking honors classes my junior year, I could take graduate-level
classes my senior year, which would double as credits for both an undergraduate and a master's degree. Of the three foreign schools Georgetown
would accept honors credits from—Oxford, Trinity, and Edinburgh—I
chose the Scottish one because my middle name, Morgan, and Amanda's,
Gordon, come from our ancestors there.

Several weeks before I left, I drove Dan up to Rochester. He was nervous,
I could tell, talking extra fast as I helped him pack sheets and towels into his
trunk. I borrowed the Stewarts' Land Cruiser, and we set out early one
morning in late August. Dan had just gotten his driver's license so I let him
drive as I played DJ. I had brought a selection of Amanda's mix tapes to listen
to on the way up. I popped one in, and Musical Youth's "Pass the Dutchie"
blared out of the speakers. Dan started to sing along, and I thrust my hand
out the window and let it ride the warm late summer air. "This is a new start
for you, Dan," I said. "College lets you be whoever you want."

"It's sort of scary, too," he said. Then he stuck his head out the window
and screamed at the top of his lungs. When he pulled his head back in, he
had an ecstatic look on his face. "That felt great!" he said. "You do it."

"I don't want to," I said. The Pretenders had just come on, and I
wanted to sing along to "Stop Your Sobbing." But Dan was insistent.

"Liz, let it all out," he said. "It's okay to just scream at the top of your
fucking lungs and let it go."

I found this annoying. It was a gorgeous, sunny day. I was relaxed. Why
was Dan pushing me to do something I didn't want to do? I ignored him
and sang, "It is time for you to laugh instead of crying."

But Dan was persistent. "Do it, Elizabeth." He was getting testy, too. I could tell by the tone of his voice. "You don't have to pretend that everything's perfect all the time."

I looked out the window at the other cars on the road. We passed one station wagon filled with large Tupperware trunks. A middle-aged man was driving; his plump blond wife sat next to him in the passenger seat; and a boy, around Dan's age, sat in the back. They were all smiling, talking in an animated fashion. I wondered what they were saying. I wondered if they were on their way to RIT, too. I wondered what Dad and Mom would say to Dan as they drove him to his very first day of college.

I stuck my head out the window and let out a scream, but what came out was more like a high-pitched squeak. I pulled back in and looked at Dan.

"You can do better than that," he said, shaking his head.

So I tried again. And this time I searched deep in my gut and found a place I had kept under lock and key for years. Somehow I managed to pry open that casket of grief and longing and missing, and the fury that had been pent up all that time came whirling up my chest, filling my lungs and then my mouth, which opened wide to let out a primal howl. I shouted so loudly it hurt my ears and strained my throat. I shouted until there was no sound left and my lungs ached.

And when I pulled my head back into the car, Dan looked at me and nodded. "That's what I'm talking about," he said.

DIANA

WHEN CAMP WYONEGONIC ended that August, I got on a bus to take me to the airport. As I waved to my favorite counselor, a gentle, hulking woman with facial hair, she pointed to her chest, drew a heart in the air with her forefingers, and pointed at me. I turned away from the window and cried right there in the bus, in front of campers. It had been a long time since I had felt loved back.

I don't remember how I got home that year, but I know that I arrived alone. Our new nanny met me at the door—a girl from Illinois named Krista who had taken over for Rhonda during her maternity leave. "I've been asked to tell you that we've had a nice, quiet summer," she said in her flat midwestern accent, "and that we'd like it to stay that way." A white scrunchie held her frizzy blond hair in a ponytail on top of her head, and she was wearing white sweat socks. When I had first met her a couple months ago, she'd seemed friendly and smiling and funny. I had thought that we could be friends. But it was clear that, in my absence, she had chosen sides.

This was a new feeling—that there were sides. School started in a few weeks, and I planned on keeping a low profile for the remainder of the summer. Still, my mom was always on me about stuff. She thought I was lazy and always told me so. She wanted me to ride my bike more, so I would, in a circle on the driveway, around and around as she watched me from the kitchen window. I just wanted to go be alone in my room. Even though I had hated it at first, I spent all my time there, dancing in front of the mirror with my hairbrush microphone or reading a book on my bed.

I liked to read by the pool, too. It was beautiful, built in the style my mom called "au naturel." The water looked black, and the diving board was a big gray stone. I got busted for being lazy there, too.

"Those are not the thighs of an eleven-year-old girl," my mom had said to me that summer, shaking her head. I was startled. My whole life, people had complimented my long legs, calling me "string bean." I hadn't changed much, as far as I could tell. But the next thing I know, she's got me doing laps. I don't remember the negotiations. I reluctantly got up, tossed my hat and sunglasses on the grass behind me, and dove in, my blue and pink ruffled one-piece straining at the straps.

I remember clearly looking up from the water at the woman I was calling "mom." She was wearing a white hat and black sunglasses, and her lumpy thighs came tumbling out of her black swimsuit, filling up the chair. Still swimming, I said to her as casually as I could: "*You* have big thighs." I felt an urgent need to point out how ironic it was for her to make me swim laps because she thought I had fat thighs while her own fat thighs just lazed around in a lawn chair reading the paper.

She flipped down the corner of her *New York Times* and looked at me, hard. "It is one thing for a woman in her thirties to have larger thighs," she said, her voice high as though she were singing a song. "It's quite another for a little girl to . . ." I didn't catch the rest. I just dove down into the soft dark water in front of me, my gliding arms a dappled green.

DAN

I WAS REALLY nervous about going to college, but walking around campus that first day with Liz got things off to a good start. All the guys were, like, "Dude, who's that?" Just as it had at Fox Lane and Trinity Pawling, it worked in my favor at RIT to have a hot blond sister. And she was so nice, saying hello, smiling back at everybody. She stayed to help me unpack and set up my room. Sure, I missed Mom and Dad at times like these, but my sisters always tried to make up for the fact they were gone. They had my back.

The best thing about RIT was that it wasn't far from Skidmore, where Lisa went to school. That first semester, I made friends with a few guys who had cars and got them to drive me there every weekend. I was making friends easily, happy to have my confidence back, but I was also broke. I had to figure out a way to make money fast. I didn't want to sell drugs anymore, so I decided to make fake IDs.

I bought a huge piece of foam board and press-on letters from an art supply store and made a giant replica of a Tennessee driver's license. It was the easiest one to copy—all straight lines, no overlapping images. I charged people thirty-five dollars to get their Polaroid taken in front of this over-sized license, which I then laminated with two pieces of tape and created the shittiest fake ID ever. The powder from the Polaroid would unglue the laminate, and people would have to come back for another one, which meant repeat business.

That semester, I made IDs for everyone in my dorm, and word spread. Soon, I started getting invited to all these parties on campus, and before long I was asked to rush Theta Xi, this fraternity that had a reputation for being bullies and tough guys. They also had parties every night and free alcohol. I agreed to rush.

For the first week, I had to wear a jacket, tie, and pledge pin, which was

easy. I'd done that every day at TP. For Hell Week, we had to drink copi-
ous amounts of alcohol every night—the idea was to build up your toler-
ance so you wouldn't act like an idiot at parties. Usually, I was able to hold
my own, but one night, we had to line up naked and pound drinks. Everyone, including me, threw up; there was literally puke splashing onto our
bare feet. It was disgusting. Another night, we were all locked naked in a
closet, packed like sardines. It was supposed to be a bonding experience.
Also, there were ridiculous games where I had to hold a carrot in my ass
cheeks and drop it in a cup. It was bizarre.

Midsemester, I moved out of my dorm room and into the fraternity
house, where I had my own room and a waterbed. For a while, I visited
Lisa every weekend, or she visited me. But soon, I started fooling around
on her. When I told her, she was so cool about it. "It's okay," she said.
"Just always be honest with me."

So that winter was about getting laid. I was at every party, hooking up
with as many girls as I could. Second semester, I was voted rush chairman,
the youngest in the history of Theta Xi. I took the job seriously. I focused
on making our parties better. My new rule was: Get all the girls inside no
matter what. If they don't have money, loan it to them. Under my reign,
that spring was the largest rush class in twenty years.

Lisa and I broke up in April. The long-distance thing was too hard; I
was fooling around on her a lot. I knew she wasn't fooling around on me,
because that wasn't her style. I loved her to death, but there were too
many opportunities for me, and I felt that I needed to experiment.

LIZ

I TURNED TWENTY-ONE in Edinburgh and celebrated at Kilimanjaro, an African club, with a few friends. I was active in the Anti-Apartheid Club and was, on that night, dancing late into the night with two members of the African National Congress. Both had left South Africa fearing for their lives, and despite their heartbreaking stories—of family members and friends being tortured or killed—they seemed so happy that evening dancing and singing and stomping to the undulating beats of Johnny Clegg and Miriam Makeba.

That was a highlight of an otherwise grim month. I couldn't afford to go home for Christmas and wound up spending it with the Raynes in London. It was lovely of them to include me, but it only fueled the hollow feeling expanding inside me. Amanda sent me a card and inside was my favorite present: two photocopied notes Dad had sent Mom that Amanda had found while unpacking the dozens of boxes she schlepped to Virginia from Bedford.

The first note, dated December 28, 1966, read: "Chops, The principle underlying all art is of a purely religious nature. I love you, your art, your nature." It was signed "Pops," and I recognized the sharp-elbowed *P*s. I missed his handwriting, his smirk, his pipe tobacco and Colgate toothpaste scent. I missed that I would never really know the man who could write such a thing.

The second note was typed and signed. It read:

Ink smudges on white—what does it mean,
putting black thoughts on paper that's clean
with a man-made and broken writing machine.
And a God-made and muddled mind.

Days into days and weeks into weeks
And never a meaningful word do we speak
And my roof and my soul and my eyes how they leak.

And no white cane to show I am blind.

On Christmas Eve, I transcribed both notes into my journal and ended the entry, "And so I cried. Merry Christmas Mom and Dad. I miss you."

I did miss them. And I missed my siblings, too, my friends, my boyfriend. Edinburgh in February was bleak. I woke up in the pitch-black darkness and stumbled to class in it too. Even the sun seemed powerless, barely able to turn the sky a dull gray by noon before giving in to a bitter cold and bruised blackness by 4 p.m. My art history class ended at 5 p.m., and I dreaded the walk back to my flat across Warrender Park, where there was no respite from whipping winds and horizontal sleet that stung any exposed skin like microscopic darts. It didn't help that I was reading Sylvia Plath. The Poem "Daddy" particularly disturbed me. Edinburgh in February felt like a boot in the face.

I needed a change of scenery and decided to do a pilgrimage. I had always wanted to go to Ireland. The Welches come from Sligo, Aunt Gail had told me. William Butler Yeats, one of my favorite poets, was buried there as well. I decided to visit Yeats's grave and look for Dad in the faces of the folks who peopled that ancient seaside town.

I arrived in Dublin on February 10. As soon as I stepped foot on Irish soil, I felt better. I belonged in this land of squinty-eyed smiles. The bus ride to Sligo was as stunning and moody as I had anticipated: lush dark-green fields popped against the pale gray skies and outlined liquid-silver lakes. The weather grew fiercer the closer I got to the coast. I spent my first night curled up in an armchair reading Sylvia Plath's *Journals* in front of a white-hot fire. That night, as wind rattled the shutters and egg-size ice cubes pounded the exterior walls, I dreamt of Dad. He was not on a boat or driving the Mercedes. In this dream, he was sitting on the bus in front of me heading for Sligo. And he was dressed not in his pressed chinos and button-down shirt but in well-worn workman clothes. His face was dirty and unshaven, and the sparkle in his eyes was dulled by the shame of my having found him.

DAN

I HAD A recurring dream of Dad, too. In it, I saw myself sitting in a movie theater watching a film. The glow of the screen illuminated my face. Dad came in dressed in a tan suit and he had long white hair, but I knew it was him. He sat three rows behind me to my left. There was no one else in the theater. And even though I knew he was there, I never turned around.

I had the same dream twice—once when Mom was alive, and the second time, that winter, when I was a freshman in college. Those dreams made me miss him. And both times I thought, in my dream, how could he be alive and not helping us, his kids? Now, I think it was his way of checking in on us, making sure we were all right.

LIZ

IT WAS STILL raining the next day when I began my trek to visit Yeats's grave. It was five miles outside of town, but I decided to walk and was drenched by the time I arrived. I'd only been to my Dad's and Mom's graves once each, for his and her burial. Yet there in Ireland, I felt as if I was visiting someone familiar. As I sat in front of the Yeats tombstone, that drum-tight pressure of longing eased up a bit.

I hitchhiked back to town and learned, from the guy who gave me a lift, that after twenty-seven years in prison, Nelson Mandela had been freed that day. The news catapulted any sadness from my body. Instead of heading back to the hostel, I went straight to a pub, ordered a pint of Guinness, and spent a festive evening celebrating the news with locals who seemed just as happy.

I returned to Edinburgh and received a five-page letter from Diana. Over the years, I always wrote her postcards and letters from wherever I traveled and rarely received anything in response. This letter more than made up for that. In purple ink, she wrote:

> Liz—
> Hi Honey! I got your postcard, it's terrific! I hope you like these poems, I decided to send them to you so you could name them. Their for you. So keep 'em close babe!

The poems were on separate pieces of paper, written in the same purple pen. The letter continues:

> When you write back, (which of course you will as soon as you get this letter!) you can tell me the titles. It's for you to decide. Anyway, I got the idea from, well you know the one about wonder and all? Well I got that

from science class. We're studying chemistry. It's HONKEY! *(great word, eh? I made it up myself!). The one about nothing (don't make that the name cause—) I got that one from a song by Edie Brickell, "Nothing". Okay, you wanted gossip, so I'm going to give you some, first: "frog baby blown up by terrorists bombing lily pad cradle" pretty spectacular, huh? Well here's the real stuff. My friend Alicia is going out with the most gorgeous guy who thinks she is a righteous babe. Hah! And also who I adore! I'm pretty bummed because he's hooked on her. This letters taking me a couple of days to write because I have absolutely no time! I was invited to a party by Harry, who's real nice and great looking and I'm going if I don't have to babysit Margaret and William. I went out with Harry last year, but that romance lasted for about two months. Then I gave the word. Get ready. Dumped. Poor guy. Actually he did not mind. We both just wanted to be friends. God Liz, you've got to come visit me soon. I've got so much to tell you! I'm not the letter writing person. So I never really get to talk to you. I've changed a lot. Liz, maybe its because I'm growing up. That sounds sort of sad, doesn't it? You and I have got to have a much closer relationship because I love you so much Liz. You are the one who took care of me when Mom was sick and all. You are the only one I really know. I ❤ you Liz. Don't forget that. I know it sounds dumb but write to me about your problems. Your letters are always happy and I know that's not all. It makes it fake. I am 12 and growing all the time. So I really will understand anything you want to talk about. I'm still your little sister but hey, everybody grows up. Do you think I'm being corny, cause if you do I'll stop. Well I guess you must because I am being corny. And I've said all the important things that really matter. And oh, I'm babbling again!! AAAAAAHHHHH!!! Sorry, tension breaker! Had to be done. I have major writer's cramp! I got my hair shaved off. I hate it. How's that for a problem? Oh Lizzie baby, U & I have to write back and forth a lot more. I guess it is because I've grown up more and I want to be close to my big sister in Scotland who loves me. Well big sister in Scotland who loves me, your little sister in Bedford loves you 10 times more. So their. One more thing I forgot to tell you—I ❤ U & MISS U LOTS!!! Love and hugs, Diana.*

PS—Amanda sent me that Felix clock that used to be in our kitchen!

PPS—I ❤ U 10×+ 5! Translated: I love you ten times plus five!

Of the two poems she sent, my favorite went like this:

Sad,
Worried,
Scared,
Nowhere to go,
Nowhere to hide,
Why should I stare at the clear blue sky?

Relieved,
Happy,
Safe,
Not lonely at all,
Friends at my side,
Anywhere to hide,
Why me?
Why me?
I wish for a happy ending.

Why me?
Why me?
Why should I weep?
Why should I cry?
Why do I stare at the clear blue sky?

I pinned that poem on my bulletin board, next to a photo of Diana when she was a little girl, maybe four. In that photo, she is wearing purple corduroys and her pink glasses that magnify her crossed eyes. Her hair is a wild, tangled mane.

On the other side of the photo, I pinned the second poem:

In the stillness
Nothing comes.
Waking me
Shaking me
Telling me to follow.

I search through the hallways
Sleeping dreams awake
The stillness comes alive
Silent games partake
As nothing stands by.

In the morning,
The sun comes up
Something there at last.

DIANA

MY MOM TOLD me that I would be going to boarding school next year, for seventh grade. I'd miss "B" and my other friends at Rippowam, but I knew I had no say in the matter. It was boarding school. Whatever. I liked summer camp.

That fall, we went to visit St. Anne's–Belfield in Charlottesville, Virginia. The school was big and white, perched on a hill overlooking a parking lot filled with new BMWs and shiny pickup trucks. The admissions counselor was nice, and the interview seemed to go well. My mom talked about my potential and how she and my teachers thought I wasn't living up to it. Then we all shook hands. It all seemed promising.

"So, what did you think?" my mom asked casually as she backed the rental car out of its parking spot. I remember that I was in the backseat, looking out the window, but I don't remember what I said. We were off-campus when she spoke next. "Your sister lives in Virginia," she said and caught my eyes with hers in the rearview mirror. I looked at her briefly before quickly turning away. If this was some sort of test, I didn't know the right response. So I said nothing and stared out the window. Then she said something about visiting Amanda for spring break, and would I like that?

Amanda. My sister. In the five years since I had seen her, the only things I'd heard about her was that she was a drug addict who lived with this guy on a farm and that they had no electricity or hot water. I heard her house was a dive.

Visiting a drug addict in a dive sounded scary. And Amanda could be scary. I remembered the time she had yelled at me in front of all her friends at my favorite restaurant in Mount Kisco, the Pizza & Brew. Amanda was pouring soda out of a plastic pitcher and talking. I wanted some and kept telling her so, until she pointed at the table in front of me and yelled, "It's right there! Jesus!" And when I looked down, I saw that she had already poured me some. It was embarrassing.

I felt my mom's eyes on me as we headed back to the airport. I breathed fog on the window and made a trail of tiny baby footprints by pressing the pinky side of my fists against the glass, then making toes with my fingertips, starting with the big toe, my thumb. It was a trick I learned when I was a kid, from Amanda's friend Sue.

"I guess that would be good," I said quietly to the passing trees, avoiding the dark eyes in the mirror.

AMANDA

I PICKED UP the phone in my bedroom upstairs. It was Nancy. I couldn't remember the last time I had spoken to her. Our only contact was through the mail; the trust had been paying Diana's tuition at Rippowam this whole time. Nancy sent me the tuition bills, and I wrote checks. I don't think she'd ever called me. After the usual pleasantries, she said, "Diana would like to come down to visit you for spring break." The next thing I remember was Nancy giving me Diana's flight information. There was no "Oh, do you mind? Is this okay with you? Will you even be around?" It was completely out of the blue. I didn't know what had changed, and I didn't think to ask. I was just like, Diana's coming for a visit? Awesome!

Then I started to panic. Not because I was nervous about seeing Di, more that I had no idea what to do with a twelve-year-old for her vacation. Young girls should have fun on their spring breaks.

DIANA

AS AMANDA CLOSED the hatchback on her beat-up beige Volkswagen Rabbit, I noticed the remnants of a "Jesus Saves" rainbow sticker that somehow had melded to the rear window. "I tried really hard to get that off," she said, rolling her eyes. "I scraped and scraped."

Amanda told me that Dad's Mercedes had finally died earlier that year, and since Liz had killed her Saab, she had to buy this clunker. The car's interior was dusty red velvet, coated in a thin layer of animal hair. There was a mix tape in the tape player, songs I recognized from long ago. As I rode shotgun, Amanda asked if I remembered her quizzing me about songs on the radio. "You'd be in your car seat with your pigtails and glasses, and I'd say, 'Who's this?'" She laughed. "And you'd be like, 'Start Me Up' by the Rolling Stones!"

I didn't remember playing this game and told her so. I did, however, remember this woman sitting next to me, my sister. Back when I knew her, she wore eyeliner, spiky hair, and rubber bracelets like Madonna. Now her hair was long and straight. In place of leather pants and a giant paisley button-down knotted at the hip, she wore black leggings and a big white T-shirt. She used to be mean to me because I annoyed her. I didn't annoy her now. When she turned to me, her big greenish eyes were timid and searching at once, I saw Mom in their shape, and in the shape of her nose, too. She was beautiful. She was familiar. She wasn't scary at all.

And her farmhouse wasn't a dive, either. The way my mom talked about it, I was expecting swinging, bare lightbulbs and rats. Separated from the paved rural road by an eight-foot boxwood hedge, her house was big and white with black shutters. Amanda planned on painting the house gray with forest-green shutters. "Like the old house," she said as she led the way through the rusty chain-link gate, down the path of cracked slate. Inside, the place was big and drafty, filled with things I remembered: the grandfather clocks, the painting of Mom. Even the couches were the same fabric. The big brass bed I slept in that night was our parents' and so was the stained Oriental rug beneath it. For the first time in as long as I could remember, I felt at home.

Even the pets were familiar: Bentley was there and so was Ralph. Amanda loved animals and often took in strays. There was a cat named Maybe, a bunny called Harold, and a giant black Great Dane named Banana, whose ears pointed up and out, at right angles. The woman who had bred her had cut her ears and taped what was left to Popsicle sticks. Amanda called it barbaric and told me that the first thing she did when she got Banana home was to remove the splints.

AMANDA

DIANA SHOWED UP with this ridiculously short haircut and these big horn-rimmed glasses. It could not have been more unflattering. I mean, she was adorable, the same goofy kid, but she seemed a lot more self-conscious. She was polite the whole time, timid at first but more and more comfortable as the week wore on. At the same time, she was very Diana, open and free and interested in trying new things, up for an adventure. We spent a long weekend at my friend Jean's cabin in West Virginia, hiking and swimming in the river. Diana was surprisingly good with Jean's baby and seemed relaxed, like she was having a great time. It was nice.

Then, when we were at the airport waiting for her plane to board, she started acting all nervous and fidgeting in her seat. Finally she said, "Um, I was supposed to talk to you about coming back down and spending the summer, if it's okay with you?"

And I was like, "Of course it's okay!" But inside, I was fuming. I couldn't believe that bitch would make Diana ask me, but what really pissed me off was that Diana felt it might not have been okay. It killed me to think that she had thought there was even a remote possibility that I would say no.

DIANA

ONE AFTERNOON I came home from school to find the Chamberlains' door locked. This had never happened before; I didn't have a key. I knocked. Nothing. Figuring no one was home, I went around to the backyard and sat on the stone wall behind the swing set until the woman I called "mom" shouted from the kitchen window. "Hey!" Her tone was pleasant. "What are you doing out there?"

"Didn't you hear me?" I shouted back as I jumped down from my perch. "I knocked!"

It was too bright outside to see her face in the window. I could only hear her voice. "Oh, I must not have heard you!" she shouted in the same pleasant tone. "I was on the phone with your Aunt Barbara!"

With those words, things started to fall into place. My mom had locked the door to keep me out so that I wouldn't get to talk to Aunt Barbara. Why else would she have locked the door while she was home? Over spring break, Amanda had backed up Liz's version of reality, the one in which she and Liz had wanted, even tried, to come see me the whole time I had been here. Amanda said that this lady I was calling "mom" wouldn't let them come, that being separated wasn't up to them, that they all three had wanted me in their lives, always. Amanda said that she had called, even though I had never heard about it. And she assured me that she wasn't a drug addict, either, and that Dan wasn't a thief.

I still didn't understand why this lady would want to keep me from my family, but, suddenly, I understood that she did.

LIZ

I SPENT A disastrous spring break in Tunisia. I decided to go there because it sounded exotic, adventurous, more exciting than, say, Germany or Spain. But then, in the taxi to the hotel in Tunis, the driver asked me to marry him. Then another man followed me from the cab to the hotel, hissing, then grabbed my arm and asked if I was looking for "a boyfriend," and I wondered if I had made a mistake.

I headed to Djerba, thinking the mythical-turned-touristy island would be less lecherous, and wound up getting chased by a band of furious teenage boys, one of whom hurled a rock at me. I think it was because I was wearing a T-shirt and not a long-sleeved shirt as my guidebook recommended.

My trip to Khartoum left me in tears until I accepted an offer from a shy bellhop in his midtwenties who offered to be my guide. I quickly learned that as long as I was with a man, I was okay. No more hissing or tongues unfurled and wiggling between parted lips. This man showed me the walled city, had his sister escort me to a women's bathhouse, and invited me to his home, where his mother hennaed my hands and then led me to a candle-lit bedroom where a feast had been laid out on the floor. And then my guide appeared, strumming a guitar. He began to serenade me as his mother slowly backed out the door. He motioned to a pillow on the floor. I sat down, dumbfounded, my mind racing. He finished his song and then knelt beside me, so close I could see the space between his two front teeth and how his black mustache covered the top peaks of his upper lip. He picked up a fig and pressed it to my lips, and I panicked. "I can feed myself," I said, leaning away from this suddenly scary man. When I balked, he shook his head and said I must learn to be obedient if I were to be his wife. I felt trapped and bluffed my way through the couscous course before feigning a stomachache. "I need to go back to the hotel," I said. I checked out early the next morning.

I kept moving—across the desert, where I saw a Bedouin tribe, to the oasis town Nafta, then back to the coast. On my last day, I decided to go to the beach. I wanted to get some sun. I sat on the white sand and rolled up my pants and long sleeves and tilted my head back. I began to sweat. The searing heat tightened my skin. I was glad for it. I wanted to bring something else back from this trip besides horror stories and a hand-loomed rug. As the sun's rays cooled, I started walking back toward my hotel, sun-dazed and sleepy. Then, from the corner of my eye, I saw a man emerge from behind a bush. I felt his hands on me, tugging my shoulders backwards and down. I screamed. He pulled, tearing my shirt. I started to swing and scratch. My vocal cords strained to the point I thought they might snap. I fought with all my might and managed, I'm not sure how, to get away. Back at the hotel, I collapsed on the bed, spent. I was incapable of tears. My throat felt raw and shredded as if I had swallowed broken glass. I could not wait to get back to Scotland.

DAN

WHEN I TURNED eighteen that March, I stopped getting Social Security checks. Before the school year ended, Karen had told me that I would need to pay her eight hundred dollars a month if I was planning on staying with her for the summer. I couldn't believe it. It just reminded me that she wasn't really family; that's not what family would do. Of course, I now understand that Manhattan was expensive and she needed the money, but back then it was like getting kicked out all over again. Frankly, I preferred to be on my own. I ended up sharing a house in Rochester with a few friends that cost me only one hundred sixty dollars, and I got a job waiting tables.

That summer, I started really missing Lisa. Then, out of the blue, she called. She was living with her parents and wanted to see me. I was so excited; I was going to win her back! My buddy had a car, so I asked him to drive me down to Manhattan. We met Lisa at a place in South Street Seaport. She was as gorgeous as ever, but I could tell something was wrong. I could see it in her eyes; she was annoyed that I brought my friend. Immediately, I wished I hadn't.

When he finally left to go to the bathroom, Lisa said, "I have something serious to tell you."

I have no idea why, but I said, "It's not like you were raped."

She nodded. After hearing the details, I got so angry I kicked a hole in the wall of the restaurant. "Who was it?" I asked. I needed to know because I was going to kill him.

Lisa refused to tell me, and to this day she still won't. But I swear to God if she had, he'd be dead and I'd be in prison. And I'd be happy about it.

By then, Lisa and I had gotten up to go outside. I asked if her parents knew, and she said her mom did. Her mother had asked Lisa if we'd had sex and was actually relieved that Lisa had lost her virginity with me.

But then Lisa told me she thought it was God punishing us for having premarital sex. I had always felt I was bad luck for people, but this was too much. I made a decision, unconscious at that point, never to fall in love again. Bad things happen to people that I love. My childhood might have knocked me down, but Lisa being raped kicked me in the teeth.

When I went back to Rochester, I started having a recurring nightmare: A motorcycle gang was tattooing a deflated balloon of Mickey Mouse on my foot, but I couldn't move because they'd drugged me. Then they put Lisa on top of me and began raping her. All I could see was Lisa being raped and me being helpless. I couldn't do anything to protect her.

After that, I started going to bars every night and picked fights. If a guy walked up to me, I'd just wallop him. No chest bumping, nothing like that, just bam! I'd hit him. And it felt good.

LIZ

THE SCHOOL YEAR was coming to an end, and most of my friends were headed back to their homes, even my two South African friends. They talked excitedly about how things were changing now that Mandela was free. Their joy was palpable and contagious. I wanted to see this hopeful new land.

One of my Edinburgh professors mentioned that a former student was running an orphanage outside of Harare, and I figured Zimbabwe was close enough. I wrote a letter to the Matthew Rusike Children's Home offering my services in exchange for room and board and received one back that simply said, "Ms. Elizabeth Welch, you are most welcome. Signed, Mr. Mangobe."

Not until I landed in Zambia did I realize I had no idea who was meeting me, if anyone at all. Waiting for my connection from Lusaka to Harare, I got nervous: I was arriving at 10 p.m. What if no one was there? Where would I sleep? Mr. Mangobe's letter had only a P.O. box for an address. As I collected my bags from the sole carousel at Zimbabwe's international airport, my mind was racing. Throngs of people were waiting outside. My eyes scanned the bazaar-like bustle—teary reunions, hustling taxi drivers, bored airport employees—and then snagged on a large white banner, framed by ten dark faces: "The Matthew Rusike Children's Home Welcomes Ms. Elizabeth Welch." Within moments, a fleshy fortress of hugs and high fives, small hands and big smiles, surrounded me.

The orphanage was a series of low, sprawling concrete buildings in Epworth, a suburb of Harare. I was shown to my own room in the girls' dorm, where I fell asleep to the sound of crickets chirping in the quiet dark. The following morning, at breakfast, I met all one hundred twenty children as well as Lucy, another volunteer.

Mr. Mangobe asked Lucy and me to open the nursery, a small one-room structure that hadn't been used in over a decade. We swept, scrubbed, and aired out the place, preparing it for the dozen or so preschool-age or- phans, most of whom spoke only Shona, Zimbabwe's national language. Mr. Mangobe wanted us to teach them English. Before we started classes, though, he suggested we read their files.

"So you know why they are here." He spoke as if he was taking a breath between each word, soft Shona sounds clipped by a formal British accent.

Lucy and I spent that afternoon going through a stack of manila files. I learned that Portia, a quiet five-year-old with a lopsided smile, was a recent refugee from Mozambique. She survived a machete attack. Her mother did not. That explained the scar that began at her temple and ended at the curve of her lip. Nedson's mother abandoned him as a toddler at the brothel where she worked. Now four, Nedson was weaned on moonshine, which had stunted his speech but not his infectious laugh or the sparkle in his mis- chievous brown eyes. Titus was found wandering the countryside with his mentally deranged father, and Artwell was found herding goats, a nomad at age seven.

"These kids are amazing," I said to Lucy. She nodded, clenching her lips tight so as not to cry.

School began and our students were hungry for words, for games, for attention, for affection. Lucy and I learned Shona, too. "Mangwanani" meant good morning, "masakati" meant good afternoon, and hearing "mu- rungus" saying such words elicited hysterical laughter from the orphans and staff alike, as did our eating *sadza*—the thick corn porridge served for breakfast, lunch, and dinner—with our hands. I relished their laughs, their language, their customs. I felt comfortable in this totally foreign place. I felt more myself than I had in years.

Then, one day at lunch, one of the kids came running into the kitchen, breathless.

"Ms. Liz," he said, bent over, his hands on his knees. "There's an ur- gent phone call for you."

His words shocked me, and a dull buzz coursed down my limbs. Before I could answer, I started to run: out the kitchen, across the packed-dirt front lawn, and down the dusty road toward Mr. Mangobe's house and the nearest phone. Someone was hurt or sick or, worse, someone had died—Dan, Amanda, or Diana. My lungs burned as I sprinted. In the distance, I saw that Mr. Mangobe's front door was open and he was standing in the foyer holding the phone toward me in his outstretched hand. "It's your sister calling from America," he said as I raced up the stairs.

I grabbed the receiver, expecting sobs or shouts or wails. Instead, I heard a hearty chuckle. It was Amanda.

"Hey, Liz," she said. "I have a surprise for you."

Then, above my panting breath and bass-drum heartbeat, I heard an unmistakable voice.

"Hey, sis!"

It was Diana.

DIANA

VISITING AMANDA THAT summer was even better than camp. She and Dennis were both so welcoming; they made me feel right at home. They referred to the bedroom I had slept in during spring break as my bedroom, and they encouraged me to decorate it however I wanted. Amanda and I painted the kitchen floor red and splattered it with yellow and gray paint while she explained to me who Jackson Pollock was. I helped her sponge the cream-colored living-room walls with varying shades of red and gray. In between projects, Amanda and I spent hours sitting on the floor of her living room, going through old family photos, as she patiently answered my unending series of questions. She identified people I didn't recognize, told me some things I remembered in a shadowy way, and described some things that had happened before I was born.

Amanda was a lot like Dad, I soon found out. One of her favorite things to do was to sneak up on me while I was reading and grab my kneecap and squeeze it hard, causing me to flail and squeal and beg her to quit over the loud boom of her laugh. It was a little trick she learned from Dad, she explained, who loved to do it to Mom while she drove.

Both Amanda and Dennis worked full-time, so I spent many afternoons over at Fran's house, their closest neighbor, who lived just a quarter mile down the road. Fran and I would sit in her double-wide trailer with the air conditioning blasting, watching daytime TV and crocheting skeins of acrylic yarn the color of Pepto-Bismol into intricate gowns and bonnets for little plastic dolls that she'd wrap in Saran wrap to keep them from collecting dust. Other times, Amanda would drop me off at her friend Janice's house, and I'd play with her kids Hannah and Beth, who were a little younger than I. They both loved watching *Full House,* listening to Paula Abdul, and playing Donkey Kong, and though they were nice to me, I was always glad when Amanda came to pick me up. I think that was the biggest difference I noticed about that summer: For the first time I could really remember, I was eager to go home.

AMANDA

DIANA HAD ARRIVED at our house that June with a trunk full of clothes. Then Nancy called. Once again, she had a surprise for me: "Okay, here's what's going to happen," she said. "We signed Diana up for school at St. Anne's in Charlottesville; she's going to board there during the week and she'll live with you on the weekends. I'll send her stuff along. Bye!" It was the same deal as spring break: no checking in to see if it was okay, no explanations. I had no idea that Diana and Nancy had come to Virginia to visit St. Anne's–Belfield earlier that spring. When Diana showed up that summer, I had no idea that it was for good.

A couple days later, the rest of Diana's stuff came in the mail. And I mean, all of it. It was crazy: They didn't just send the rest of her clothes; they sent everything. What really freaked me out is that they sent every photograph ever taken of Diana while she lived with them. It was as if they were erasing her from their hard drive.

DIANA

WHEN THE CHAMBERLAINS sent all my stuff, it really solidified what I had felt for so long—that it really was better for them when I wasn't there. I felt hurt, because I had tried so hard to be loved by them and I had failed. It has taken me nearly twenty years to realize how hard they had tried, too, to be loved by me.

So often, people ask me why Nancy Chamberlain did the things she did. I have no way of explaining her actions. I can venture to guess, though it seems unfair. As a teenager, I felt about her as most teenagers do about grown-ups: She was a crazy, mean bitch who tried to ruin my life. But now, as I approach the age Nancy was when she took me in, I can see that there must be more to it than that. She was a middle-class girl from Albany who married into the Bedford blue-blood country-club scene, a young mother who acted on her instincts and took in a little girl who needed a home. I can think of her as a mama bear, fiercely protecting her cubs, trying desperately to maintain a sense of normalcy in her household. It just so happens that her idea of normal doesn't match mine.

I got my period one afternoon that first summer, while waiting for Amanda to get off work. When I told her, in the car, on the way home, she asked me if I knew what getting my period meant. I told her I did. She asked me if I had cramps, I told her I didn't. Then she stopped off at the drugstore and bought me a big squishy pack of menstrual pads that read "Made for Teens" in pink type on the purple packaging. Even then, at twelve going on thirteen, I thought it was adorable that my twenty-four-year-old sister bought me special pads for teens. I could see how hard she was trying to navigate these crazy waters she found herself in. More than anything, I couldn't believe my luck that I was with her, of all people, when that happened. We're similar birds, my sister and I. She doesn't make a big deal out of stuff; things are what they are. It's hard to explain. Everything just felt right.

LIZ

MAMA SENZE DROVE me to the airport the morning of August 10. At breakfast, the children all sang a song for me, and then a dozen or so accompanied me to the airport and waited on the observation deck, bouncing and waving, until the plane made its way down the cracked runway. I sank back in my seat and waited for the tears. I thought saying good-bye would be harder than it was. All I felt was a tingly sense of excitement.

Amanda had called me that day with lots of thrilling news: Diana was moving in with her. We were all going to be together on Fire Island that August for Amanda's twenty-fifth birthday. Karen had rented a house in Davis Park, and for the first time in nearly six years, all the Welch kids were going to be together. Auntie Eve and Uncle Harry were coming, and Amanda and Diana were going to pick me up at the airport. It was the longest airplane ride of my life.

Diana, with her shock of red hair, was easy to spot in the bustling crowd at JFK. It also helped that she was a full head taller than Amanda. I squeezed both sisters so hard I thought we'd all bruise. Then we all started to laugh. We laughed and laughed. It felt good to be home.

DIANA

THERE WAS NO crying when the Welches finally got together again.
Well, Auntie Eve cried a little, but nobody else did. It was as though we
had no time for tears. Or maybe the happiness of all being together again
completely pushed any sadness out of the way. For a whole week, we ate
delicious meals together on the wide wooden deck of a Fire Island beach
house that Karen had rented. I was allowed to drink wine with everybody,
and they all laughed at my jokes. Amanda, Liz, and Dan were all so comfortable around each other; it was contagious. I just slipped right in. I
don't remember any awkward silences. I remember laughter, mainly.

I was nervous at first, though. Not sure what to expect. Liz was just
as I remembered her, smiling at everybody, so easy to talk to, so pretty,
and so loving. Mainly, I was scared to see Dan. We hadn't seen each other
in so long, and when we lived together, we fought. Like brother and sister. One time, he bit me so hard for petting his dog Ralph without his
permission that he left brace marks on my forearm. But this Dan, who
was taller and thicker than I remembered, wasn't mean to me at all. When
he saw me, he hugged me so hard my feet left the ground. And he cracked
everybody up by greeting Auntie Eve with "Hey, sexy." She pursed her
lips and rolled her eyes, her signature move. Everything about her was exactly the same as I remembered; when you're in your seventies, six years
doesn't change much. And Uncle Harry smelled the same way he did
when I was little, a tobacco-scented mountain I remembered climbing up
to fall asleep on his chest. I remembered Karen as the mean lady I avoided
when I was little. I never would have thought that she of all people would
be the tenuous link that had held my siblings together all those years. But
here she was, offering us all a meeting place. She always had, Amanda explained to me on the car ride up from Virginia. Her New York apartment
was where they had spent all their Christmases while I was gone, where

they all stayed when they had nowhere else to go. And now that Amanda had her place in Virginia Karen came down there for all the holidays, along with Dan and Liz. It seemed to me that Karen needed the Welches as much as they needed her. More, even.

DAN

WHILE WE WERE on the ferry heading back from Fire Island to the mainland, I told Liz what had happened to Lisa. I had to tell somebody. Up until that weekend with my family, I was drinking nonstop. I immersed myself in liquor. I kept going to bars and picking fights. I was just so angry. I felt like such a bastard: If I hadn't cheated on Lisa, she wouldn't have broken up with me, she wouldn't have gone on that date, she wouldn't have gotten raped. That's really what I believed, and what a part of me still believes. Liz told me over and over again that Lisa's rape wasn't my fault. It's just that I wanted so badly to protect Lisa. Like I wanted to protect my sisters.

But that weekend, I saw that my sisters are tough. Our strength is in our laughter. We are all fighters. And Diana was like a beam of light, like sunshine. Her coming home marked the end of the darkest period in my life. That week I realized that I am not alone in the world. I realized that my sisters will always love me, no matter what. And that I will always love them right back.

DIANA

THOUGH I STILL called them Mom and Dad, the Chamberlains ended our relationship the same way they had tried to end my relationship with my family: by cutting me off, completely. For a while, after I moved in with Amanda, I wrote them letters and asked to visit, but my requests went unanswered. That fall, Liz brought me back to Bedford for my friend Alicia's bat mitzvah. We ended up staying with the Stewarts, because the Chamberlains hadn't responded to my requests to stay at their house. So I was surprised to see them at the synagogue. Still, I went over to say hello. Mr. Chamberlain stood silently smiling as Mrs. Chamberlain gathered her children to her legs and said, pleasantly, "Hello, Diana. How are you?" It was the first time I'd seen them since I had moved out, yet nobody made a move to embrace me. It was very formal and strange. I was stunned.

LIZ

DIANA WAS SO excited about seeing all her old friends at the bat mitz-vah. I helped her get ready at the Stewarts'—Daisy and Montgomery always made me, and my siblings, feel welcome whenever I went back to Bedford. Diana borrowed a white scoop-neck dress of mine that was big on her; you could see her bra straps. Her breasts were small bumps, just starting to grow, but she insisted she needed something to cover them. I suggested Band-Aids, as a joke. She thought I was serious and actually put Band-Aids on her little nipples. You could see their outline through the dress. But she felt grown-up—I could see that. I put a little blush on her cheeks, and she used my lip-gloss. She was giddy when I dropped her at the synagogue.

I went to get her a few hours later and was giddy myself waiting to hear her stories about seeing her best friend "B" and her ex-boyfriend Harry. But when she climbed into the car, I could tell something was wrong. She looked spooked.

"How was it?" I asked.

She looked at me, then started to tremble.

"What happened, Di?" I asked.

"The Chamberlains were there," she said, bursting into tears.

Between deep, jagged breaths, Diana told me that she ran up to say hello to Margaret, who got red in the face, nervous. And that when Diana asked Margaret what was wrong, Margaret said, "My mother said I'm not supposed to talk to you," and ran off.

I knew that Diana had been fighting back these tears all night, that this tough little thirteen-year-old wasn't going to break down in the middle of the party, in front of all her friends and those people she was still calling mom, dad, and brother and sister. I pulled her close to me and there, in my arms with her head buried in my shoulder, she began to cry. And so did I. I could not understand how Mrs. Chamberlain could be so cruel.

DIANA

ONCE I WAS back in Virginia, I got angry. I felt as though I had lost another mother, another father. I wrote them letters telling them so. I heard
nothing back. One afternoon while waiting for Amanda to get off work,
I decided to give them a call.

Nancy answered. In a shaking voice, I began to tell her how hurt I was.
I asked her why she no longer wanted me in her life. She cut me off. "We
will not be treated like a bus stop, Diana," she said, her voice quick and
angry. "I will not have you flitting in and out of our lives without a care
in the world." Then she hung up. The conversation was over, and that
was the last time I ever spoke to the woman I had called "mom."

When I looked up, it was to see Amanda standing there, waiting. "I
didn't mean to be eavesdropping, Di," she said, her eyes soft and appre-
hensive, "but I have to tell you something." Her lips quivered and grew
tight. "You are not treating them like a bus stop." As simultaneous tears
began to burn our eyes, Amanda hugged me. In the back of that retail
store, I cried for a long time into my sister's soft shoulder.

AMANDA

I DROPPED DIANA off as a boarder at St. Anne's-Belfield, because that was what Nancy arranged. At that point, I just did whatever Nancy said. Once Diana was settled in her dorm room, the admissions woman wanted to talk in private, so Diana went off to check out the tennis courts. The woman started asking me questions, about guardianship, about how things were going to work. I didn't know any of the answers. And right there, in the office, I started to cry because I had no idea what was going on. I hadn't seen Diana in all these years, and I was like, ask Nancy, because I don't know anything about any of this! I was so lost; I had no control over anything that was going on. It killed me to think that this must have been how Diana had felt for the last six years, just wondering what the fuck was going on.

The transition from living with the Chamberlains to living with Dennis and me must have been weird for Diana. We had no money. I mean, I was making six dollars an hour working retail, and Dennis was just starting out as a stockbroker, making cold calls to people. Without Diana's monthly Social Security checks, it would have been hard for us to cover her expenses. Meanwhile, she was going to this fancy private school, and my yearly salary wouldn't even cover the tuition. The trust was still in good shape; Mom had been so smart in setting that up. Still, when I dropped Diana off at school every Monday morning, and picked her up every Friday night, it was in my old International pickup truck with its "Farm Use" plates. We'd be in this long line of BMWs and SUVs creeping up the hill, and poor Di would shrink in her seat. But, I figured, hell—it was good for her. Builds character.

Eventually, she told me that she hated boarding and asked if she could live with me and Dennis full-time. Slowly, we took control of our situation, of being together. I began the guardianship transfer, but because

Diana was still considered a "ward of the state," I had to be approved by the state of Virginia. It almost didn't happen.

The state appointed for Diana a guardian *ad litem*, who advocated for Diana to move in with us but suggested that Dennis not come with me to the actual hearing. He was concerned that the conservative Virginian judge might have an issue with Dennis and me not being married. So it was just Diana and I that day in the judge's chambers, but when the judge asked who else lived in the house, I couldn't lie to him. I told him that I lived with my boyfriend. He was quiet for a while and then said, "Well, I don't like that." I think he actually might have used the words "living in sin." I was like, Jesus Christ, what are you going to do, send her to another fucked-up foster home just because I'm not married? But I didn't say anything. I didn't want to piss him off. Diana and I just looked at each other, like, oh shit. Eventually, he acquiesced—thank God. On the way home, Diana and I started laughing uncontrollably in the car, probably from relief. We didn't give a fuck whether that old judge liked it or not. We were family.

For the five years that Diana lived with me, I never asked her about what happened while she lived with the Chamberlains. I figured if there was anything she wanted to tell me, she would. So I didn't hear any of the stories on these pages until Diana wrote them all these years later. And it was hard to hear. I think the best thing Nancy ever did for Diana was to send her to live with me. I don't know how to say this in a nice neat way, but maybe Nancy finally realized that cutting us off from Diana was wrong.

I think the Chamberlains did what they thought was best. And I think that Diana would never have bent to Nancy's will, no matter what Nancy did or said. Diana has always had a fun-loving, carefree spirit. It's not surprising that she didn't fit into the Chamberlain model of the perfect family. She's way too stubborn; she does what she wants when she wants. Believe me, it can be frustrating, but I understand it. Diana is a Welch.

DIANA

MY FAVORITE THING about being back with my family was hearing the stories. I got the most during holiday meals, where we always gathered around Mom and Dad's table, eating good food, drinking wine, and laughing.

"Tell that story again," I'd beg them. "The one where Amanda convinced Liz to eat soap by telling her it was cheese." And they would, through laughter that often rocked their bodies to the point of tears.

Hearing these tales, seeing my siblings' eyes lit up with their memories, I would dissolve, slamming down my fork, leaning forward, and laughing with my family. The time that the mean goose at Leonard Park chased Dan and ripped off his diapers. The time Mom called Amanda upstairs to help her investigate the ghost beneath her bed. It was actually Dan, making the mattress rise up and down with his back. Knowing this, Amanda took a running jump and landed spread-eagle on the bed.

"Then I heard the saddest little whimper," Amanda would say through laughter, somewhat amazed by the depths of her childhood cruelty. "And Mom totally freaked out, screaming, 'You could have killed him!'" Somehow, even Dan found the story hilarious.

They told me stories of Mom and fallen soufflés, failed piecrusts, and blueberry pancakes on Sunday mornings. They told stories of me, a chubby cross-eyed kid who was always on someone's hip or lap. Mom was forty-two years old when I was born, an unplanned pregnancy. "You were the love child," Liz would say every time I joked that I was a mistake. "Mom called you the best surprise."

Liz's favorite story to tell was a bedtime story that Dad told each of us about the one-legged pheasant that patrolled the grounds of the gray house while we slept. "Dad would pretend his pointer finger was the pheasant, and he would poke up our legs and into our bellies so that our last waking memory was a fit of giggles," Liz explained, poking her finger on the table for effect.

"Tell me that story again," I'd ask, hungry for more.

And they would, every time.

acknowledgments

The authors would like to extend deep gratitude to our agent, Brettne Bloom, and our editor, Julia Pastore. Brettne's enthusiasm and diligence about this book has not waned since the start. We simply cannot thank her enough, or our brilliant and gifted editor, Julia, who believed in this book from its first one hundred pages. She trusted us completely and we trusted her. We are grateful to everyone at both Kneerim Williams and Harmony Books for making this experience such a great one.

This memoir began in Hettie Jones's workshop—Liz wants to personally thank Hettie for her initial support and guidance—and it took shape in Lynda Barry's Writing the Unthinkable workshop, at which both Diana and Liz discovered the right way to tell this story. Thank you, Lynda, for inspiring us.

We were lucky to have such fine minds read (and reread) all or portions of this book on its long journey out into the world, namely—Rebecca Bengal, Susanne Sanchez, and Karen Braziller, whose Little Red House Workshop lovingly shepherded this book to its final form. Clyde "Skip" Wachsberger, Charles Dean, LB Thompson, and Paula Mauro, we thank you for being such thoughtful and generous readers.

A huge thank-you to Cathy and Joe Zicherman, Janey Rayne, Jim and Kathy Walters, Bernie Sykes, and Mary Farley, who offered us beautiful places to write in Bedford, New York; in Greppo Corgno, Italy; in Big Sur, California; in the Outer Banks, North Carolina; and in Marfa, Texas.

Liz would like to thank Elizabeth Peyton, Jonathan Horowitz, and

Rob Pruitt for cheering her along every step of the way; Nahama Broner for her guidance; Liz Subin and Birgithe Lund Henriksen for their life-long friendships; Cathy Zicherman for being there always; Kate Lewis for her enthusiasm and sage advice; and Emily Young, Genevieve Field, Christine Muhlke, T. J. Wilcox, and David Cashion for their final votes of confidence. Thank you, Gideon D'Arcangelo, for making every day feel like a gift—I love you.

Diana would like to thank Rebecca Johnson, Matt Houston, Virginia Poundstone, Justine Kurland, Sarah Rosenthal, and Morgan Coy for their support during the writing of this book. Thank you, B Chatfield, for being such a good friend then, now, and in-between. And thank you, Jesse Hartman, for making home such a radical place to be, in every sense of the word.

The Welch kids also would like to thank Karen Kayser Benson for being such a dedicated friend to our mom, and for always giving us a place to crash.

Finally, Diana and Liz would both like to thank Amanda and Dan for their honesty, bravery, and love. We are so proud to be your sisters.

about the authors

Diana Welch is a writer and musician living in Austin, Texas, where she works with the collaborative, multimedia label Monofonus Press and plays in the band Storm Shelter. Her reportage, fashion, and travel writing has appeared in the *Austin Chronicle, Nylon,* and *Night Magazine,* her six-word memoir was included in the collection *Not Quite What I Was Planning* from *Smith Magazine.* This is her first book.

Liz Welch is an award-winning journalist who writes regularly for *Glamour, Real Simple,* and *Inc.* Her work has also appeared in *O, The Oprah Magazine, Vogue,* the *New York Times,* and many other publications. She lives in Brooklyn, New York, with her husband. This is her first book too.

Amanda Welch still lives on a farm in Virginia with her husband, Dennis, two horses, two dogs, and a bunch of bees. She makes a living gardening and making soaps and bath products marketed as Grubby Girl.

Dan Welch works as a location manager and scout for film and television. He lives in Brooklyn, New York.

Visit them at www.thekidsareallrightbook.com.

To find out just how all right Amanda, Liz, Dan, and Diana are, visit them at **www.TheKidsAreAllRightbook.com**

WHERE YOU CAN:

—view a photo album of the people, events, and places mentioned in the book

—watch old family movies

—read their "Morgan Fairchild Killed Our Mother" blog

—see clips from *Loving, The Edge of Night, Search for Tomorrow,* and *The Guiding Light* featuring Ann Williams

—listen to *The Kids Are All Right* playlist of songs referenced in the book

—find out what other people mentioned in the book remember about the Welch kids and events recounted in the book

—share your own story or comments about *The Kids Are All Right*